MW00560019

Voodoo
WordPerfect
for Windows

TIPS & TRICKS WITH AN ATTITUDE

Voodoo WordPerfect for Windows

TIPS & TRICKS WITH AN ATTITUDE

Kay Yarborough Nelson

Ventana Press Voodoo™ Series

Voodoo WordPerfect for Windows: Tips & Tricks With an Attitude
Copyright© 1992 by Kay Yarborough Nelson
The Ventana Voodoo™ Series

Library of Congress Cataloging-in-Publication Data
Nelson, Kay Yarborough
      Voodoo WordPerfect for Windows : tips & tricks with an
attitude / Kay Yarborough Nelson. -- 1st ed.
               p.   cm.
     Includes bibliographical references and index.
     ISBN 0-940087-97-9 (pbk.)
     1. WordPerfect (Computer program) 2. Word processing--Computer programs. 3. Desktop publishing--Computer programs. 4. Windows (Computer programs) I. Title.
Z52.5.W65N489 1992
652-5'5369--dc20   91-48142
                                       CIP

Book design: Karen Wysocki
Cover design: Thea Tulloss, Tulloss Design; John Nedwideck, Sitzer & Spuria
Cover illustration: Lynn Tanaka, Lynn Tanaka Illustration
Desktop publishing: John Cotterman
Editorial staff: Diana Cooper, Linda Pickett, Pam Richardson, Margaret Sloane,
 Laura K. Wenzel
Production staff: Rhonda Angel, Karen Wysocki
Technical review: Martha Mellor

First Edition, First Printing
Printed in the United States of America

For information about our audio products, write us at
Newbridge Book Clubs, 3000 Cindel Drive, Delran, NJ 08370

Ventana Press, Inc.
P.O. Box 2468
Chapel Hill, NC 27515
919/942-0220
FAX 919/942-1140

Limits of Liability and Disclaimer of Warranty

ABOUT THE AUTHOR

Kay Yarborough Nelson, author of over a dozen computer books, knows how to extract the essence from complex programs and operating systems and present it to readers in simple, plain English. She is the author of the acclaimed *Voodoo DOS: Tips & Tricks With an Attittude,* published by Ventana Press. Ms. Nelson has also written encyclopedias and macro handbooks for advanced readers (*Encyclopedia WordPerfect* and *WordPerfect 5.1 Macro Handbook,* Sybex), instant references for all audiences (*DOS Instant Reference* and *WordPerfect Instant Reference,* Sybex), and beginner books (*The Little DOS 5 Book* and *The Little Windows Book,* Peachpit Press). Her books have been translated into many languages, including French, German, Spanish, Italian, Portuguese, Dutch and Swedish.

TRADEMARKS

Trademarked names appear throughout this book. Rather than list the names and entities that own the trademarks or insert a trademark symbol with each mention of the trademarked name, the publisher states that it is using the names only for editorial purposes and to the benefit of the trademark owner with no intention of infringing upon that trademark.

ACKNOWLEDGMENTS

Many thanks to all the people who made this book possible. At Ventana, special thanks to Linda Pickett, my project editor, and to editorial assistant Pam Richardson (thanks a lot for those 30-page faxes on Fridays, Pam). Seriously, these folks are a lot of fun to work with.

I'm grateful also for the help from everybody behind the scenes— Lee Weisbecker and Fran Phillips in marketing; Karen Wysocki, John Cotterman and Ruffin Prevost in production; and Joy Metelits, for making those daily calls a pleasure. Credit also goes to technical reviewer Martha Mellor, for a painstaking and thorough review.

In addition, I'd like to thank Elizabeth and Joe Woodman at Ventana for not saying "*What?*" and hanging up when a strange lady called about doing a series of books with an unusual title, to say the least.

Contents

Anything I don't understand completely is magic to me, and I'll never fully understand computers. I just try to get as much work out of them as I can, and probably you do, too.

Enter *Voodoo WordPerfect for Windows.* To truly master this powerful program demands something beyond a tutorial—but a lot more palatable than a 1,000-page brick of a computer book. I wrote *Voodoo WordPerfect for Windows* so you could browse through it and learn all sorts of neat WordPerfect for Windows tricks and shortcuts—to suit your pace and needs.

What makes them *voodoo* is that they get results without your having to understand the theory behind them. Instead of digging through the techno-jargon of long boring books, you'll find tips presented here in a format that lets you quickly find the ones that apply to what you're doing, or what you'd like to do but never had time to bother with before. These tricks also show you a few things you can do that you probably never thought possible.

Voodoo WordPerfect for Windows isn't sequential. You don't "learn" a topic in Chapter 1 and then learn more about it later in Chapter 2. Think of it as a cookbook you can thumb through whenever you need to concoct some WordPerfect magic.

By the way, I mean no disrespect to anyone's religion—or politics. I call this book *voodoo* to get your attention and because it's full of magic tricks.

USING THIS BOOK

To get the most out of this book, you need to know the very basic basics of WordPerfect and Windows—like how to use the mouse, open and close windows, pick commands from menus and things like that. But you certainly don't have to be an advanced user. If you've used WordPerfect and Windows even just a little bit, you're ready for this book.

WHAT'S INSIDE

Here's a quick preview of the voodoo herein.

Chapter 1: Be a WordPerfect Wizard

Here you'll find tricks for all levels of users, from getting the program installed and running the way you want it through tips for using WordPerfect and Windows together. If you're upgrading from Word-Perfect DOS, you'll see in this chapter the hidden ways WordPerfect for Windows differs from the WordPerfect you're used to.

Chapter 2: Magic 101

In this chapter, we step back and take a look at the very basic tricks you need to know for working in WordPerfect for Windows. If you're new to the program, be sure to check out this chapter before you go on to some of the more arcane tricks in later chapters.

Chapter 3: Customizing WordPerfect

Tailoring the program to work the way you want it to will save you tons of time and money. Even if you're new to WordPerfect for Windows, you can customize it to suit yourself by using the tips in this chapter.

Chapter 4: Editing Alchemy

This chapter is full of tips and shortcuts for selecting and deleting text, using the Speller and Thesaurus, editing long documents and other useful editing techniques.

Chapter 5: Formatting Secrets

All you ever wanted to know about formatting in WordPerfect for Windows, including many hidden mouse shortcuts, tricks to use in tables and hints for supercharging the Ruler.

Chapter 6: Tricks for Managing Your Documents

WordPerfect's File Manager is better than Windows's File Manager, any day. Here are all sorts of tricks for keeping your files in order, sharing directories between WordPerfect DOS and WordPerfect for Windows, accomplishing magical searches and so forth.

Chapter 7: Spells for Your Special Problems

Quite candidly, this chapter is the one that has everything that wouldn't fit anywhere else: alphabetizing lists; making indexes; using tables of authorities, automatic lists and concordance files; making cross-references; numbering lines; using footnotes and endnotes; outlining . . . and more. If you can't find it in any other chapter, it's probably here.

Chapter 8: Spinning Straw into Gold: Printing

Printing can be a nightmare or can work like a charm. In this chapter, you'll delve into the mysterious differences between "WordPerfect printing" and "Windows printing" and find some secrets that the manual never tells you.

Chapter 9: Desktop Publishing Sorcery

This chapter was the most fun to write! Here, in quick how-to steps, are tricks that show you exactly how to get those special effects—like drop caps, pull quotes, rules and reversed-out text—into your documents.

Chapter 10: The Magic of Macros

If you can do it in WordPerfect for Windows, you can record a macro that will do it so you don't have to do it again. Macros aren't hard when you got your mojo workin'. Here they're demystified so you can start using them.

A word or two about the conventions used in this book. What *you* type is set in boldface or in a shaded box. If capitalization doesn't matter, I've shown what you type in lowercase letters, just because it saves you (and me) from having to press the Shift key. File names and directory names are UPPERCASE.

USE THE INDEX!

You'll find tricks related to a certain topic grouped together, but because WordPerfect for Windows has so many commands that let you do so many things, you may want to check out the index to locate tricks on a particular topic. Formatting shortcuts, for example, are scattered throughout the book, even though a whole chapter is devoted to formatting tricks.

HARDWARE/SOFTWARE REQUIREMENTS

The tips in this book apply to Windows 3.0 and 3.1.

For starters, you'll need at least a 286 computer and 2 Mb of RAM to run WordPerfect for Windows. But let's be honest: you'll really need a 386 machine and 4 Mb of RAM (8 Mb is even better) to get the most from the program. You'll also need a mouse and a hard disk with at least 10 Mb of free space on it for a full installation.

In the examples in the text, I assume your Windows directory is C:\WINDOWS, your WordPerfect for Windows directory is C:\WPWIN and that WordPerfect DOS (if you have it at all) is in a directory named C:\WP51. These directories are where the respective installation programs normally put them.

YOUR FAVORITE TRICK?

If you've got a favorite trick that's not covered here, send it to me or to Ventana, and we'll try to get it in the next edition. If we include your trick, the next edition is yours, free. Be sure to include your name and address.

If you like this book, stay on the lookout for the other Voodoo books, such as *Voodoo DOS* and *Voodoo Windows*. They're all designed to help you make magic with the most popular software.

You can write Ventana Press, P.O. Box 2468, Chapel Hill, NC 27515, 919/942-0220 or fax 919/942-1140, or get me on CompuServe (72000,1176) or America Online (KayNelson).

—*Kay Nelson*

CHAPTER ONE

Be a WordPerfect Wizard

WordPerfect needs no introduction. It's been the leading word processing software for an eternity—in computer years, anyway. Users have had a multitude of sources and sorcery to cull from.

Enter WordPerfect for Windows. It does what WordPerfect does, only better. And there's more of it. So, it's time to start fresh with sources and sorcery that will let you unleash the power of this remarkable program.

This chapter has all kinds of tips and secrets for using WordPerfect for Windows and Windows together. If you're upgrading from WordPerfect DOS, you'll be interested in the many pointers about how the Windows version of WordPerfect is different. Some features are really new and some you already know about, but probably under a different name. You'll also find lots of help for starting up the program and running it under Windows.

INSTALLATION TIPS

WordPerfect for Windows comes with a self-installing program, which you have to use. You can't just copy the files directly onto your hard disk; if you do, they won't be usable because they're compressed. The installation program expands them as it puts them on your hard disk.

To start the installation, put Disk 1 in drive A or drive B and type **a:install** or **b:install**. You don't have to be running Windows first; in fact, you should be at the DOS prompt. Then follow the instructions on your screen. Here are some tips that you might want to read over before you begin the installation process.

Do you have what you need? WordPerfect for Windows comes on high-density disks (1.44-Mb 3.5-inch disks), so you'll need to have a high-density disk drive. If you don't have one, you can order the program from WordPerfect Corporation (800/ 321-4566) on 720K 3.5-inch disks. You can also order 1.2-Mb 5.25-inch disks.

You'll need a mouse to use WordPerfect for Windows efficiently. A graphics monitor is also required, but it doesn't have to be a color monitor. And you'll need a hard disk and, of course, Windows 3.0 or higher. Don't try installing WordPerfect for Windows on an XT-class computer; you'll need at least a 286 (AT-class) machine.

Make sure you've got enough memory. As the installation program begins, it checks your hard disk to see how much space is available. The full installation of WordPerfect for Windows (all the files, everything) takes between 9 Mb and 10 Mb of hard disk space. Practically speaking, that means you need at least about 12 Mb of free space to store the documents you create—which means you'll probably need a 40-Mb hard disk to give you room for Windows and storing all the other work you do, like spreadsheets and graphics. We'll take a look at the files you can delete or not install later in this chapter.

You'll want at least 4 Mb of RAM, but 8 Mb is even better. Adding more RAM to your system is relatively inexpensive. If you're not sure how much RAM your system has, issue the MEM command at the DOS prompt before you run anything. If you're running DOS 5, you can use the /C switch, like this: **mem /c**. Then read the "Total bytes available to programs" line. If it says 400K or so, you're fine.

Although you can run WordPerfect for Windows with only 2 Mb of RAM, that's the bare-bones minimum. And it will be slow. You won't like it.

Use DOS 5 to get the most from memory. Although you can run Windows (and therefore WordPerfect for Windows) with DOS 3.3 or 4, DOS 5 gives you the most memory because it takes up less space in RAM. It also has some memory-management features that aren't available in the earlier versions of DOS. Windows wants all the memory it can get, so consider upgrading to DOS 5 if you haven't already. (*Voodoo DOS*, the first book in this Voodoo series, is a good source of information for getting your memory in order.)

Do a Basic installation. The installation program lets you choose among several different types of installations (Basic, Custom and so on). Choose a Basic installation; you can always delete unwanted files later. There's a tip later in this chapter that will help you find out which files you can probably live without.

Custom installation trap. The Basic installation automatically puts files in the C:\WPWIN and C:\WPC directories. A Custom installation lets you specify which directories you want files to be put in. If you do a Custom installation, don't install your WordPerfect for Windows files in your Windows directory, because if you upgrade to a newer version of Windows later, files might be overwritten.

Updating WordPerfect for Windows. WordPerfect Corporation occasionally issues "interim releases" of WordPerfect for Windows. These are "bug" fixes and performance upgrades. If you call in to report a problem, ask which version is the current release. You may want to obtain a more recent version, depending on what kind of problem you're having and whether the newer version has fixed it. You can see the date of your release by choosing About WordPerfect from the Help menu.

If you get an interim release, use the Interim option to install so only the changed files will be affected. There's also a Printers option that will install just the printer drivers, because these also are updated from time to time.

Installation problems? The magic number for installation problems is 800/228-6076, but you don't see it until you start the installation program. If you're having problems with Disk 1, for instance, you may not know about this number.

Which keyboard should you choose? During the installation process, you'll be asked whether you want to use the CUA (Common User Access) keyboard or the WordPerfect DOS-style keyboard. It doesn't matter which you choose, because you can switch to the other at any time (use the Preferences command on the File menu). If you're planning to use WordPerfect for Windows with other Windows programs, though, I recommend that you choose the CUA keyboard right from the beginning. Go cold turkey. You might as well get used to the Windows-style keystrokes, like Shift+Ins for Paste and Ctrl+Ins for Copy.

Use the Name Search feature to find your printer. When you choose your printer, use the Name Search feature, especially if you have a Xerox Memorywriter. You won't have to go through the whole long list of printers. Just press F2 and type the first letter of the printer manufacturer's name.

Select a printer, even if you already selected one through Windows. Just because you've installed a printer in Windows doesn't mean that WordPerfect knows about it. You have to install your printer through WordPerfect, too.

Also, if you're going to be downloading soft fonts on disk, you'll need to use the Printer Setup dialog box (see Figure 1-1) when you're through with the installation program to tell WordPerfect the name of the directory where your soft fonts are stored. Choose Select Printer from the File menu, highlight your printer's name and click Setup. You'll see "Path for Downloadable Fonts and Printer Commands"; fill it out with the path to your fonts directory. For example, if your soft fonts are stored in a subdirectory named FONTS under your WordPerfect 5.1 directory, the path name is C:\WP51\FONTS. You can click on the tiny folder icon to see your directory structure. Then just click on your fonts directory.

Figure 1-1: When you install a printer that uses soft fonts or fonts on cartridges, you'll need to specify where they're stored.

Click the Cartridges/Fonts button if you've bought soft fonts or fonts on cartridges; then select all the fonts you have. Mark them to indicate whether they'll be present when a print job begins or whether WordPerfect can load them while printing is going on. The fonts that you mark as present when a print job begins are the soft fonts that you need to put in the printer's memory by downloading them or inserting their cartridge before you print. (To download fonts, choose Print from the File menu and then select Initialize Printer.) See Chapter 8, "Spinning Straw into Gold: Printing," for more on printing and fonts.

What you can delete to save disk space.   You can probably do without the Printer program. It's necessary only if you're planning to modify printer resource files (.PRS files, also called printer drivers) or use Autofont support. If this sounds meaningless to you, go ahead and delete the Printer program's files: PTR.EXE, PTR.ICO and PTR.HLP.

If you don't plan to work through WordPerfect's lessons, you can delete the Learning and Workbook files: SPREAD26.PLN, WPLEARN.WWB, WPWORK.PRS and all the files that end in .WKB (you can delete *.WKB, because * stands for "everything"). They're in the C:\WPWIN\LEARN directory. Then delete the C:\WPWIN\LEARN directory.

If you don't plan to use any graphic images supplied by Word-Perfect, you can delete all the files that end in .WPG (delete *.WPG, which stands for all the WordPerfect graphics files). They're in the C:\WPWIN\GRAPHICS directory. Then delete the directory itself.

If you're not going to use macros (a pity), you can delete the macro facility and its associated files: MFWIN.EXE, MCWIN.EXE, MXWIN.EXE, WPWPUS.WCD and WPM2WCM.DLL. If you delete these files, though, you can't use the macros supplied with the program (and there are some neat ones for labels, envelopes, and so forth). Delete *.WCM (all the macro files) if you decide to delete the macro facility. They're in the C:\WPWIN\MACROS directory. Then delete C:\CPWIN\MACROS.

Make backup copies of your disks. Just because you can't run WordPerfect for Windows from your floppy disks doesn't mean that you shouldn't make backups of them. If something goes wrong with your hard disk, you'll probably have to reinstall WordPerfect for Windows (unless you've got a tape or floppy backup of the whole hard disk), and if you find that one of the original floppies has been left too close to a stereo speaker or other magnetic source, you're out of luck until you can order a replacement disk. So use the DOS DISKCOPY command to make duplicates of your program disks—and store them somewhere away from the original set.

Type **diskcopy a: a:** (or **diskcopy b: b:**, depending on which drive you want to use) at the DOS prompt (or run this command from the Windows Program Manager's File menu). You'll be prompted to insert the original disk (the "source") and a blank disk (the "target"). The blank disk doesn't have to be formatted; DOS will format it for you as it makes the copy. You'll be asked to switch disks again, so stick around.

WordPerfect for Windows modifies your AUTOEXEC.BAT and CONFIG.SYS files. WordPerfect for Windows needs to have certain information in your AUTOEXEC.BAT and your CONFIG.SYS files. During installation, it checks and changes these files if the information it needs isn't there. First, it puts the path to the C:\WPC and C:\WPWIN directories in the path statement in the AUTOEXEC.BAT file. It also makes sure that the CONFIG.SYS file has enough files and buffers specified. You may need to restart your computer after installation for these changes to take effect.

If you don't like what you see, try a Windows VGA driver. Some people who use special video drivers report problems with WordPerfect for Windows. If you're using one of these special video drivers at 800 x 600 or 1024 x 768 resolution and you don't like the looks of WordPerfect on the screen, try changing to the Windows VGA driver, which uses a standard 640 x 480 resolution. Double-click on the Windows Setup icon in the Main group to choose the VGA driver.

UPGRADING SECRETS

If you're upgrading to WordPerfect for Windows from WordPerfect DOS, this section will help you sort out what's new and what's not. At a very basic level, some of the terminology has changed. The cursor is now called the insertion point, for example. You don't exit from a document; you close a document window. List Files is now the File Manager. Instead of Moving, you Cut, Copy and Paste. View Document is Print Preview, and Compose is now called WP Characters. That's just a start—here's more. Keep an eye open for more tips about changes throughout the book.

What's *not* in WordPerfect for Windows. If you could do it in WordPerfect DOS, you can probably do it in WordPerfect for Windows. The feature set is virtually the same, and documents created with either program can be used interchangeably, with no conversion required. But there are a couple of subtle things that aren't in WordPerfect for Windows. The Esc key doesn't repeat things. And you can't make calculations on columns that aren't in tables. Also, you can't fine-tune Graphics box borders to specify exactly how thin is "thin," for example. These features may be added in later interim releases, though.

What You See Is What You Get, almost. You may have heard of WYSIWYG (it's pronounced "wizzywig"), which stands for "What You See Is What You Get." In WordPerfect for Windows, this is almost true. You'll see columns of text and graphics on the screen, italics will look like italics, boldface will be bold and so forth. But you'll only be able to see page numbers, headers and footers, and footnotes in the Print Preview window. And unless you've purchased a font management program like Adobe Type Manager, the fonts you see on the screen will be only representations of the actual fonts your printer uses. (The same is true even if you have a font management program, but they'll be *closer* representations!)

What *is* in WordPerfect for Windows.   Cutting, copying and pasting is vastly improved in WordPerfect for Windows, because you can just double-click with the mouse to select a word, triple-click to select a sentence, or click four times to select a paragraph. There are also neat keyboard shortcuts that you can *remember*, like Ctrl+G for Go To, Ctrl+B for Bold and Ctrl+I for Italic. And these Ctrl key shortcuts work the same on the WordPerfect DOS-style keyboard or the CUA Windows-style keyboard.

The Ruler lets you set and change tabs, set margins, switch fonts, apply styles and create tables and columns just by clicking the mouse. The Button Bar lets you assign almost any task—from carrying out a menu command to assigning a complex macro—to a button, which you then play by clicking on the button with the mouse. Graphics appear on the screen as they will in your printed documents. You simply double-click on a graphic to edit it. You can drag a graphic to place it wherever you want, and text will reformat around it. In most cases, what you see is what you get. Italics look like italics, 14-point type looks like 14-point type and so forth.

Which keyboard should you use?   As you saw when you installed WordPerfect for Windows, you can choose between two predefined keyboards—the CUA (Common User Access) keyboard and the WordPerfect DOS-style keyboard. If you're upgrading to WordPerfect for Windows basically to get the improved graphics interface, and you're planning only to do word processing in Windows, with WordPerfect alone, you might as well choose the DOS-style keyboard. You won't have to learn very many new keyboard shortcuts.

I say "very many" because some of the old keyboard shortcuts just won't work because of the keystrokes that Windows preempts for itself. It is a little disconcerting to press Alt+F4 to turn on block marking (called "selecting text" now) and find that the program thinks you want to exit from your document (called "closing a document" now). Shift+F7 is another big surprise. It doesn't print any more; it centers text.

But if you're planning to use WordPerfect for Windows with other Windows programs, choose the CUA keyboard. It's really not *that* hard to get used to, and it uses keystrokes—like Shift+Ins for Paste—common to other Windows programs.

Chapter 2, "Magic 101," looks in more detail at how keyboard shortcuts differ on the two keyboards. As you'll see, not all of your favorite WordPerfect DOS shortcuts survived.

Watch your fingers. The worst mistake you can make while adjusting from WordPerfect DOS to WordPerfect for Windows is to press Alt+F4 to turn on block marking and then type N in response to the dialog box that's asking you if you want to save your document. Alt+F4 is the Windows key combination for Exit. You'll exit, losing your work. Press Esc or choose Cancel to get out of this dialog box. (And set yourself up for automatic timed backups, so if you mistakenly exit, you can still get some of your work back. Chapter 3, "Customizing WordPerfect," shows you how to do this.)

You can reassign key functions. If there are WordPerfect DOS key combinations that your fingers just can't forget, you can reassign them and make a custom keyboard that's a mix of the WordPerfect DOS and WordPerfect for Windows keyboards. For example, F1 is Help on both keyboards in WordPerfect for Windows, but you might want to reassign it to F3 on the CUA keyboard, as it was in WordPerfect DOS. (See Chapter 3 for keyboard secrets.)

Text can disappear unless you're aware of this new feature. When you select text and press a key in WordPerfect for Windows, the text is deleted. In WordPerfect DOS, if you turned on block marking and then typed a character, the selection extended to that character.

To undelete text you've deleted by mistake, choose Undelete from the File menu or press Ctrl-Z to Undo the deletion.

Getting around the previous trap. Press F8 to turn on a hidden "WordPerfect Select" mode. (I say "hidden" because I had used the program for quite a while before I realized it was there.) Once you press F8, you'll see "Select" on the status line, and Word-Perfect for Windows will work the way WordPerfect DOS did: you can type a character to extend the selection to it.

 F1 isn't Cancel or Undelete any more. In WordPerfect DOS, F1 works as the Cancel key or the Undelete key, but in WordPerfect for Windows, F1 gets you Help now.

 Use the Esc key to cancel. In WordPerfect DOS, Esc can cancel some operations and also can repeat an operation any number of times. In WordPerfect for Windows, Esc just cancels; it doesn't repeat.

 The new Undo feature. The WordPerfect for Windows Undo command is new. It lets you undo the last thing you did, like resizing a graphic image or resetting a tab. If what you did last was delete, Undo restores that deletion (although there's an Undelete feature, too).

Keep in mind that Undo can undo only the very last thing you did. It can't undo the next to the last thing. And it doesn't undo things that don't affect the document, like scrolling or moving the insertion point. For instance, it won't resort text you've sorted, and it won't magically change columns of text to tables or vice versa.

The Undo shortcut is Ctrl+Z (on both keyboards). To remember the shortcut, imagine Undo as a benevolent wiZard.

 You can also Undelete. Undelete works as it did in Word-Perfect DOS: you can restore your last three deletions.

Be careful about pressing Enter in dialog boxes. If you're used to WordPerfect DOS, your fingers may want to press Enter after you type text in a dialog box. In WordPerfect for Windows, pressing Enter in a dialog box usually accepts all the default selections and closes the box. So if there are buttons or list items you need to check in that box, don't press Enter until you've filled out the whole box.

WordPerfect for Windows is slower than WordPerfect DOS. WordPerfect for Windows runs in graphics mode, which means it's slower than the DOS version. If you can't stand it, you can use Draft mode for the bulk of your typing and switch back to Graphics mode when you're ready to format. Buying more RAM is a good idea, too. I have 8 Mb of RAM on a 386 computer, and it runs pretty fast.

A couple of other things you can do to speed up the program are in the Display Settings dialog box. In the Document Window group, turn off Auto Redisplay in Draft mode. If you work with text in columns, you can turn off Display Columns Side by Side so that WordPerfect displays just one column at a time. You can turn it back on again before you print.

If you want to spell-check faster, you can uncheck the Suggestions box in the Speller. Just manually correct your typos.

You can turn off Undo (use the Environment Settings dialog box) to speed things up. If you're working with large blocks of text that have to be kept in a memory buffer, turn off Undo temporarily. Before you do that, though, save your unchanged document under another name so you can get the original back if you need to undo anything.

You can also make sure that Fast Save (in the Environment Settings dialog box) is checked. When it's checked (or on), the program saves your document without checking its format. When it's not checked (or off), WordPerfect goes to the end of the document and checks page breaks and so on before saving it.

Some things in WordPerfect for Windows can only be done with a mouse. Get a mouse! All sorts of features in Word-Perfect for Windows are accessible only with a mouse. The Button Bar. The Ruler. Resizing graphics easily. Selecting text (double-click to select a word, click three times to select a sentence, click four times to select a paragraph).

See Chapter 4, "Editing Alchemy," for tips about where hidden mouse secrets lie on the screen if you click in just the right places. Here's a preview: click just above the bottom of the scroll bar. Then drag upward. Aha! The Reveal Codes window appears.

You can make menu selections via the keyboard. To open a menu without using the mouse, press Alt and type the underlined letter in the menu's name. For example, Alt+F opens the File menu.

Then, to select a menu item, type the underlined letter in its name. Type O after opening the File menu to choose Open, for instance.

These mnemonic shortcuts may be the best to use until you get used to the Windows interface. And there are lots more of them—Chapter 2 shows you more keyboard shortcuts than you'll ever need to use.

Make the most of all those document windows. Now you can have *nine* document windows open, not just two. Make the most of them. Use a document window as a scrap heap for the text you're cutting; you can get it back later if you need to. Keep a list of headings in another window so you can see the structure of your document as you develop it. Keep a list of terms you've defined in another document window to remind you which have been de-fined. Be creative. You get the idea.

You can create directories in WordPerfect for Windows when you specify the location of files. You may remember from WordPerfect DOS that one of the first things you did after installing the program was go into the Setup menu and specify how you wanted things to work. In WordPerfect DOS for Windows, that Setup menu is called the Preferences menu, and it's on the File menu.

The Preferences menu lets you specify where certain types of files are to be stored (that's the Location of Files choice on the menu). The basic installation program figures that you want just about everything stored in a directory called C:\WPWIN, but that may not be the case. (In fact, you can store your WordPerfect documents along with your WordPerfect for Windows documents, as you'll see in the next tip.)

Now here's the magic. If the directory in which you want to store a certain type of file—like macros or document files—doesn't exist, you can create it by just typing a path name for it in the Location of Files dialog box. You couldn't do this in WordPerfect DOS; you had to create that directory first.

Keep your WordPerfect DOS files and WordPerfect for Windows files in the same directories. Documents you create with WordPerfect DOS and WordPerfect for Windows are completely compatible. So don't bother messing up your hard disk with a complicated directory structure. Just keep your WordPerfect for Windows program files in the directories the installation program puts them in (C:\WPWIN). The shared program files are in the C:\WPC directory. Then use the Location of Files dialog box to tell the program where you want your document files kept. That could be in your C:\WP51\DOCS directory (where you keep WordPerfect DOS documents), or wherever you like.

WINDOWS & WORDPERFECT

If you're new to Windows, here are some tips to help you get the most from WordPerfect for Windows. You'll find ideas for starting and stopping the program, manipulating windows and icons, making yourself a WordPerfect for Windows shortcut key combination, and more. You could say that the tricks in this section "come with Windows" because they're part of the standard Windows interface. You'll find plenty more tricks in the next chapter for the basic things you do in WordPerfect.

The fastest way to start WordPerfect and Windows at the same time. At the C:\ prompt, type **win wpwin**. That will start both programs at the same time. If you want both Windows and WordPerfect to start each time you turn on your computer, put that line as the last line in your AUTOEXEC.BAT file.

To start both programs *and* open a WordPerfect document (named CHAP2, in this instance), type **win wpwin chap2.** (The document must be in the directory you specified to hold your documents in the Location of Files dialog box. Use a full path name if the document isn't in that document directory.

If you're already running Windows, just double-click on the WordPerfect group icon to open the program group and double-click on the WordPerfect icon. Or use the Program Manager's Run command (on the File menu) and enter **wpwin**.

If you have Windows 3.1, you can just put WordPerfect in your Startup group to start it each time you run Windows.

Start WordPerfect for Windows *and* a macro? Sure. You can have a macro start each time you start WordPerfect by putting this line in the Properties dialog box:

    c:\wpwin\wpwin.exe /m-c:\wpwin\macros\macro.wcm

In this example, I assume that WordPerfect for Windows is stored in C:\WPWIN and that the macro (MACRO.WCM) is in a directory named C:\WPWIN\MACROS. Make sure there's a space between the .EXE and the /M-C parts. Without it, the macro won't run.

To get to the Properties dialog box, highlight the WordPerfect for Windows program icon in the Program Manager and then choose Properties from the File menu.

If you want to start WordPerfect for Windows and a macro "manually" (from the DOS command line), use this pattern:

    win wpwin /m-*macroname*

The fastest way to exit from WordPerfect, Windows and anything running under Windows. Don't bother to close each document and exit from WordPerfect, or to exit from each program you've got running. Just press Ctrl+Esc, highlight Program Manager and select End Task from the Task List. If you've forgotten to save anything, you'll be asked whether you want to save it before exiting from Windows. This is a lot faster than saving and exiting everything step by step.

Another fast way out is to minimize WordPerfect (or any other program) by clicking on its Minimize icon (the one that looks like a downward-pointing arrow in the upper-right corner of the window). Then exit from Windows by double-clicking on the Program Manager's Control menu icon (the one that looks like a tiny filing cabinet drawer in the upper-left corner of the window).

You can start WordPerfect from the File Manager. Word Perfect for Windows has its own File Manager that's preferable to the Windows File Manager because it has so many more features. You'll see tips for using it in Chapter 6, "Tricks for Managing Your Documents."

You can start WordPerfect from either File Manager by double-clicking on WPWIN.EXE or by choosing WordPerfect from the WordPerfect File Manager's Applications menu.

In the WordPerfect File Manager, you can just double-click on the name of a WordPerfect document to open the document and start WordPerfect, too.

Want to open your WordPerfect program group each time you start Windows? If you have a lot of program groups, it can be tedious to locate your WordPerfect program every time you start Windows. To make sure it's open when you start, open it before you exit and then click the Save Changes box when the Windows Program Manager tells you you're ending your Windows session.

Lost? Try the Window menu. If you're having trouble locating your WordPerfect program group, select Window from the Program Manager menu. It lists all your program groups and you can pick the one you want from it. It's a lot faster than shuffling through all the windows you may have opened.

You can add programs and accessories to your Word-Perfect program group. You don't have to leave your WordPerfect program group as you found it, with just the program, the Speller, the Thesaurus and the File Manager. If you work with a graphics or spreadsheet program regularly, you can add their icons to your WordPerfect group. Or you might want to keep a copy of the Windows Calculator or Calendar accessories in your WordPerfect program group.

To put a program or desk accessory in your WordPerfect group, just copy its icon from the Windows group it's in by pressing Ctrl and dragging the icon to your WordPerfect group. To move it there instead of making a copy of it, just drag it without pressing Ctrl.

You have to see into both groups to do this, so open both the group that has the icon you want to copy and the WordPerfect group. If your screen is too cluttered to see into both groups, choose Tile from the Program Manager's Window menu. Then you should be able to see into both groups.

You can put a document in your WordPerfect program group. If there's one document that you want to start your work with every day, make an icon for it so that double-clicking on it will start WordPerfect for Windows and open the document at the same time. (You can do this from the command line, as explained earlier in "The fastest way to start WordPerfect and Windows at the same time," but that's not much fun. Windows uses icons, so why shouldn't you?)

Open the WordPerfect group and choose New from the Program Manager's File menu. Click Program Item and OK. In the Description box, enter what you want the icon's name to be. In the Command Line box, enter **c:\wpwin**, followed by the file name of the document that you want the icon to represent. For example, to open a document named CH1, you'd enter **c:\wpwin ch1**. (I'm assuming that it's in your documents directory as specified in WordPerfect's Location of Files dialog box; if it's not, use its entire path name, such as C:\DOCS\VOODOO\CH1.)

Click OK, and you've got an icon that will start WordPerfect for Windows and open CH1 at the same time.

Don't put a lot of document icons in your WordPerfect group. Because clicking on an icon that you've set up to start the program and open a document at the same time starts a new copy of the program running each time you open the icon, don't make very many of these icons, or you'll run out of memory by starting multiple copies of WordPerfect each time you click on a document icon. Just make one document icon and use it to start your daily document; then open additional documents from within WordPerfect, which is already running.

You can change your icons. This is a neat trick if you're making a document icon as explained in the previous tip. WordPerfect for Windows comes with several other icons. To see what they are, highlight the WordPerfect program icon in its program group. Then choose Properties from the Program Manager's File menu. Click on Change Icon; then choose View Next to review the available icons and pick another one, if you like.

Your selection of WordPerfect icons is limited, but you can get programs that let you choose other icons. Or you can use this trick: in the File Name box, enter **c:\windows\progman.exe**. Then click OK. You'll see lots of icons you can use.

Running slow? Try Standard mode. If WordPerfect for Windows is running too slow for your taste on a 386 or higher computer (and you aren't using a lot of other Windows programs with it), try running Windows in Standard mode. Give the startup command as **win /s**.

Take a peek at how Windows is using memory while you're running WordPerfect. Choose About Program Manager from the Program Manager's Help menu. You'll see how Windows is using memory. The "Free Memory" number includes all the disk space that it's able to use as memory, too, if you're running Windows on a 386 computer in Enhanced mode.

"Free System Resources" indicates an amount of memory that Windows is using to manage itself. If this falls to 15 percent, you won't be able to open any more windows.

What can you do about low system resources? Close windows. Minimize the windows you really need but aren't using right now. You can also consolidate your program icons into fewer groups. The fewer groups the Program Manager has to take notice of, the better. If there are program icons that you rarely use, consider deleting them.

In WordPerfect for Windows, the items that use the most system resources are the Ruler, the Button Bar and the scroll bars. If you don't use them, don't display them. Even after you hide them, they take up resources; quit WordPerfect and start it again without them.

Not enough memory? The most obvious thing you can do if you get "Out of memory" messages is to buy more RAM. It's relatively inexpensive. If you don't want to get more RAM, though, here's a trick you can use: start WordPerfect for Windows first, then start your other programs. WordPerfect tends to grab a lot of memory and hold onto it.

Avoiding UAEs when you start WordPerfect for Windows. Some folks report a UAE (Unrecoverable Application Error) when they first start WordPerfect for Windows. If this happens to you, try this (I don't know why it works). In your CONFIG.SYS file, increase your DOS environment space to a large number, such as 512 or 1024. To do this, change the /E parameter in the SHELL= command, or add one before the /P switch if it's not already there:

```
shell=c:\dos\command.com /e:1024 /p.
```

Then restart your computer.

If you move WordPerfect for Windows to another drive, you may have trouble. If you buy a new hard disk and move WordPerfect for Windows to it, it will continue to look for certain files back on drive C (if that was where it was before). What to do? Well, if you want to avoid a hassle, just reinstall WordPerfect on your new hard drive instead of moving it. Then copy your documents over to the new drive. This is another good reason to keep documents in a directory of their own, because you can just copy that directory.

To copy any macros and styles you've created, copy the files ending in .WCM (macros) or .STY (if you've used the .STY extension for style files).

If you decide to move WordPerfect for Windows to your new hard drive anyway (instead of reinstalling it), follow these steps.

In your C:\WPWIN directory is a file called WP{WP}.ENV that contains the line \WPC=C:\WPC. You'll need to change that C: to a D: (or to the letter of your new drive). You'll also need to edit the WPC.INI file in your Windows directory, because it will also contain references to files that were on drive C. You may also need to edit WPWP.INI and WPFM.INI.

Use the Windows Notebook, not WordPerfect for Windows, to edit these files; if you change settings for WordPerfect while Word-Perfect is running, it may cause unexpected results.

Assign WordPerfect for Windows a shortcut key combination. If you want to be able to switch quickly to WordPerfect for Windows from another Windows program, assign it a shortcut key combination. Assuming you're using Windows 3.1, highlight the WordPerfect program icon and choose Properties from the File menu. Then, in the Shortcut Key box, enter the key combination you want to use. You have to use either the Alt key, the Ctrl key or the Shift key. You can use all of them if you want to, like Alt+Ctrl+Shift+W. Shift+Ctrl+W is my favorite.

The fast switch.   The fastest way to switch between programs is to press Ctrl+Esc. That brings up the Task List, and you can choose which program you want to switch to from those that are running. You don't have to go out to the desktop and hunt for them, or locate the Program Manager to start a new one. Just highlight Program Manager, click Switch To, and *then* start the new program running.

You can press Alt+Esc to cycle through all the programs you've got running, but it's a lot slower than Ctrl+Esc. Or, if you can see any part of a program's window on your screen, you can click in it to switch to it.

Using the Control icons.   The Control icons (the tiny file drawers in the upper-left corner of a WordPerfect for Windows window) are pretty useless, in my opinion, except for one basic task: closing a document. They also open a menu that lets you move and resize windows and switch to the next document, but there are faster ways to do those things (see the next tip).

There are two Control icons, one for WordPerfect (on the top, with the program's title bar) and one for the document (on the document's title bar). Double-click on the program's Control icon (the top one) to exit from WordPerfect. Double-click on the document's Control icon to close the document window.

Pressing Alt+hyphen is the keyboard shortcut for opening the Control menu, if you ever want to. I just keep it closed and double-click on the icon.

Moving and resizing windows.   To move a window, drag it by its title bar. To resize a window, click in a border and drag the border inward or outward. Click in a corner to expand or shrink a window in two directions at once.

If you're moving and sizing several document windows, use the Window menu instead of doing each window one by one. Choose Cascade to see your documents arranged with only their title bars showing. Choose Tile to see a peek of each document in a tiny window of its own.

Shortcuts for switching documents. Press Ctrl+F6 to go to the next document, if you've got more than one document window open. This shortcut is easy to remember because the keys are right next to each other, if your function keys are on the left side of your keyboard.

Pressing Ctrl+Shift+F6 takes you to the previous document. Now that one *is* hard to remember.

Drag any window that has a title bar. Any window, including any dialog box, that has a title bar can be repositioned on the screen by dragging the title bar. That includes the Undelete and Search dialog boxes and the Speller window, which sometimes get in the way of what you want to see on the screen.

Use the Minimize, Maximize and Restore icons to your advantage. In the upper-right corner of a window are tiny icons that look like arrowheads. These are the Maximize and Minimize icons that let you reduce to icon size and increase to full-size again WordPerfect itself, or the document you're working on (see Figure 1-2). Even though something is minimized, it's still in memory, ready to use again as soon as you double-click on it.

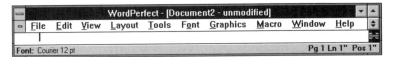

Figure 1-2: The Minimize, Maximize, and Restore icons in the upper-right corner of a window let you control the size of windows, too.

If a window is already full-screen size, it will have a Restore icon. Clicking on it resizes the window to less than full-screen size, but it's still big enough to see into.

You can minimize a document to keep it in memory, but out of your way, not cluttering up the screen. You can also minimize the whole WordPerfect for Windows program if you want to go out to another program and keep your screen uncluttered. These are both neat tricks to use if you're planning to return to a document or to WordPerfect later.

Minimized icons are stacked at the bottom of your Windows desktop (see Figure 1-3) so you can get at them again easily.

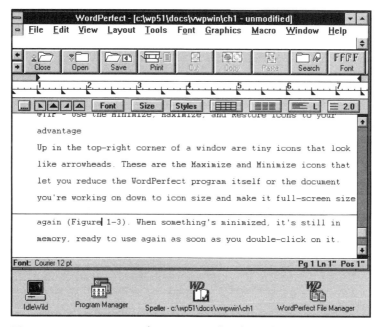

Figure 1-3: Minimized icons can be found at the bottom of your Windows desktop.

Minimizing a document doesn't save it. You might think that making a document into an icon would automatically save it, since it's being held in memory somewhere. But it's not saved until you save it.

Minimize the Speller or the File Manager if you plan to use them again. The WordPerfect File Manager, the Speller and the Thesaurus are all stand-alone programs that come with WordPerfect for Windows. You can minimize them to keep them in

memory if you're planning to use them again soon. You can minimize Help windows, too, to speed up access to Help.

**To see what you've minimized, click WordPerfect's Restore
icon.** If you're running WordPerfect full-screen size, there's
a Restore icon in the upper-right corner. Click it to make the program
window smaller so you can see what's on your Windows desktop.

MOVING ON

Now we've covered the basics of getting WordPerfect installed and
running. You've learned some fundamental tricks that let you inter-
act with the program through the Windows interface. The next
chapter explores the WordPerfect for Windows basics.

Magic 101

Welcome to Magic 101, required voodoo reading. This chapter features some of the basic ways to operate in WordPerfect for Windows. Just because they're "basic," though, doesn't mean they're always obvious, even to longtime WordPerfect fans.

OPENING & CLOSING DOCUMENTS

One of the most basic things you do in WordPerfect for Windows is open and close documents. I'll start out with a really hidden trick, one that's not on any menu, just to get your attention.

The hidden Clear shortcut. You can press Ctrl+Shift+F4 to clear the current document out of the window you're working in. This is the same as selecting Close from the File menu and then opening the File menu again and selecting New.

Closing and Exiting are two different things. Choosing Exit from the File menu exits you from WordPerfect and gives you a chance to save any documents you haven't saved yet. This is often faster than closing all your open documents one by one.

Clicking on the Close button or choosing Close from the File menu just closes the active document. It also gives you a chance to save the document if it hasn't been saved yet.

Opening and Retrieving are a little different.   If you're used to WordPerfect DOS, you're used to "retrieving" a document into the editing screen. With WordPerfect for Windows, you "open" a document. If you choose Retrieve when there's a document in the active window on the screen, the document you retrieve will appear *in* the document you're working on.

This may not be what you want. On the other hand, if you're assembling a large document from parts stored as separate files, it may be exactly what you want.

Hidden options in the Open File dialog box.   You can delete, copy and rename files by clicking on the Options button in the lower-left corner of the Open File dialog box.

There are options for finding files by name (click Find) or locating files that have specific words in them, if you don't remember their file names (click Find Words). These features work the same way as in WordPerfect's File Manager (see Chapter 6, "Tricks for Managing Your Documents," for details about them).

Saving and Saving As.   The CUA keyboard shortcut Shift+F3 saves a document. To save it under a different name, choose Save As from the File menu or press F3.

Choose Save As to save a document in a different format, like Microsoft Word or WordStar. Then, next to the Format box in the Save As dialog box (see Figure 2-1), click on the arrow and scroll through the options until you see the program whose format you want to use.

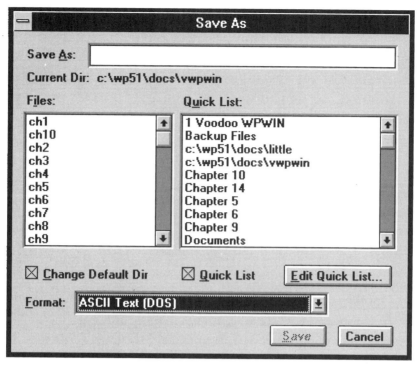

Figure 2-1: Use the Format pop-up list in the Save As dialog box to choose a different document format.

Use the Save button for a fast save, with no prompt. Clicking the Save button on the Button Bar will save the document (if it's been saved before) without prompting you to confirm that you want to save it under the same name.

There's no Text In/Out menu any more. If you're upgrading from WordPerfect DOS, you'll remember that you used to use Ctrl+F5 (Text In/Out) to create and edit DOS text files (ASCII files). To edit text files in WordPerfect for Windows, use the Save As command, click the Format button and pick ASCII Text (DOS).

Don't open several copies of the same document. With so many window opportunities, it's easy to retrieve two copies of the same document into two windows. WordPerfect doesn't warn you that you're doing this; it just lets you do it. Be careful not to edit two windows of the same document at once. You won't get all your changes when you save them (assuming you save both copies under the same name).

How to tell whether you've saved a document. If a document's title bar has a document title *and* says "unmodified," you've saved it and you haven't done anything else to it after that. If it just says "unmodified," it hasn't been given a name and saved yet.

Quickly opening a document you've already worked with. At the bottom of the File menu, you'll find a list of the last four documents you've opened. If you need to get a document back, even if you've already closed it, just choose the one you want from that list.

Make yourself a Quick List. The Quick List (see Figure 2-2) is really handy for getting at frequently used files. Instead of typing a path name to a document (like C:\WPWIN\DOCS\CHAP1) or opening several subdirectories, just click on a document's name in your Quick List.

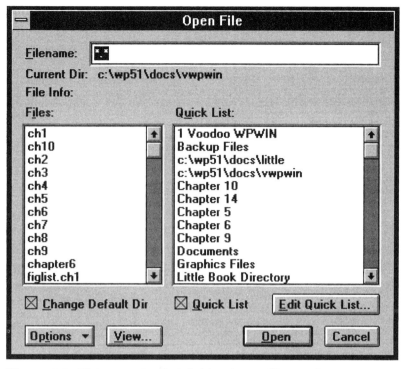

Figure 2-2: This sample Quick List shows files and directories that are worked with most often.

To set up your own Quick List, you'll need to open a directory dialog box first. Choose Open, Retrieve or Save As from the File menu to do this. Then check the Quick List box, select Edit Quick List and choose Add (see Figure 2-3).

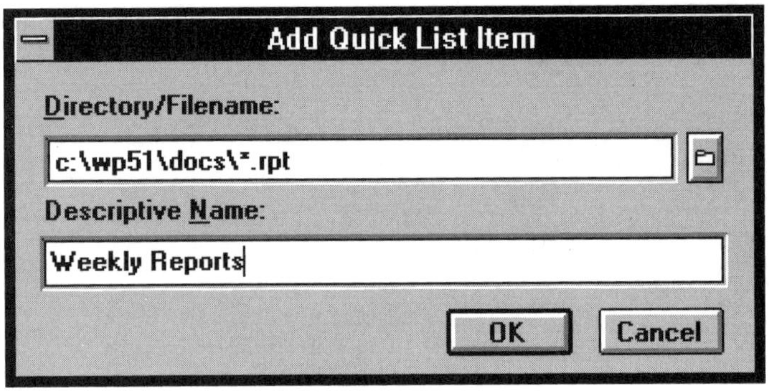

Add Quick List Item

Directory/Filename:

`c:\wp51\docs\*.rpt`

Descriptive Name:

`Weekly Reports`

OK   Cancel

Figure 2-3: Make a Quick List of files you work with frequently.

See the tiny folder icon? Click on it to see all your directories on the current drive. To see what's on another drive, just double-click on the drive letter (click on [-b-] to switch to drive B, for instance). You'll see the Select Directory dialog box (Figure 2-4).

Click on [..] at the top of the list to go up one level in the directory tree—where you can change over to another branch and go down again. For example, if you want to look in your C:\WP51 directory but you're viewing the contents of C:\WPWIN, click on [..] to go up one level (in this case, to your root directory); then click on [wp51]. If the directory you want is several levels down, it's probably faster to type the path to the directory you want in the Directory Name box instead of clicking with the mouse. But if you don't know the exact path name, click until you see the directory you want.

The name of the directory you're looking in will be listed in the Directory Name box (see Figure 2-4).

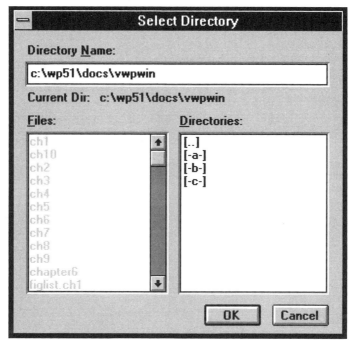

Figure 2-4: Click on [..] to go up the directory structure, or type the path to a different directory in the Directory Name box.

Once you've opened the right directory, click on the OK button. You'll see the directory's path name in the top box. Click in the box next to Directory Name and see if you can give the directory a more meaningful name than its DOS name.

You can add individual files to your Quick List. Type the file name at the end of the path name. For example, to add a document named CHAP20 in your C:WP51\DOCS\VOODOO directory to your Quick List, add **\chap20** to the path name so that it reads

c:\wp51\docs\voodoo\chap20

In the lower box, under Descriptive Name, type the name that you want to be displayed in the Quick List. You'll see the DOS-style cryptic path name in that box, but just type over it with something meaningful, like *Voodoo Chapter 20*. Click the OK buttons to close all these dialog boxes.

Once you've added an item to your Quick List, you'll see it when you choose Open, Retrieve or Save As; when you use the File Manager; when you want to play a macro and so forth. It's a real timesaver.

If you want to see things that *aren't* in your Quick List, just uncheck the Quick List box.

Put directories in your Quick List.   If you want to have access to lots of documents through your Quick List, put directories there and give them descriptive names (like *Voodoo Word-Perfect*, which holds all these chapters).

Start the descriptive names of directories that you use a lot with a letter that's near the beginning of the alphabet, or use a numeral first, like *1 Voodoo WordPerfect*.

Group documents together by naming them creatively.   If you want documents to be listed close together, just start their descriptive names with the same letter or number, such as *b August Report* and *b June Report*.

You can also use wildcards with directory or file names.   When you add an item to your Quick List, you can use the wildcard characters ***** (to stand for any number of characters, or none at all) and **?** (to stand for any one character). Entering ***.txt** as a directory or file name in the Add Quick List Item dialog box represents all files with that extension. Entering **lttr??** represents files with names like LTTR01, LTTR22, LTTRMY and so forth. (Remember, you can use a "real" descriptive name in the Descriptive Name box—you don't have to deal with these cryptic DOS-style names once your Quick List is set up.)

Use extensions to your advantage.   Some programs use a three-character extension on files they create to indicate that the files "belong" to that program. Lotus 1-2-3 assigns its spreadsheets the extension .WK1. WordPerfect doesn't require extensions on file names, but you can set up your own extension system.

For example, if you assign the extension .RPT to all your reports and store them in one directory (called DOCS in this example), you can set up a Quick List entry for all your reports. Use *Reports* as the descriptive name and give the file name as **c:\wpwin\docs*.rpt.** Do this for different types of documents, and you'll have fast access to them through your Quick List. For instance, you could use a client's initials as an extension for all documents pertaining to that client or you could abbreviate a project's name to three letters.

Changing the default directory.   At the bottom of the Open File dialog box is a tiny box that says "Change Default Dir." If you keep that box checked, each time you look in a different directory that directory becomes the default directory. (The default directory is the one in which WordPerfect automatically saves and opens files.) Keep that "Change Default Dir" box unchecked if, like most folks, you don't want to change the default directory each time you look into a different directory.

The Quick List lets you see what's in files.   WordPerfect for Windows has a great View feature that lets you look at the contents of any file. If you're upgrading from DOS WordPerfect, you'll remember this as the Look feature in List Files. Well, List Files is now a stand-alone program called the File Manager (see Chapter 6, "Tricks for Managing Your Documents"), but you can look in files without using the File Manager.

To see how the View feature works, choose Open from the File menu or click the Open button. You'll see a Quick List. If you don't, check the Quick List box. If you haven't customized your Quick List to show the files you use most frequently, it will show just the standard types of files, like Documents, Graphics files and so forth. Click on a name in the Quick List to open it; then click on a file name under Files on the left. Then—here's the magic—click View to see what's in the file (see Figure 2-5).

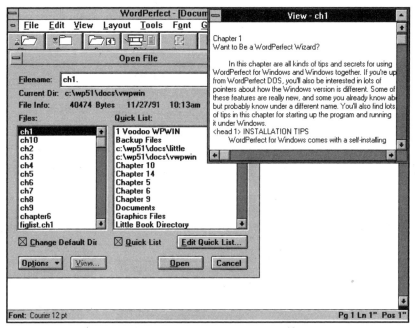

Figure 2-5: Use the View feature in the Quick List to view
file contents.

You can view graphics files with the Quick List, too. The
Quick List's View feature is a great way to review graphic
images you've stored on disk, because you can see what's in them—
in color, too!

USING THE CLIPBOARD

The Clipboard is a special area that Windows provides for temporarily storing the last thing you cut or copied. To see what's currently on
the Clipboard, go out to Windows and open the Program Manager's
Main group. Then just double-click on the Clipboard's icon. You
can paste what's on the Clipboard into your WordPerfect documents
or into any other Windows program.

Use the Clipboard to bring in graphics.   You can select a graphic in another program, copy it and paste it in your WordPerfect documents. You can copy and paste spreadsheet data, text, database records—whatever you like—from one Windows program to another. (To see how to copy from a non-Windows program, read Chapter 9, "Desktop Publishing Sorcery.")

Whatever you cut or copy replaces what's on the Clipboard.   The Clipboard normally holds one item at a time. Whatever you've most recently cut or copied replaces what was on the Clipboard before. See the next trick for a way around that, though.

Use Append on the Edit menu to append selections to the Clipboard.   If you select text or graphics in a document, you'll see that the Append command on the Edit menu becomes available. (If nothing's selected, it's dimmed.) Choosing Append *adds* a copy of the selected text or graphics to the Clipboard instead of replacing what's already there. You can use this feature to assemble selections to paste into WordPerfect documents or other Windows programs.

Don't confuse appending to the Clipboard with appending documents to each other.   To append text or graphics to the end of an existing document, select the text or graphics and choose Save from the File menu. You can also create a new file with Append. Click on the name of the file you want to append the selection to, or type in the new file name in the Save As box. When you click Save, you'll be asked whether you want to overwrite the existing file or append the selection to it.

You can "build" documents this way, by selecting paragraphs and appending them to files. It's sort of the reverse of retrieving documents that already exist into the document you're working on.

You don't have to do anything special to send selections to the Clipboard. Whatever you copy or cut goes to the Clipboard. Whatever you delete with the Delete or Backspace keys doesn't.

Cutting, copying and pasting shortcuts. Windows has a set of keyboard shortcuts for cutting, copying and pasting that are common to all Windows programs. Press Shift+Del to Cut, Ctrl+Ins to Copy, and Shift+Ins to Paste. The Cut and Paste shortcuts are easy to remember because they shift things from one place to another.

WordPerfect has its own mnemonic set of keyboard shortcuts for these operations, and they're a lot easier to remember. You can use them in WordPerfect and in some other Windows programs. Press Ctrl+X to Cut, Ctrl+C to Copy and Ctrl+V to Paste.

MAGIC SHORTCUTS

WordPerfect for Windows gives you several different ways to do just about everything, so you're going to learn shortcuts throughout this book. This chapter focuses on a few tricks for very basic operations, like selecting from menus and using dialog boxes. Chapter 4, "Editing Alchemy," shows you lots more shortcuts for moving through your documents, selecting text and so forth.

MOUSE SHORTCUTS

You can do all sorts of things in WordPerfect for Windows with the mouse. In fact, there are a few things you *can't* do without it, like using the Button Bar and the Ruler. Following are the basic mouse tricks (you've seen a few of these in Chapter 1).

Double-click in a window's title bar to make it full-screen size. If you've made a window less than full-screen size, just double-click its title bar to blow it up to fill the whole screen again.

Double-click in a window's Control icon to close the window.
This is much faster than opening the Control menu and
choosing Close. Of course, you can also use the keyboard shortcut
Ctrl+F4.

Click a window's Restore icon to make it smaller than full-
screen size.   When a window fills the whole screen, clicking
on its Restore icon (the one with the double arrowheads) will make
it smaller than full-screen size. This is useful for seeing what may be
buried under a window.

More mouse shortcuts.   Here are more hidden mouse shortcuts. Double-click on a word to select it, click three times to
select a sentence, or click four times to select a whole paragraph.

Look at Figure 2-6. You can click in the tiny area just below or
above the scroll bar to open a Reveal Codes window. Just drag the
line to make the window as large or as small as you want it.

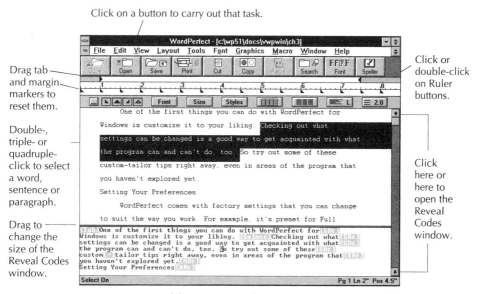

Figure 2-6: Hidden mouse shortcuts.

On the Ruler, just drag a tab icon to move a tab setting. Drag it completely off the Ruler to delete it. Drag one of the other kinds of tabs to set a decimal, center or right-aligned tab.

To set a tab with a dot leader, click on the dot leader icon (the one with ...) and then drag the kind of tab you want to the position you want it.

Drag the right and left margin markers to reset the right and left margins. They're preset at one inch each.

To reset top and bottom margins, double-click on a right or left margin marker. Then enter the new top and bottom margins that you want.

And, of course, you can click or double-click on all the boxes on the Ruler. Clicking once usually has one effect and clicking twice usually brings up a dialog box.

You'll see many more formatting shortcuts in Chapter 5, "Formatting Secrets."

KEYBOARD SHORTCUTS

The most basic of all keyboard shortcuts are the mnemonic shortcuts built into the WordPerfect for Windows program. Press Alt and the first letter of a menu's name to open that menu. For example, pressing Alt+F opens the File menu. Once the menu is displayed, you can type the underlined letter to carry out the command; pressing Alt+F and typing **O** (either uppercase or lowercase will do) selects the File menu and chooses Open.

But there are lots of other keyboard shortcuts, too—probably more than you care to know about. And they're different, depending on whether you're using the Windows-style (CUA) keyboard or the DOS-style (WordPerfect 5.1) keyboard. (By the way, to switch keyboards, choose Preferences from the File menu; then click Keyboards. Click Select and choose WPDOS51.WWK to use the DOS-style keyboard.)

Different kinds of keyboard shortcuts. You've already seen how the mnemonic shortcuts work. There are also function key shortcuts normally listed on the menus. (Well, some are; others are hidden, as you'll see later.) In addition, some Ctrl key shortcuts let you bypass the menu system. For example, Ctrl+P prints the document that's on the screen without any prompting or filling out of dialog boxes.

The Ctrl-key shortcuts are the same on both keyboards. You can use the following shortcuts on either the standard or the DOS-style keyboard:

Command	Shortcut
Copy	Ctrl+C
Bold	Ctrl+B
Line Draw	Ctrl+D
Justify Full	Ctrl+F
Go To	Ctrl+G
Italics	Ctrl+I
Justify Center	Ctrl+J
Justify Left	Ctrl+L
Normal Font	Ctrl+N
Print	Ctrl+P
Justify Right	Ctrl+R
Underline	Ctrl+U
Size	Ctrl+S
Paste	Ctrl+V
WP Characters	Ctrl+W
Cut	Ctrl+X
Undo	Ctrl+Z

Some Ctrl-key shortcuts can't be used if you've opened a menu. If you've opened a menu and there's a shortcut listed on it, use it. Don't use the Ctrl-key shortcut. For example, if you're displaying the Edit menu, WordPerfect wants you to use Shift+Del to cut, not Ctrl+X. The Ctrl-key shortcuts are designed to bypass the menu system.

You can choose not to display the menu shortcuts on the menus. If you don't use keyboard shortcuts and don't want to be reminded of them, go to the Preferences menu (it's on the File menu), choose Environment and uncheck the Shortcut Keys box.

 Don't try to memorize all these shortcuts! Most of the time, you won't use all of these shortcuts. (And there are even more of them, too!) But if you do something frequently, you'll appreciate a shortcut for it. Come back to these tables whenever you find you'd like to learn more ways to bypass the menu system. If there's no shortcut available, or if you don't like the one that's available, you can set up your own. See Chapter 3, "Customizing WordPerfect," which shows you how to edit your keyboard.

 Shortcuts for the File menu.

Command	CUA Keyboard	DOS Keyboard
New	Shift+F4	
Open	F4	Shift+F10
Close	Ctrl+F4	F7
Save	Shift+F3	F10
Save As	F3	F10
File Manager	Alt+F, F	F5
Preferences	Ctrl+Shift+F1	Shift+F1
Print	F5	Shift+F7
Print Preview	Shift+F5	Alt+Shift+F7
Exit	Alt+F4	F7

Shortcuts for the Edit menu.

Command	CUA Keyboard	DOS Keyboard
Undo	Alt+Backspace	Alt+Backspace
Undelete	Alt+Shift +Backspace	Alt+Shift +Backspace, or F3
Cut	Shift+Del	Shift+Del
Copy	Ctrl+Ins	Ctrl+Ins
Paste	Shift+Ins	Shift+Ins
Search	F2	F2
Search Next	Shift+F2	Shift+F2
Search Prev	Alt+F2	Alt+Shift+F2
Replace	Ctrl+F2	Alt+F2
GoTo	Ctrl+G	Ctrl+G or Ctrl+Home

 Shortcuts for the View menu.

Command	CUA Keyboard	DOS Keyboard
Ruler	Alt+Shift+F3	
Reveal Codes	Alt+F3	Alt+F3

Shortcuts for the Layout menu.

Command	CUA Keyboard	DOS Keyboard
Layout		Alt+F7, Ctrl+F7 or Shift+F8
Line	Shift+F9	Shift+F8
Center	Shift+F7	Shift+F6
Flush Right	Alt+F7	Alt+F6
Paragraph		
Indent	F7	F4
Double Indent	Ctrl+Shift+F7	Shift+F4
Hanging Indent	Ctrl+F7	F4 Shift+Tab
Margin Rel	Shift+Tab	Shift+Tab
Page	Alt+F9	Shift+F8 P
Page Break	Ctrl+Enter	Ctrl+Enter
Columns	Alt+Shift+F9	Alt+F7 C
Tables	Ctrl+F9	Alt+F7 T
Document	Ctrl+Shift+F9	Shift+F8 D
Footnote		Ctrl+F7 F
Endnote		Ctrl+F7 E
Margins	Ctrl+F8	Shift+F8 M
Styles	Alt+F8	Alt+F8

Shortcuts for the Tools Menu.

Command	CUA Keyboard	DOS Keyboard
Tools menu		Shift+F5 or Ctrl+F9
Speller	Ctrl+F1	Ctrl+F2
Thesaurus	Alt+F1	
Date		
Text	Ctrl+F5	
Code	Ctrl+Shift+F5	
Outline		
Paragraph #	Alt+F5	
Define	Alt+Shift+F5	
Sort	Ctrl+Shift+F12	
Merge	Ctrl+F12	Shift+F9
End Field	Alt+Enter	Alt+Enter or F9
End Rec	Alt+Shift+Enter	Alt+Shift+Enter
Mark Text	F12	Alt+F5
Define	Shift+F12	
Generate	Alt+F12	Alt+Shift+F5
Line Draw	Ctrl+D	

 Shortcuts for the Font menu.

Command	CUA Keyboard	DOS Keyboard
Font	F9	Ctrl+F8
Normal	Ctrl+N	Ctrl+N
Bold	Ctrl+B	Ctrl+B
Italic	Ctrl+I	Ctrl+I
Underline	Ctrl+U	Ctrl+U
Size	Ctrl+S	Ctrl+S
WP Characters	Ctrl+W	Ctrl+W

Shortcuts for the Graphics menu.

Command	CUA Keyboard	DOS Keyboard
Graphics	Alt+G	Alt+F9
Figure		
Retrieve	F11	
Edit	Shift+F11	
Text Box		
Create	Alt+F11	
Edit	Alt+Shift+F11	
Line		
Horizontal	Ctrl+F11	
Vertical	Ctrl+Shift+F11	

 Shortcuts for the Macro menu.

Command	CUA Keyboard	DOS Keyboard
Play	Alt+F10	Alt+F10
Record	Ctrl+F10	Ctrl+F10
Stop	Ctrl+Shift+F10	Ctrl+Shift+F10

 Shortcuts for the Help menu.

Command	CUA Keyboard	DOS Keyboard
Help	F1 for index	F3
	Alt+H for menu	

 Get Help on keyboard shortcuts. To get help on keyboard shortcuts, choose Keyboards from the Help menu. It shows you the template for both keyboards and lists the Alt-key combinations, Ctrl-key combinations and so forth.

Instead of learning keyboard shortcuts, make a button. You can make a button for any menu item—it's even more magical than memorizing keyboard shortcuts. Chapter 3 has plenty of tips about making buttons.

DIALOG BOX TRICKS

A basic way Windows operates is through dialog boxes. These are special boxes that request additional information that the program needs to do what you ask it to. Any time you choose a menu item that has an ellipsis (. . .) next to it, you'll get a dialog box.

You'll find several different kinds of dialog boxes in WordPerfect for Windows: list boxes (which you see when you choose Open, for example), text boxes (in which you type text) and check boxes (in which you can choose several options). Dialog boxes also have command buttons that you choose (like Close, Cancel and OK) and radio buttons that let you pick from a list of features. See Figure 2-7 for a typical dialog box that contains most of these boxes and buttons. We'll look at tricks for using them in this section.

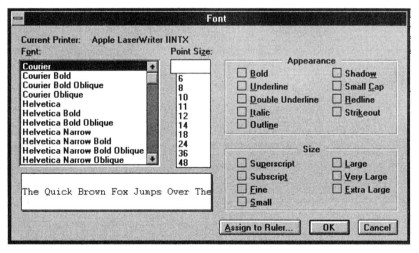

Figure 2-7: Dialog boxes let you perform all sorts of neat tricks.

Moving in dialog boxes. You can just click with the mouse to move from area to area in dialog boxes. If you'd rather use the keyboard, Tab moves you from area to area; Shift+Tab moves you backward.

The selection cursor in dialog boxes. You can tell which area of a dialog box you're in by looking for the selection cursor. It's the dotted text or highlighted rectangle that indicates where you are. Sometimes it looks like a regular insertion point.

Press Esc to cancel a dialog box. To get out of a dialog box without making any selections, even if you've already filled out the box, just press Esc or click Cancel.

WordPerfect DOS keyboard shortcuts don't work in dialog boxes. Even if you choose the DOS-style keyboard, dialog boxes don't use any shortcuts that you're used to. You have to use the Windows-style shortcuts in dialog boxes.

Double-click to choose an item and close a dialog box at the same time. Lots of dialog boxes, like the Open and Font dialog boxes, let you double-click on an item to select it and to close the dialog box at the same time.

Quick selecting in list boxes. In a list, type the first letter of an item's name to move directly to it. The trick is to make the list part of the dialog box active first. For example, if you're looking at the Open File dialog box (see Figure 2-8), type Alt+I or click in the area under Files to make the list active; then you can type the first few letters of a file name to go to it directly.

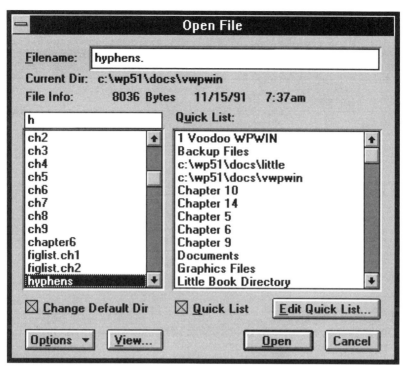

Figure 2-8: There's a hidden speed-select feature in list boxes: just type the first few characters of a file name to go to it.

Just press Enter to choose the default option. In many dialog boxes, you'll see "three-dimensional" buttons that have a darker outline around them. This is the default choice, the one the program is preset to carry out if you don't choose anything else. If you just press Enter, you accept that default choice. You don't have to reach for the mouse and click on it.

Grayed items aren't available. Grayed menu choices and buttons in dialog boxes can't be used at this time. You probably have to select text or do something else before you can use them.

You can cut, copy and paste in text boxes. WordPerfect for Windows lets you cut, copy and paste in a lot more places than WordPerfect DOS did. For example, if you want to put text into a text box, like the Search text box, just copy it from your document and paste it in the box.

Selecting text in text boxes. To select a word that's in a text box, double-click on it. Drag over the text with the mouse to select more than one word.

To replace highlighted text in a text box, just type over it. You don't have to delete text in a text box before you replace it. If the text is highlighted, just type over it. A very hot tip.

No mouse? Here's how to check a box. If you don't have a mouse (say *what?*), use the space bar to make checks in check boxes. You can usually check more than one check box in a group. If an item's checked, there's an X in the box next to it.

You can only select one radio button at a time. Unlike check boxes, only one radio button can be selected in a group.

Hidden pop-up lists. There are hidden lists that appear when you choose a pop-up button. These buttons are usually marked by a triangle, like the Options button in Figure 2-9. Once you've displayed a list, you have to hold the mouse button down to keep it displayed.

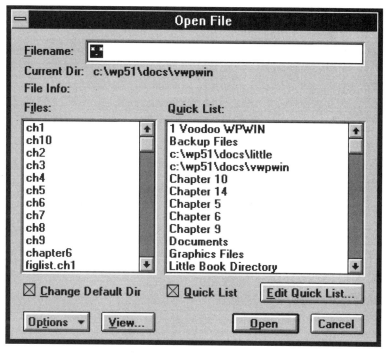

Figure 2-9: Click on the Options button to display the hidden pop-up list.

Sometimes you'll also see a downward-pointing arrow next to a text box. If you click on the arrow (in Figure 2-10, it's next to the Format text box), you'll see a list that you can make additional choices from.

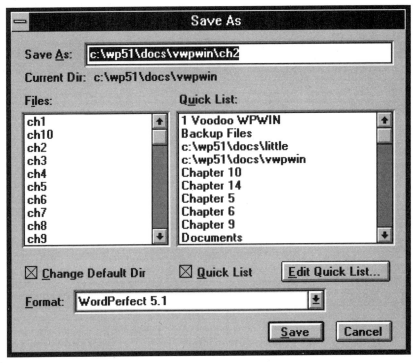

Figure 2-10: Downward-pointing arrows like the one next to the Format text box hide lists, too.

No mouse? Here's how to work pop-up lists. Press Tab to move to the pop-up list; then use the space bar to open it and the arrow keys to move through it.

Keeping your hands on the keyboard. It can be very frustrating to have to stop typing and reach for the mouse just so you can fill out a dialog box, especially if you're a touch typist. Here are some magic ways to work dialog boxes with your hands on the keyboard. You've seen some of these already, but here's a handy list to help you type your way through dialog boxes.

◆ Press Tab or Shift+Tab to move from area to area in a dialog box.
◆ Press Alt and type the underlined letter to select an underlined choice.

- Type the first letter of an item in a list to move directly to it. (Use Tab to move to lists, check boxes, radio buttons and pop-up lists.)
- Press the space bar to turn a check box off or on.
- Use the Down Arrow or Up Arrow keys to turn a radio button off or on.
- Press Alt+Down Arrow or Alt+Up Arrow to open a pop-up list.
- Press Enter to choose OK and to close the dialog box.

MISCELLANEOUS BASIC TRICKS & TRAPS

Defying categorization, the following tricks are still basic to most of the work you do.

The status bar measures from the edge of the paper, not from the margins.   The cryptic "Ln" and "Pos" on the status bar stand for "Line" and "Position." Lines are measured from the top of the invisible paper you're using (the page size) and the position is the amount of space, in inches, from the left edge of the paper, not from the left margin.

You can override the units of measurement that are in effect.   WordPerfect's factory settings use inches as the standard unit of measurement. You can use centimeters, points ($^1/_{72}$ inch) or "WordPerfect units" ($^1/_{1200}$ of an inch, useful only if you need to fine-tune the placement of graphics).

Use the Preferences menu (see Chapter 3, "Customizing Word-Perfect") to change the standard units of measurement. But to override the standard units, just enter a measurement followed by " or **i** for inches (if you've switched to another standard), **p** for points, **c** for centimeters or **w** for WordPerfect units. For example, entering **10c** tells the program "ten centimeters," no matter what unit of measurement is in effect.

Don't bother calculating decimal equivalents. When you enter measurements, just enter them in the form of fractions (like $7/8$) and WordPerfect will figure out the decimal for you. So don't waste your time.

Want to see the Ruler all the time? Go to the Preferences menu (it's on the File menu), select Environment and check the Automatic Ruler Display box. That way, the Ruler will always be there when you open a new document.

Get Help when you need it. Just press F1 to get context-sensitive help, which is help about whatever the program senses you're doing. For example, if you've opened the Fonts dialog box, F1 gives you help on fonts.

Use What-Is Help, too. There's a new kind of help in Word Perfect for Windows, called *What-Is Help*. This is the help to use if you want to know what a mysterious icon or button is for. Instead of pressing F1 for Help, press Shift+F1. The mouse pointer will switch to a question mark and you can click on any item that you want help on.

A hidden secret of What-Is Help is that you can find out what a key combination does just by pressing that combination. For example, to find out what Alt+Backspace does, first press Shift+F1 or choose What-Is from the Help menu. Then press Alt+Backspace. You'll get a Help window about the Undo feature, which is what Alt+Backspace does.

The program doesn't always guess right about what you want help on. It's often better to use the Help Index if you know the name of the topic that you want help on. Instead of pressing F1, press Alt+H or choose Help Index from the Help menu.

Use the Back and Browse buttons. While you're in the Help system, don't forget the Back and Browse buttons. Browse gets you related topics, and Back takes you to the Help screens you looked at previously.

There are hidden pop-ups in Help. Words that have dotted lines under them are actually *pop-up definitions* (see Figure 2-11). Click on one and a screen will pop up, defining the term for you.

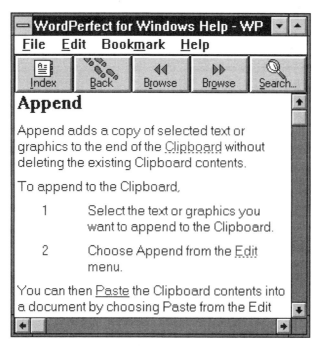

Figure 2-11: Terms that are underlined or have dotted lines under them are hidden pop-ups.

Words that are underlined are *jump topics*. If you click on one, you'll go straight to a help screen on that topic.

It's usually faster to search for a Help topic than to use the Index. The Help system has its own Search feature that's much faster to use than scrolling through the list of Help topics in the Index. If you don't know the exact name of what you need help on, click Search instead of using the Index. The Help system will list phrases and key words that you can search for (see Figure 2-12), and you can type your own guesses about what a feature's called until you can find some help on it. WordPerfect does have its own special vocabulary, and it may take some guessing to figure out that a form letter is actually called a primary file, for example.

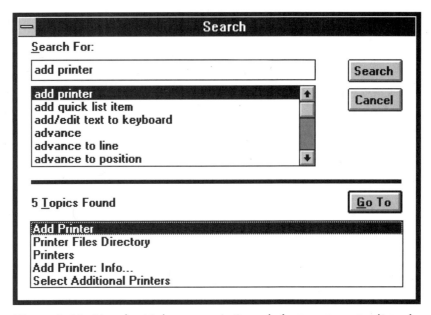

Figure 2-12: Use the Help system's Search feature to get a list of key words you can search for.

You can create custom Help. There's more hidden Help magic. Help has its own Edit menu, with Copy and Annotate commands. Choose Copy to put a copy of the Help topic you're reading onto the Clipboard. Once it's on the Clipboard, you can paste it into a document window and change it to suit yourself, adding details about your particular situation or deleting long stretches of text you already know about.

And you can annotate Help, too. If there are topics that you want to make notes on, choose Annotate. Then just type your notes into the space provided (see Figure 2-13). When you finish and click OK, a tiny paper clip will appear next to the Help topic to remind you that you've annotated it.

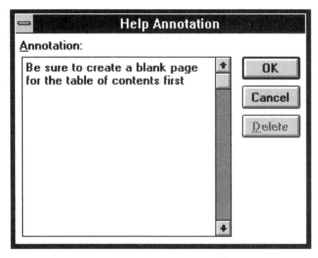

Figure 2-13: You can annotate Help topics.

This trick is a great way to remind yourself about procedures you don't do very often, such as setting up a table of contents. You can even annotate the Help topic to remind yourself of what you always tend to forget. For instance, I always forget to create a separate page for the table of contents before generating it, so that it doesn't run together with the first page of text.

MOVING ON

This chapter explored a lot of basic WordPerfect for Windows tricks, enough to help you get some voodoo out of the program. But even though you passed Magic 101, you've only scratched the surface. In Chapter 4, "Editing Alchemy," we'll look at editing tips; in Chapter 5, "Formatting Secrets," you'll conjure up some formatting magic. But Chapter 3 digresses to show you how to tailor WordPerfect to suit your particular needs.

Customizing WordPerfect

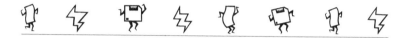

O ne of the first things you can do with Word Perfect for Windows is customize it to your liking. Checking out what settings can be changed is a good way to get acquainted with what the program can and can't do. So don't be afraid to try some of these customizing tips right away, even in areas of the program you haven't explored yet.

Of course, you don't *have* to change any settings at all in order to use WordPerfect. You can just go ahead and use it exactly as it comes out of the box. But you'll probably want to make WordPerfect conform to your preferences and work habits.

SETTING YOUR PREFERENCES

WordPerfect comes with default settings you can change to suit the way you work. For example, it's preset for full justification, which means that text is evenly spaced between the left and right margins and aligns along both of them for a nice "square" look. I don't like that. I like to have text aligned on the left margin (left justified) and uneven on the right, often called "ragged right."

Other things you can change include the time that elapses between automatic backups, where your files are stored, the units of measure the program uses and so forth. All these settings can be changed by using the Preferences menu (on the File menu).

Instead of going down the Preferences menu item by item, I'll just give you a sampling of some of the tricks you can pull, since after all these will be *your* personal preferences.

Press Ctrl+Shift+F1 to get the Preferences menu.   Here's an undocumented keyboard shortcut. (At least, it's not listed on the menu.) Instead of choosing File and then Preferences, just press Ctrl+Shift+F1 to bring up the Preferences menu directly. On the DOS-style keyboard, the shortcut is Shift+F1.

Set up a logical filing system through the Location of Files dialog box.   The installation program, if you did a Basic install, decided you wanted most of your files in a directory named C:\WPWIN. That directory can get very, very cluttered if you put all your document files in it.

My advice is to keep document files in a separate directory, perhaps named C:\WPWIN\DOCS, and to make separate subdirectories under that for specialized documents like letters, reports and invoices. Or you could keep client files in separate subdirectories or organize your files by project. Use a scheme that lets you keep track of where your files are. Believe me, if you put everything in C:\WPWIN, you'll get tired of looking in that huge directory all the time, and it will be hard to find things.

Having documents in separate directories also makes backups easier. I keep files in subdirectories by project, and since I normally work on only one project a day, I can easily make a backup of my daily work on a floppy disk: I just copy the files in the current directory that have the current date. (See Chapter 6, "Tricks for Managing Your Documents," for details on using the File Manager for things like this.)

If you use both WordPerfect DOS and WordPerfect for Windows, remember that their documents are interchangeable. See Chapter 1 for tips about setting up a mutual directory structure for them.

Create a directory in the Location of Files dialog box.
You don't have to go out to the File Manager or to DOS to create a new directory when you're in the Location of Files dialog box in WordPerfect for Windows (see Figure 3-1). Just type the path name to the new directory you want to create in any of the text boxes. (I know this was mentioned in the upgrading tips in Chapter 1, but you may have missed it, and it sure does save time.)

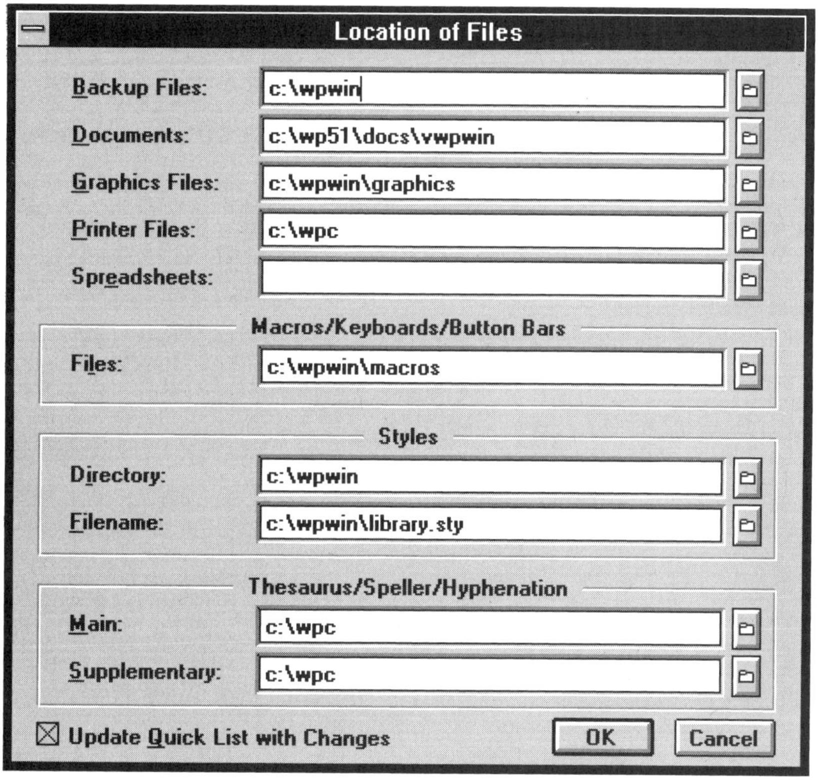

Location of Files		
Backup Files:	c:\wpwin	
Documents:	c:\wp51\docs\vwpwin	
Graphics Files:	c:\wpwin\graphics	
Printer Files:	c:\wpc	
Spreadsheets:		
Macros/Keyboards/Button Bars		
Files:	c:\wpwin\macros	
Styles		
Directory:	c:\wpwin	
Filename:	c:\wpwin\library.sty	
Thesaurus/Speller/Hyphenation		
Main:	c:\wpc	
Supplementary:	c:\wpc	

☒ Update Quick List with Changes   [OK] [Cancel]

Figure 3-1: Set up directories for your documents in the Location of Files dialog box.

Keep Update Quick List checked. If you change a directory name listed in the Location of Files dialog box, be sure to keep the Update Quick List with Changes box checked. That way, the program automatically updates the path for directories on your Quick List, if you change them in the Location of Files dialog box.

Set the right interval for backups. If you live in an area where the power goes out often, set a short interval between timed backups. WordPerfect for Windows's factory settings are for backups every 20 minutes, but I wouldn't want to lose 20 minutes of work. I set mine for 5 minutes, which is about all I can remember of what I've typed.

Timed backups aren't backups. Don't think you can get away with not making backups just because WordPerfect for Windows has an "automatic backup" feature. Automatic backup files are just duplicates of what you've been working on. Say the power goes out. The next time you start WordPerfect you'll be asked whether you want to open, rename or delete the backup files of your work. If you think that the backup is more recent than your last-saved version, open it, compare it and, if it's more recent, save it with the same name as the last-saved version. If it's not more up-to-date, close it without saving it. You could also choose Rename and give the automatic backup file a name that lets you know it's a copy, so you can check it later. If you choose Delete, though, it's gone for good.

   But if your hard disk crashes and you haven't made real backups (copies on a separate disk, stored preferably in another location), those automatic backups will go down with your hard disk. So make backups on floppy disks or backup tape drives of the work you want to keep. Those hard disks aren't immortal; I've gone through a few of them myself.

Original backups and timed backups aren't the same.
   Original backups are duplicates of the previous version of a document. Think of them as the father generation whose child version you're saving now. The child version is the one that's usually overwritten when you save a document under the same name.

If you check the Original Document Backup box, WordPerfect makes a duplicate of the previous version of your document (but with the extension .BK!) every time you save a document. So you can get that previous version back if you have to. If that's important for the kind of work you do—if you need to be able to get a previous version of a document back because a committee has changed its mind, for example (these things *do* happen)—turn this feature on, because it's normally off.

By the way, original backups aren't real backups, either. They'll crash with your hard disk, too.

How can you tell original backup files from timed backup files? Timed backup files follow the pattern WP{WP}.BK*n*, where *n* is the number of the document window. So if your power went out and you're looking for the backup of the document that was in the Document 4 window, it will be named WP{WP}.BK4. (You'll probably need to view all of these cryptically named backup files in a Quick List window to tell which is which.) Do yourself a favor and keep backup files in a separate directory (use the Preferences menu's Location of Files dialog box) so you can locate them easily if you ever need them.

Don't uncheck Allow Undo in the Environment Settings dialog box. Environment settings are preset and are usually just fine. They control things like when the program beeps at you and so forth (see Figure 3-2). If you experiment with changing any of these settings, be sure to keep Allow Undo checked, or you won't be able to use WordPerfect for Window's neat Undo feature that lets you change your mind about something you just did. (For instance, you can undo a Search and Replace.)

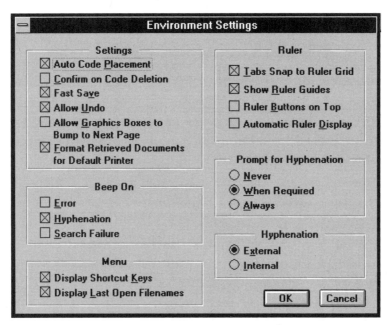

Figure 3-2: Keep Allow Undo checked if you want to use the Undo feature.

Auto Code Placement may confuse you. Auto Code Placement is a new feature in WordPerfect for Windows. If you're upgrading from WordPerfect DOS, be aware that Auto Code Placement makes the program work differently.

When Auto Code Placement is on, many format settings, such as margin changes and tabs, go into effect at the beginning of the paragraph or page in which you make the change instead of where the insertion point is. If you change fonts, though, this doesn't happen: font changes are made exactly where the insertion point is.

Keep Fast Save checked if you usually print from the screen. Keep Fast Save checked if you usually print the document that's displayed on the screen instead of specifying a file name to print a document that's stored on disk but isn't open. Uncheck Fast Save if you normally print from disk. You'll print faster.

When Fast Save is checked, WordPerfect doesn't check the document's format every time you save. If Fast Save is unchecked, the program checks all the formatting before it saves the document—so documents saved on disk are ready to print.

Use a horizontal scroll bar if you need one. In the Display Settings dialog box, choose a horizontal scroll bar if you normally use a small point size and the entire line of type isn't visible all at once on the screen. That way, it's easy to scroll over and see the rest of the line.

If you don't want to have to constantly scroll to see the entire line, type your documents in a point size bigger than the one you plan to print in. You can switch to a smaller point size just before you print.

Use a paragraph symbol as a hard return character. Some typists prefer to see a special character on the screen every time the Enter key is pressed for a hard return. The favorite symbol seems to be the paragraph symbol (¶), but it's a little tricky to get that symbol in the Hard Return Character Display As box. First click the Display As box. Then press Ctrl+W to bring up the WordPerfect Characters dialog box. Click on the arrowhead under Sets and choose Typographic Symbols from the pull-down menu. Click on the paragraph symbol and choose Insert and Close.

Draft mode is a little faster. In Draft mode, WordPerfect for Windows runs a little faster than it does in the normal graphics WYSIWYG mode. If you have lots of columns, graphics or tables in a document, you may want to switch to Draft mode (choose it from the View menu) while you work in one of these documents.

It also speeds things up a little to turn off Auto Redisplay in Draft mode so WordPerfect won't rewrite the screen each time you make changes.

Customize Draft mode colors.   If you find that you're working in Draft mode very often, you can go to the Display Settings dialog box and click on Draft Mode Colors to choose different colors for italics, bold and so forth. There are sets of default colors for different types of computers, such as laptops with LCD displays. To see them, click next to Predefined Display Colors.

You can change the color sets by clicking on the buttons for appearance and sizes and then clicking on the color buttons. If you get all mixed up, choose Reset to put things back the way they were.

There's no way to make Draft mode the default.   Even if you want to make Draft mode the default so WordPerfect for Windows always starts in character-based mode, you can't. So don't spend a lot of time trying to figure out how. You can record a macro that switches to Draft mode and executes it when you start Word-Perfect, though (see "Playing a macro every time WordPerfect starts," in Chapter 10).

WordPerfect Corporation may issue interim releases of Word-Perfect for Windows that will let you set Draft mode as the default. If this feature is important to you, call them and see if they have.

You can change the Reveal Codes colors.   To customize your Reveal Codes screen, click Reveal Codes Colors in the Display Settings dialog box and change the colors used for the cursor, codes and text. You can also change the background and foreground colors for each setting.

Initial Codes can cause confusion.   What are initial codes? Well, they're formatting codes you insert in the Initial Codes window (see Figure 3-3). Once you put these codes in the Initial Codes part of the Preferences menu, they affect every document you create from then on.

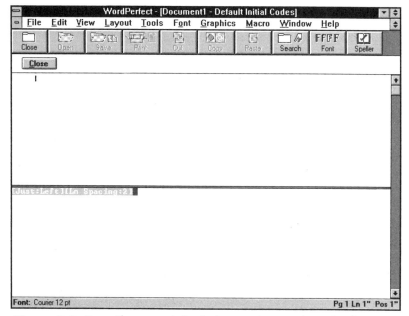

Figure 3-3: Specify your default formatting settings in the
Initial Codes window.

Say, for example, that you want all your documents to be double
spaced. Instead of changing the line spacing each time you begin a
new document, just put the code for double spacing in the Initial
Codes window: click on the Line Spacing icon on the Ruler and
choose 2. The code appears in the Initial Codes window, beneath the
line, just as if it were in a Reveal Codes screen.

You can do this for any format setting you want to apply to all of
your documents. For example, you can choose a base font, change
margins or line spacing, choose how text is justified and so on. To
override these settings, just choose new ones.

You can't put text in the Initial Codes window, just codes.

Now, here's the initial codes secret: they don't show up in the
Reveal Codes screen. (Maybe a better name for initial codes is hidden codes.) This can truly make you crazy if you've forgotten that
you set an initial code and you're looking in the Reveal Codes window to see what codes are in effect. If something isn't formatted the
way you think it should be, check your Initial Codes window.

It gets more complicated. If you create a document with a set of initial codes, it retains those codes when you open it later, even if you've changed to another set of initial codes. So if you're swapping documents back and forth with Mary and Joe and they're using different initial codes, you may have to do some "local" formatting at your own computer to get things looking the way you want.

Document Initial Codes are different than Preferences Initial Codes. The initial codes you choose by selecting Document from the Layout menu aren't the same as the initial codes you set on the Preferences menu. The ones you set in the Preferences menu affect all the new documents you create; the ones you set in the Layout menu affect just the current document. (Be warned: these codes don't show up in the Reveal Codes window, either.)

Personally, I know of no reason to use Document Initial codes unless you're doing mail merge. WordPerfect Corporation says that the option exists to keep the Reveal Codes screen from getting too cluttered, but it also keeps you from seeing which codes are really in effect. Also, WordPerfect for Windows very tidily cleans up excess codes, unlike its predecessors, which stacked them all up, including the ones not in effect any more, and your Reveal Codes screen no longer gets cluttered that way. So why bother with Document Initial Codes at all? (There *are* a couple of tricks you can do with them when you do a merge operation, as you'll see in Chapter 7.)

The Reveal Codes window has no permanent setting. Unfortunately for those of you who like to work with the Reveal Codes window always open, there's no permanent setting you can tweak to keep that window always open to a certain size.

But you can drag just above or below the scroll bar to open it, or press Alt+F3, or make a button for it.

To insert the time as well as the date, set up a custom style. When you choose Date from the Tools menu, you can insert the current date in your document. Some offices use a time stamp on documents as well as a date stamp, but you may not want to format the date and time every time you choose Date. Use the Document Date/Time Format dialog box (see Figure 3-4) to set up a custom format for your time and date stamp.

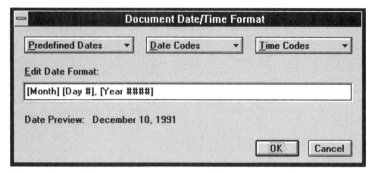

Figure 3-4: Set your custom date/time stamp here.

THE AMAZING BUTTON BAR

Imagine being able to carry out a sequence of complicated tasks just by clicking on an icon. WordPerfect for Windows lets you do just that, if you add custom buttons to the Button Bar. In fact, if you can do it in WordPerfect for Windows, you can record it as a macro; if you can record it as a macro, you can assign it to a button. You can make just about any task, complicated or simple, into a button that you can click on with the mouse. It's magic.

The program comes with several different Button Bars, such as the main Button Bar (if it's not on your screen, choose Button Bar from the View menu); a Print Preview Button Bar; a different one in the Equation Editor; a table Button Bar for editing tables; and another specialized Button Bar in the Figure Editor.

You can make completely new Button Bars as well as edit the ones that are already there.

You need a mouse to use a Button Bar. Sorry, Button Bars don't work from the keyboard. This is one area of the program where you have to use a mouse.

Create a custom Button Bar by editing an existing one. The main Button Bar already has buttons for all the basic tasks like Save, Open, Print and so forth. If you want some of these tasks on your custom Button Bar, first save the main Button Bar under a different name (choose Button Bar Setup from the View menu; then choose Save As). That way, you can keep the original intact and work on the copy with the different name. Using the copy, delete the buttons you don't want and add new buttons. It's faster than creating a Button Bar from scratch.

Another way of accomplishing the same thing is to choose Select from the Button Bar Setup menu. When you see the list of Button Bars, highlight the one you want to edit. Then, in the Select Button Bar dialog box that appears, make a copy of it under a new name by clicking on the Options button and choosing Copy (see Figure 3-5). You can give the copy a different name and then select that Button Bar to edit.

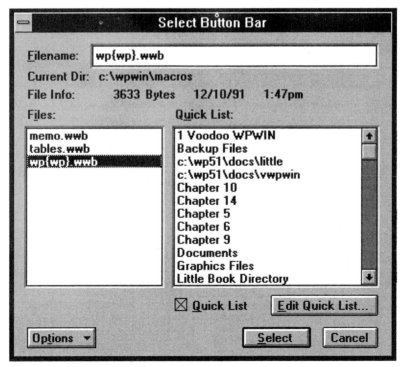

Figure 3-5: Make a copy of a Button Bar by clicking on Options and choosing Copy.

You can't edit all of the Button Bars. You can make duplicates of the main Button Bar (WP{WP}.WWB) and the table Button Bar (TABLES.WWB), but you can't duplicate the Print Preview, Figure Editor or Equation Editor Button Bars. You can edit all of them, though, to add new buttons or remove buttons you don't use.

And, of course, you can make copies of all the Button Bars that you create.

Editing a Button Bar. To edit a Button Bar, choose Button Bar Setup from the View menu. Then choose Edit, and you'll get the Edit Button Bar dialog box (see Figure 3-6).

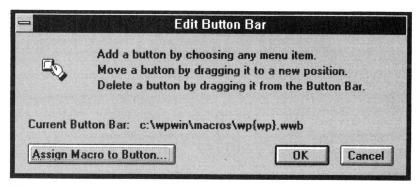

Figure 3-6: Whenever the Edit Button Bar dialog box is open, you can edit the Button Bar.

Once that dialog box is open, you can drag buttons to move them or delete them. The pointer will change to a little hand holding a button. You can also create new buttons, as you'll see in the following tricks.

Creating a Button Bar from scratch. Instead of choosing Edit after you choose Button Bar Setup, as you saw in the previous trick, choose New to create a completely new Button Bar.

Adding a menu item to a Button Bar. To add a menu item as a button, select it with the mouse. You can make a button for anything that doesn't already have a keyboard shortcut.

Click outside the Edit Button Bar dialog box for some special effects. Once you click *outside* the Edit Button Bar dialog box, you can create buttons by pressing function keys and using the mnemonic menu shortcuts. This is the best way to add a button for a menu item that has a right-pointing arrowhead next to it (indicating that another menu will come up if you choose that item). If you click on an item like that to make a button of it, the next menu will come up, and you'll have to make a selection from it. For example, instead of clicking on Preferences in the File menu to make a button that will take you to the Preferences menu, press Alt+F and type **e** (the shortcut for Preferences).

Click OK for your changes to take effect. If you close the Edit Button Bar dialog box without clicking OK, the changes you made to the Button Bar won't be saved. Instead of clicking Cancel if you've added a button you don't want, drag the button off the Button Bar. That way, you can continue editing the Button Bar until you've got it the way you want it. Then click OK.

Assign macros to buttons. You can assign macros to buttons so they'll play back when you click the button. For example, say you've recorded a macro named PARA.WCM that inserts a standard boilerplate paragraph in 10-point Helvetica italics, centered between the right and left margins. Click on Assign Macro to Button to get a dialog box (see Figure 3-7) that shows all the macros in the macros directory (WordPerfect for Windows assigns macro files a .WCM extension). Double-click on the macro's name (in this case, it's PARA.WCM) to make it a button. Click on [..] to go up one level in your directory structure and go back down a different branch until you find the directory where your macros are stored. If you did a Basic installation, they're in C:\WPWIN\MACROS.

If you're keeping macros in your Quick List, check the Quick List box to see it.

For more information about recording and playing macros, see Chapter 10, "The Magic of Macros."

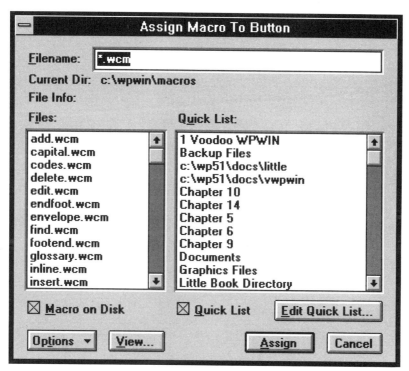

Figure 3-7: Choose a macro from the list of macros you've already recorded.

You can set up a hierarchy of Button Bars with macros.

Now we're getting into some true sorcery. Think about this one. You can have a bunch of Button Bars—say, one for mail merge, another for creating reference aids like indexes and tables of contents, another for boilerplate text and specialized document formats—and, on your main Button Bar, put buttons that take you to each one. To do this, record a macro that selects each different Button Bar and then assign the macro to a button. Then you can just click on your Mail Merge button to bring up the Mail Merge Button Bar you've created. Click on your Special Formats button to get your custom formats Button Bar.

Then—and here's some more magic—on each custom Button Bar include a button that will take you back to the main Button Bar when you're done.

If you edit a macro, add a new button for it. WordPerfect doesn't keep track of changes you make to your macros once you've assigned them to a button. If you edit a macro and want the macro button to reflect the editing changes, be sure to delete the old button for it and add the new one.

Sometimes you have to exit WordPerfect for changes in new buttons to take effect. If your new macro-as-a-button isn't working, exit WordPerfect and start it again. Sometimes there are things that the program has to read before a macro button will take effect, and restarting forces it to read them.

Too many buttons? Here's a trick. As you add buttons to a Button Bar, you'll soon get too many to see all of them at the top of the screen at once. When all the space fills up, you'll see arrows on the right end that you can use to scroll the Button Bar. But there's a neater way to set up a big Button Bar.

Choose Button Bar Setup from the View menu. You'll get the Button Bar Options dialog box, where you can choose different arrangements for your Button Bar—Picture Only, Text Only, Picture and Text and Left, Right, Top and Bottom. Choose Text Only and you'll be able to display a lot more buttons.

Rearrange the buttons. Just drag a button to move it to a new position. You may want to keep frequently used buttons on the right of the bar (or on the left if you're left-handed) so you don't have to move the mouse pointer to the other side of the screen very often.

To delete a button, drag it completely off the Button Bar.

For the maximum amount of buttons, choose Text Only and Left. To cram the most buttons onto your screen, choose Text Only and Left from the Button Bar Options dialog box. You can get about twenty buttons on your screen this way (see Figure 3-8).

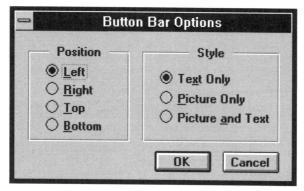

Figure 3-8: The settings Text Only and Left let you see the most buttons on the screen.

Button ideas. You might want to make buttons for the Reveal Codes window, the File Manager, the Ruler (if you turn it off and on a lot) and any dialog box that you use frequently.

Some others, which you'd need to record macros for, might be for setting up special formats (such as a memo or an envelope), marking a selected item for an index or table of contents entry, or starting a mail merge that uses the files you specify.

Remember, anything you record as a macro can be assigned to a button. So make all your favorite macros into buttons, if you can cram them onto your Button Bars (see the previous trick).

You can create Button Bars in the File Manager, too. The File Manager lets you create Button Bars that only work within it. See Chapter 6, "Tricks for Managing Your Documents."

CUSTOMIZE YOUR KEYBOARD

Now for more magic. You can make your own custom keyboard (not a real one, of course: you just modify the real keyboard to work the way you want it to). You can reassign keys to different functions—for example, you can put Help back on the F1 key, like it was in Word-Perfect DOS. In addition, if you take the time, you can make key combinations generate special characters for specialized typing, like foreign-language or mathematical typing.

Don't like using menus? Fine. Assign menu commands to keys. Want to play a macro by pressing a key combination? You can do that, too. Want to type boilerplate text like your letterhead or a standard contract paragraph when you press a key combination? Go right ahead. Here's how.

Edit a copy of a keyboard. You don't want to mess up the original keyboard definitions that came with WordPerfect, so the secret in editing keyboards is to edit a *copy* of a keyboard. That way, you can always get the original back, unchanged.

Choose Keyboard from the Preferences menu, then click Select. You'll see a list of all the existing keyboards. Choose a keyboard that's closest to what you want to use it for. To customize the DOS-style keyboard, for example, highlight WPDOS51.WWK. Click on Options and choose Copy. In the From box, accept the keyboard's original name (WPDOS51.WWK), and in the To box, type the name you want your new keyboard to have (such as NEW.WWK). You'll want to use a name that helps you remember what your new keyboard is for (math, German, Spanish, typographical symbols or whatever). Then click OK.

That brings you back to the Select Keyboard dialog box, where you'll see your new keyboard listed. Highlight its name and click Select. Then click Edit to get the Edit Keyboard dialog box.

Under Item Type, choose what you want to assign to a key combination. (It could be a command, a menu, a macro or text. See the following tips for hints about each.)

Say, for example, you want to assign the command CaseToLower to Ctrl+T so you can convert selected text from uppercase to lowercase just by pressing Ctrl+T. Under Item Type, choose Command, select CaseToLower and press Ctrl+T. Then click Assign.

 Unused key combinations. A great many key combinations are taken, but here are some you can use:

Available Key Combinations	
Ctrl+A	Ctrl+E
Ctrl+H	Ctrl+K
Ctrl+M	Ctrl+O
Ctrl+Q	Ctrl+T
Ctrl+Y	Alt+Shift+Del
Ctrl+Shift+Enter	Ctrl+Shift+Backspace
Alt+Shift+F10	Ctrl+Shift+F8
Ctrl+Shift+F2	Alt+Shift+F1

Assigning a macro to a key combination. The trick here is that you have to record the macro first. After you do that (see Chapter 10, "The Magic of Macros"), select Macro under Item Type and choose Add. You'll get an Import Macro to Keyboard dialog box. Just click on the macros you want to add, and they'll appear in the Assignable Items box.

Assigning text to a key combination. You can assign text to a key combination, too, so that the program will magically type boilerplate text when you press that key combination. The trick here is to follow the same procedure as in the preceding tricks but to choose Text as the item type and click Add. Then give the text a name that describes what it does. After that, you can type the text in the text box (but see the next trick).

Paste text instead of retyping it.   Instead of retyping text, copy it from an existing document and paste it in the Add box; it's much faster than typing it again here. Choose Text as the item type; choose Add; then paste your copied text with Ctrl+V or Shift+Ins. (It's better to use the Ctrl-key shortcuts; they're the same on both the CUA and the DOS-style keyboards!)

Formatting codes aren't included when you assign text to key shortcuts.   Formatting codes aren't copied when you paste text from a document into the Add Text dialog box. If you want to create formatted text, record it and the codes used to format it as a macro. *Then* you can assign that macro to a key shortcut (or to a button, too). Sneaky.

Mapping a special symbol to a key combination.   The trick here is to press Ctrl+W to get the WP Characters dialog box. Then pick the character set that has the symbol. Choose Insert and Close.

It's a little tricky to assign text to keystrokes, so I'll give you a step-by-step example. Say that you want to assign the Greek letter Omega (Ω) to Ctrl+M (a key combination that's not taken). First, choose Preferences from the File menu and select Keyboard. Then select the keyboard you're going to assign the text to and click Edit. Choose Text from the pop-up menu under Assignable Items; click Add. Type a name for your symbol (such as "Omega") and then press Tab to move to the text box. Press Ctrl+W; choose the Greek character set, click on the Omega, and click Insert and Close. Click OK. Highlight the name of the symbol. Then press Ctrl+M (or the keystrokes you want to assign to the item). Click Assign and then click OK until you get back to your document, saving the changes to your keyboard along the way.

You can't edit the CUA keyboard.   WordPerfect won't let you edit the CUA keyboard, but you can copy one of the others and edit it, or you can create a brand-new keyboard.

Assign dialog boxes to shortcut keys. If you choose Menus as the item type in the Keyboard Editor dialog box, you can assign any of the menus to a keyboard shortcut. But if you choose Commands, you can assign shortcuts to dialog boxes that are several levels deep in menus, which can save you several keystrokes or clicks with the mouse.

There's a speed-selecting secret in list boxes. You can just type the first letters of a command or a menu's name to go directly to it in these list boxes. For example, typing **col** takes you right to the command ColumnDefineDlg.

What's the "Home Key Works Like DOS WP 5.1" option in the Keyboard Editor dialog box? In WordPerfect DOS, the Home key means "very" when you use it to reposition the cursor. For example, Home Left Arrow takes the cursor to the beginning of the line (very left) and Home Right Arrow moves it to the end of the line (very right). Home Up Arrow moves the cursor to the top of your screen, and Home Down Arrow takes it to the bottom. Home Home Up Arrow takes you to the beginning of your document (very very up), and Home Home Down Arrow takes you to the end (very very down). And Home Home Home Up Arrow takes you to the very very very beginning of your document, before any invisible formatting codes.

Keep the Home Key Works Like DOS WP 5.1 box checked if you want to be able to do this on your new keyboard.

Remember to switch back to the keyboard you want to use. After you've defined a new keyboard, remember that if you're not planning to use it right away, select the keyboard you *do* want to use.

To switch back to the CUA keyboard, just click the Default (CUA) button and OK when you see the Keyboard dialog box showing you the current keyboard (see Figure 3-9).

Figure 3-9: Just click Default (CUA) and OK to go back to the default keyboard.

Make a macro that switches between keyboards. If you find that you switch back and forth between keyboards very often, why not record a macro that switches you back and forth? You can assign it to a button, too, so you can just click on it.

CUSTOMIZING WORDPERFECT THROUGH WINDOWS

Use the Windows Control Panel instead of WordPerfect to set some preferences, like mouse speed and screen colors. Select the Colors icon to set screen colors, the Mouse icon to change the "feel" of the mouse (to switch it from a right-handed to a left-handed mouse) and the Keyboard icon to adjust the key repeat rate.

Setting screen colors. You set the screen colors for Draft mode and the Reveal Codes window in WordPerfect by choosing Display from the Preferences menu, but you use the Windows Color Control Panel to set screen colors in WYSIWYG mode. (There is a way to change the color of text in your editing screen, but you have to cheat. See the tip "Text in color on the screen? Sure," in Chapter 8.)

To set screen colors, go to the Windows Control Panel in the Main group and click on the Color icon. Choose from several pre-defined color schemes (see Figure 3-10) or create your own.

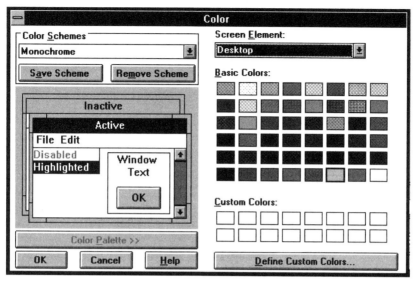

Figure 3-10: Use the Color Control Panel to change Windows screen colors.

When you're viewing this screen, you can just press the Down Arrow key to see a preview of the predefined color schemes. If you like one of these, press Enter or click OK when it's displayed. (In Windows 3.1, try Hotdog Stand or Black Leather Jacket for an "interesting" effect.)

You can mix your own color scheme, too. First, pick a color scheme that's close to what you want; then click on Color Palette. (Of course, you have to have a color monitor to do this.)

Now, this part is a little tricky. Click in the Screen Element box at the top of the Color screen and press the Down Arrow key to see a list of the items whose colors you can change, like the desktop, the title bar text, the menu bar text, the scroll bars and so forth. Next, in the color palette part of the window (see Figure 3-10), click on the color you want to use for that element. Choose Save Scheme and give your color scheme a name. If you don't save it, you won't be able to use it again!

Customize the feel of the mouse. You'll be using the mouse a lot in WordPerfect for Windows—set it so it feels right in your hand. Click on the Mouse icon in the Windows Control Panel to get the Mouse dialog box (see Figure 3-11).

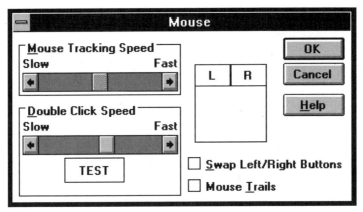

Figure 3-11: The Mouse dialog box lets you adjust the speed of the mouse.

You might want to change the tracking speed, for example. The tracking speed controls the rate at which the mouse pointer moves on the screen as you move the mouse on your desktop. Old hands at mousing generally like a fast speed. Keep it slow until you get used to the mouse; then speed it up.

You'll also double-click often in WordPerfect for Windows. If your double-clicks are interpreted not as double-clicks but as two single clicks, change the double-click speed. Test it by double-clicking in the TEST box. How can you tell when you've got it right? The box will switch from white to black (or to white, if it's black already) when your double-clicks are interpreted as double-clicks.

If you're left-handed, you can also make your mouse into a (please excuse the expression) "southpaw" by switching the actions of the right and left mouse buttons.

Customize the repeat rate on the keyboard. Use the Windows
Keyboard Control Panel (see Figure 3-12) to change the rate
a key repeats when you hold it down. You may prefer a light touch
or a heavy one. Either way, you can test out your choice in the Test
Typematic box.

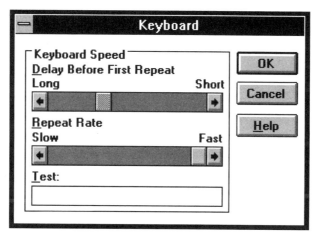

Figure 3-12: Use the Keyboard Control Panel to
change the feel of the keyboard.

WordPerfect has .INI files. The choices you make from
the Preferences menu are stored in the file WP{WP}.SET. But
some preferences are stored in special .INI files that all Windows
programs have. You can see what's in your WordPerfect .INI files
and edit the settings you find there. In fact, there are separate .INI
files for the Speller (WPSP.INI), the Thesaurus (WPTH.INI), the
File Manager (WPFM.INI) and WordPerfect for Windows itself
(WPWP.INI).

If you're fairly advanced with Windows, you may want to edit
these files to change some of the settings in them. Before you do,
make a duplicate copy of the file under a different name (such as
WPWP.OLD), so you can get the original back if you need to. Then,
for the absolutely fastest way to edit them, go out to Windows and
type **wpwp.ini** (or the name of the .INI file you want to edit) in the
Program Manager's Run box. The Notepad automatically comes up
because all .INI files are associated with it, and you can use it to

change the settings (see Figure 3-13). You can edit these files in WordPerfect for Windows, too, but I thought you might like that little Windows trick.

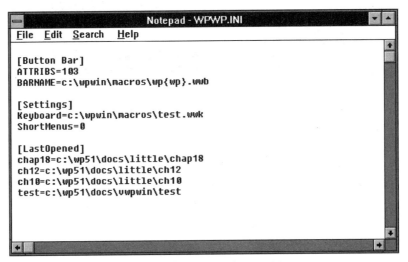

```
Notepad - WPWP.INI
File   Edit   Search   Help

[Button Bar]
ATTRIBS=103
BARNAME=c:\wpwin\macros\wp{wp}.wwb

[Settings]
Keyboard=c:\wpwin\macros\test.wwk
ShortMenus=0

[LastOpened]
chap18=c:\wp51\docs\little\chap18
ch12=c:\wp51\docs\little\ch12
ch10=c:\wp51\docs\little\ch10
test=c:\wp51\docs\vwpwin\test
```

Figure 3-13: Use the Notepad to edit .INI files.

Share a computer? Customize WordPerfect anyway.   Here's a neat trick for setting up WordPerfect just the way you like it and getting it to run that way each time you start it, even if you share your computer with other users who change preferences to suit themselves.

At the DOS command line, start both Windows and WordPerfect at the same time with the command **win wpwin /nt=0**. This tells WordPerfect that you're on a network even though you're not. When it starts, you'll be asked who you are. Enter your initials. Then, as soon as the program starts, go to the Preferences menu and set it up the way you like it. You'll only have to do this the first time. From then on, use the WIN WPWIN /NT=0 command to start WordPerfect. After you enter your initials, the program comes up with your own particular preferences in effect. Tell your office mates about this one so they can do it, too.

Lagniappe: If you can't be bothered to remember the command, you can make a batch file (named MYWP.BAT here—name it something else if you like) that will remember it for you. At the DOS command line, type

> **cd ** [and press Enter]
> **copy con mywp.bat** [and press Enter]
> **win wpwin /nt=0** [and press Enter]
> [then press F6]

Now you've got a batch file named MYWP.BAT that executes whenever you enter **mywp** at the command line. It starts both WordPerfect and Windows and asks you who you are.

MOVING ON

These are just some of the ways to customize WordPerfect for Windows. There are lots of others. Remember the customizable Quick List you saw in Chapter 1? The File Manager lets you set preferences for using it, too (see Chapter 6, "Tricks for Managing Your Documents"). You can also tailor WordPerfect for Windows to your needs with macros (see Chapter 10, "The Magic of Macros"). Stay tuned throughout the book to learn more about making WordPerfect suit you and all the different ways you like to work.

CHAPTER FOUR

Editing Alchemy

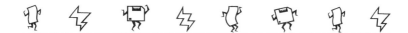

I t's quick and easy to edit your documents once you discover WordPerfect for Windows's many hidden shortcuts. In this chapter you'll see all kinds of sneaky ways to use keyboard and mouse shortcuts to select and delete text; find your place in documents; use bookmarks; capitalize and hyphenate text; and use the Speller and Thesaurus.

This chapter is especially important for those who are upgrading from WordPerfect DOS to WordPerfect for Windows—not all of the shortcuts you remember still work, and there are lots of new ones.

What's the difference between *editing* a document and entering it from scratch? Well, you can edit a document at just about any time in the process, but a lot of people find that simply getting the words typed (we can't say "on paper" anymore) and then going back to refine them later works best. In short, use these techniques whenever you need them, whether you call it "editing" or not.

MOVING THROUGH DOCUMENTS

It's important, if you ever edit a large document, to know how to move around in it easily, how to find things and how to find your place again. Here's a little bag of tricks to keep you from getting lost in the maze.

Ctrl+Home and Ctrl+End. The absolutely fastest way to go to the beginning or end of a document is to press Ctrl+Home or Ctrl+End. (On the DOS-style keyboard, you can use Home Home Up Arrow and Home Home Down Arrow.)

Press Ctrl+G for the Go To dialog box. Ctrl+G brings you the Go To dialog box, where you can specify the page you want to go to in your document.

If you click on the pop-up list arrow under Position in the Go To dialog box, you can select Go to Page Number, Top of Current Page and Bottom of Current Page, but it's easier to use keyboard short-cuts. To get to the top of the page, press Alt+Home; to get to the bottom of the page, press Alt+End.

Finding your place. Press Ctrl+G and click the Last Position box to go back to your last location. Press Ctrl+G; then press Tab twice and press Enter for a keyboard shortcut for this. It also makes a very useful macro that you can turn into a button or assign to a key combination for getting back to where you were.

Use the scroll bars for speedy moving. Often, the fastest way to move in a document is to drag the scroll box on the scroll bar, especially if you're not sure of the exact page number you want to go to. Drag it to the top of the scroll bar to go to the beginning of your document, to the bottom of the scroll bar to go to the end, and anywhere in between to go to that relative place.

The insertion point doesn't move when you scroll. When you scroll with the scroll bars, the insertion point stays where it was. If you start typing without clicking in your new location, WordPerfect displays the page where the insertion point is and inserts the text there. So if you scroll, be sure to click to reset the insertion point before you start typing.

Click on the scroll boxes to scroll line by line. To move line by line through a document, click on the tiny arrowheads at the top or bottom of the scroll bar.

Just drag text to scroll. The quickest way to scroll is to drag downward or upward through the text with the mouse. When you get to the top or bottom of the window, the text continues to scroll.

Keyboard shortcuts for moving through documents. Here are a few keyboard shortcuts you can use for moving through documents.

Destination	CUA Keyboard	DOS Keyboard
End of line	End	End
End of document	Ctrl+End	Home Home Down Arrow
Top of document	Ctrl+Home	Home Home Up Arrow
A specific page	Ctrl+G	Ctrl+G or Ctrl+Home twice
Up one screen	PgUp	Alt+PgUp
Down one screen	PgDn	Alt+PgDn
Up one page	Alt+PgUp	PgUp
Down one page	Alt+PgDn	PgDn
Next document	Ctrl+F6	Shift+F3
Previous document	Ctrl+Shift+F6	Alt+Shift+F3

PgUp and PgDn don't move by pages. In WordPerfect for Windows, PgUp and PgDn move you one screen at a time, not one page, as they do in WordPerfect DOS. Don't expect to move the way you did in the DOS version of the program.

The DOS keyboard and the Home key. Here's another difference between the two keyboards. If you're using the DOS-style keyboard, the Home key can work just as it does in WordPerfect DOS. See the tip "What's the 'Home Key Works Like DOS WP 5.1' option in the Keyboard Editor dialog box?" in Chapter 3 for the nuances of moving with the Home key.

SELECTING TEXT

One of the most basic techniques in WordPerfect for Windows is selecting text. Before you can edit text—or cut it, copy it, delete it or do anything else with it—you have to select it. In fact, some menu choices are dimmed if you haven't selected text first.

You can select text with the mouse by itself, the keyboard by itself or both the mouse and the keyboard. Sometimes one way is better, and sometimes the other's faster. In my opinion, your best bet is to double-click on a word to select it, triple-click to select a sentence or click four times to select a paragraph. You can drag across text to select it, too, or use the Shift-click method: press and hold the Shift key down, click at the beginning of the selection, and then click at the end of the selection.

Here's a list of more shortcuts.

To Select:	CUA Keyboard	DOS Keyboard
Sentence	Click three times	Ctrl+F4
Paragraph	Click four times	Ctrl+Shift+F4
To the end of the line	Shift+End	Shift+End
To the beginning of the previous word	Ctrl+Shift +Left Arrow	Ctrl+Shift +Left Arrow
To the beginning of the next word	Ctrl+Shift +Right Arrow	Ctrl+Shift +Right Arrow
Up one line	Shift+Up Arrow	Shift+Up Arrow
Down one line	Shift+Down Arrow	Shift+Down Arrow

To Select:	CUA Keyboard	DOS Keyboard
Previous paragraph	Ctrl+Shift +Up Arrow	Ctrl+Shift +Up Arrow
Next paragraph	Ctrl+Shift +Down Arrow	Ctrl+Shift +Down Arrow

Just type over selected text to replace it.   You don't have to delete selected text before typing the new text. Just start typing. This speed trick is great to use in dialog boxes that are presenting you with selected text.

This can be a trap, too, if you're expecting WordPerfect for Windows to work the way WordPerfect DOS did. In WordPerfect DOS, typing another character extended the selection to it. In WordPerfect for Windows, selected text is *replaced* by the next thing you type. (But see the next tip.)

WordPerfect has a Select mode.   Press F8 to turn on Select mode (on the DOS keyboard, use Alt+F4). Once it's on, you just type the character that you want to extend the selection to. For example, to select from the insertion point to the end of a sentence that ends in a period, press F8 and then type a period.

SHORTCUTS FOR DELETING, COPYING & PASTING TEXT

Since you have to use the keyboard at some point to delete text, even if you select it with the mouse, there are lots of shortcuts for deleting text. And because copying and pasting are basic to the whole concept of Windows programs (after all, copying and pasting between applications is Windows's number-one selling point), there are plenty of shortcuts for that, too. Note that all of the shortcuts aren't available on both keyboards.

Ctrl+Backspace deletes one word at a time. Ctrl+Backspace deletes the word that the insertion point is in. On the DOS-style keyboard, use Ctrl+Backspace for the word to the left of the cursor and Ctrl+Del for the word to the right of the cursor.

Ctrl+Del deletes to the end of the line. The Ctrl+Del shortcut clears the rest of the line, without your having to select anything first. On the DOS keyboard, it's Ctrl+End.

Ctrl+Shift+Del deletes to the end of the page. On the CUA keyboard, pressing Ctrl+Shift+Del deletes text from the insertion point to the end of the page. Get rid of it in a hurry!

Deleting part of the current word (DOS keyboard only). On the DOS keyboard, delete to the beginning of the current word with Home+Backspace and to the end of the current word with Home+Del. Unfortunately, this shortcut doesn't work on the CUA keyboard.

To deselect, just click somewhere else, or press an arrow key. To quickly deselect a selection, click in an area that's not selected or press an arrow key.

You can copy the screen to the Clipboard. In both Word-Perfect DOS and WordPerfect for Windows, the contents of the screen are copied to the Clipboard when you press PrtSc. Once they're on the Clipboard, you can paste them into other applications.

You can copy the whole window to the Clipboard, too. Press Alt+PrtSc to copy the entire active window to the Clipboard. This is an easy way to put illustrations of WordPerfect screens into other programs.

OTHER EDITING TRICKS

There are shortcuts for undeleting text you've deleted by mistake, too—and for converting lowercase text to uppercase (and vice versa). Here are a few more editing shortcuts you'll find useful.

Paste text you've cut but Undelete text you've deleted. The Undelete buffer stores the last three deletions you made with the Backspace or Delete keys. It doesn't hold text you cut with Ctrl+X or Shift+Del (or by choosing Cut from the Edit menu). Text that you cut goes to the Clipboard; you can get it back by pasting.

The Undelete dialog box. Sometimes the Undelete dialog box covers what has been deleted. If it gets in the way, move it. Just drag it by its title bar. You can put it "upstairs," near the window's title bar.

Deleted text can be undeleted several times. If you delete text, you can undelete it several times, even in different locations. For example, you can restore a deleted paragraph in various places in your document, or even in other documents, as long as you're within WordPerfect.

To put deleted text in other application programs, undelete it, select it, copy or cut it, and then paste it into the other program.

You can delete codes and undelete them, too. As you'll see in Chapters 7 ("Spells for Your Special Problems") and 9 ("Desktop Publishing Sorcery"), this is a voodoo trick for moving equations and figures: you just delete their codes and then undelete them in the new location.

What's Typeover good for? Use Typeover when you're editing data in tables that have roughly equal-sized entries, or in columns of numbers where the number of digits stay the same. You can just type over what's already there and replace it with the new data, without having to select or delete any text first.

Press the Ins key to toggle Typeover mode on and off. You'll see "Typeover" on the status line when it's on.

 Typeover won't let you type over codes. Use Typeover only when there aren't a lot of formatting codes around your text. If you encounter a code in Typeover, it's pushed ahead of the insertion point and text is inserted, just as in Insert mode.

Switching from uppercase to lowercase and back. Word-Perfect for Windows has a built-in Convert Case command that lets you change text from uppercase to lowercase and vice versa. This is really helpful if you've pressed the Caps Lock key by mistake, or if you want to change a heading to all caps.

Highlight the text you want to convert and choose Convert Case from the Edit menu. WordPerfect will keep "I"s that begin words capitalized (as in "I'm").

Highlight the ending punctuation from the preceding sentence when you're converting a sentence to lowercase. When you highlight a sentence to change it to lowercase, be sure to highlight the ending punctuation of the previous sentence, too. This tells WordPerfect for Windows to keep the first letter in the highlighted sentence capitalized, so you convert whole paragraphs or blocks of text from uppercase to lowercase while keeping the capitalization at the beginning of each sentence. Neat.

SEARCHING & REPLACING

The fastest way to find a certain word or phrase in your document is to use the Search feature. But the Search feature goes beyond just finding things. You can search for every occurrence of a word or phrase, for instance, and change it to something else (Search and

Replace). You can remove all occurrences of a word, phrase, formatting code, punctuation mark or number, among other things, from a document.

If you use macros, you'll often set them up to search for things so that they can go to specific places in your document, do their job and then move to the next place.

The often-neglected Search feature is a powerful editing tool.

F2 is the Search shortcut on both keyboards. Shift+F2 is Search Next. Press F2 to start a search, or choose Search from the Edit menu. Then fill out the Search dialog box (see Figure 4-1). Once you've located the first occurrence of what you're searching for, press Shift+F2 to look for the next occurrence of the same thing. Or press F2 and Enter; this does the same thing, but a little slower than using Shift+F2.

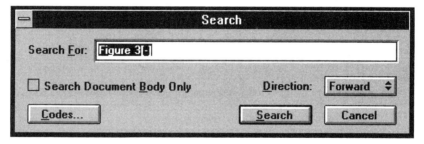

Figure 4-1: The Search feature finds things faster than you can.

How you enter the search pattern determines what WordPerfect finds. WordPerfect for Windows locates every form of the string of characters you enter unless you use spaces to tell it you're looking for an entire word. If you enter **book**, for example, it locates *books, Bookman, bookstore* and so forth. To indicate that you're looking for a word by itself, put a space before and after the word.

Using spaces before and after a word doesn't always work.
If the word you're looking for is at the beginning of a paragraph, or if it's followed by a period or a comma (or any other punctuation), WordPerfect won't locate it if you use the previous trick. To be absolutely sure that you locate every instance of your word, search for it without spaces around it and ignore the words that don't apply.

You can search backward or search for the previous occurrence of what you're looking for. To search for the previous instance of what you're looking for, press Alt+F2.

To start a backward search by using a keyboard shortcut, press F2 and then press Tab Tab Down Arrow. That switches the direction to backward. You can click on the arrow next to Direction in the Search dialog box, too, but I find this keyboard shortcut is faster.

You can search through *everything*. To do an extended search, uncheck the Search Document Body Only box in the Search dialog box. WordPerfect then searches headers and footers, footnotes, endnotes, Graphics box captions, text boxes and all the rest.

Avoid typos: paste text in the Search dialog box. Use WordPerfect for Windows's copy-and-paste features to put what you're looking for in the Search For box of the Search dialog box. You won't make any typos this way. Just copy the word or phrase you want to search for from the document (with Ctrl+C) and paste it in the Search For box (with Ctrl+V).

Don't search for a common word. Try to keep the search pattern as unique as you can. If you search for a common word like *and* or *but*, you'll find a lot of them!

Use your own system of bookmarks so you can have as many as you want. Although there's a built-in bookmark feature that lets you set four bookmarks, you can use your own system to set as many bookmarks as you like. If you want to return to a certain part of a document later, mark it with a unique pattern of characters, such as ****** or **@#**. You can easily search for those patterns later to find your place.

Drag that Search dialog box out of the way. The Search dialog box often obscures what the program has located. So drag it out of the way by its title bar.

Keep the Search dialog box open while you edit. Once you find what you're searching for, just click in the document to edit it. The dialog box won't close until you click Close or double-click on its Control icon. (But you can move it out of the way; see the previous trick.) If you're making minor editing changes, you can search, edit your document and keep on searching.

Click Search Next in the dialog box to resume your search.

Searching for codes. To search for a formatting code, click the Codes box in the Search dialog box. Then select the code you want to look for.

There's a speed-select feature in the Codes list: just type the first letter of the code you want to search for to go directly to that part of the alphabet.

If you're searching for a code, keep the Reveal Codes window open. If you don't open the Reveal Codes window, you won't see where the insertion point is relative to the invisible code. It's always placed *after* the code or the text you're looking for.

Searching for special characters. Search for special characters by pressing Ctrl+W when the insertion point is in the Search For box. You'll see the WordPerfect Characters dialog box (see Figure 4-2). Select the character set that has the character you want to search for, highlight the character and click Insert and Close.

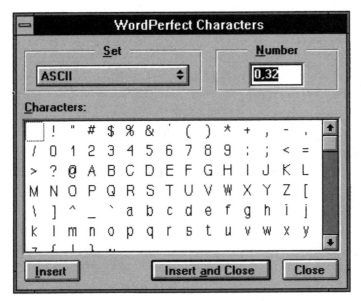

Figure 4-2: Use the WordPerfect Characters dialog box to search for special characters.

Use Ctrl+F2 as a shortcut for Replace. To search for something and replace it, use the program's built-in Replace feature. Press Ctrl+F2 or choose Replace from the Edit menu.

You can search and replace all at once. To tell the program to go ahead and replace all occurrences of something, click the Replace All button in the Search and Replace dialog box (see Figure 4-3). Otherwise it stops at each instance of what you're searching for.

```
┌─────────────────────────────────────────────────────────────┐
│ ▬                    Search and Replace                       │
├─────────────────────────────────────────────────────────────┤
│ Search For:    ┌──────────────────────────────────────────┐  │
│                │ Figure 3[-]                              │  │
│                └──────────────────────────────────────────┘  │
│ Replace With:  ┌──────────────────────────────────────────┐  │
│                │ Figure 4[-]                              │  │
│                └──────────────────────────────────────────┘  │
│                                                               │
│ ☐ Search Document Body Only        Direction: ┌─────────┐     │
│                                               │ Forward ↕│     │
│ ┌────────┐ ┌────────────┐ ┌─────────┐ ┌─────────────┐ ┌───────┐│
│ │ Codes..│ │ Replace All│ │ Replace │ │ Search Next │ │ Close ││
│ └────────┘ └────────────┘ └─────────┘ └─────────────┘ └───────┘│
└─────────────────────────────────────────────────────────────┘
```

Figure 4-3: Click Replace All to replace everything all at
once; click Replace to stop at each replacement for
confirmation.

Be sure to search in lowercase if you want to find everything.
WordPerfect locates all occurrences of a word if you enter the
search pattern in lowercase letters. If you use uppercase and lowercase letters, it will match that exact pattern.

Enter the replace pattern exactly as you want it. Use
uppercase and lowercase in the Replace With box exactly as
you want the text to appear in your document. WordPerfect enters
your replace text exactly as you do.

Use Replace to strip out text and codes. A quick way to
remove all instances of something from a document is to
search for it and replace it with nothing. For example, if you want to
remove all the italics from a document, enter the [Italics On] code in
the Search For box and don't make any entry in the Replace With
box.

Use Search and Replace as your own special shorthand.
Instead of typing complicated names like *Warshawski International Consortium,* use abbreviations like *wic@* and replace them later
with the entire phrase. It saves typing time.

You can reverse the effects of a Search and Replace with Undo. If you mess up and replace every instance of a word with the wrong word, you can Undo the Search and Replace operation by pressing Ctrl+Z (or choosing Undo from the Edit menu) as soon as the operation is over and you see that it didn't do what you wanted.

If you do something else before you use Undo, such as reformatting a paragraph or deleting a word, *that* operation will be undone, not your search-and-replace operation. Undo works on the very last thing you did.

Use Search and Replace to reformat a document. Searching for formatting codes and replacing them is a neat trick to use for changing formatting in a document. For example, to insert a blank line between every paragraph in a document, search for one [Hrt] and replace it with two [Hrt]s.

Use the File Manager for major searching. If you're looking for a document or group of documents whose name you've forgotten except for a word or phrase, use the File Manager's Search features. (See Chapter 6, "Tricks for Managing Your Documents.")

You can use all these Search features in the File Manager, too. The File Manager's View window lets you do all the same searches and search-and-replacements we've been discussing here. So you can search *for* documents and then search *within* documents (as you saw here) in the File Manager.

HYPHENATION

Hyphenation is a feature that's often overlooked, but it's a very effective tool for improving the looks of your documents.

Turn hyphenation on for better results with full justification.
If you justify your text, you probably know that you often get
big spaces between words as WordPerfect fills out lines to align both
the right and left margins. If you use hyphenation, this problem will
clear up, because the program can then break words at the ends of
lines.

To turn on hyphenation, select Line from the Layout menu; then
select Hyphenation and OK.

Hyphenation is turned on at the point in the document where
you use this command, so go to the beginning of your document
(Ctrl+Home) if you want to hyphenate the whole document.

If you always want hyphenation to be on, put it in your Initial
Codes on the Preferences menu.

Turn hyphenation off in narrow columns. You'll get too
many word breaks if hyphenation is on and your text is in
narrow columns. To turn hyphenation off, position the cursor at the
point in your document where you want to turn it off and then
choose Layout, Line and Hyphenation Off. You can turn it back on
again after the columns.

Type your document; then turn on hyphenation. It's
easier to let WordPerfect hyphenate a document after you've
typed it so you won't be interrupted for word breaks. After typing
your document, go to the top of the document and turn on hyphenation; then go to the end of the document, and WordPerfect will
hyphenate it along the way.

**If you don't like the way WordPerfect has hyphenated a
word, you can change it.** If you're being prompted for
where to put the hyphen and you don't like the place WordPerfect is
suggesting, use the Left and Right Arrow keys to move to the place
where you *do* want the hyphen; then click Insert Hyphen. If you
don't want the word to be hyphenated at all, click Ignore Word.

There are soft hyphens in WordPerfect. Soft hyphens appear only when a word is broken at the end of a line. If the word doesn't have to be broken at a line ending, you'll never see the soft hyphen (you can see its code in Reveal Codes, though).

WordPerfect inserts soft hyphens automatically when hyphenation is on, and normally you never have to put them in. The only time you might want to insert a soft hyphen is when you're not using automatic hyphenation and you want to hyphenate a word for a better line break. If you later edit the document and the line doesn't break there any longer, the soft hyphen disappears.

To get a soft hyphen, press Ctrl+Shift (on both the CUA and the DOS keyboards) and type a hyphen at the appropriate place in the word.

Use hard hyphens to keep a hyphenated word from being broken. If you want a word like *daughter-in-law* to be hyphenated, type the hyphens. If you want to make sure that it's always hyphenated and won't be broken at the end of a line, use hard hyphens. To get a hard hyphen, press Ctrl and type the hyphen. (On the DOS-style keyboard, use Home+hyphen.)

Use different kinds of dashes to give your documents a professional look. En dashes are longer than hyphens and are often used as minus signs. Strictly speaking, they should be used only to indicate ranges of inclusive numbers, as in "pages 22–25" or "during the period 1941–45."

Em dashes are longer than en dashes—like this one. They're also called long dashes, and they usually indicate a break in thought.

To insert either an em dash or an en dash, press Ctrl+W for WP Characters and choose your dash from the Typographic Symbols set. Record a macro for each of them, if you use them a lot. Then make a button for them if you'd rather point-and-click to insert them.

Use a hard space to stop a phrase from breaking. A hard space prevents a phrase from being broken at the end of a line. This is a really professional touch to use in your documents. I've noticed that some book publishers aren't even aware of it.

If you don't want a certain phrase to be broken at the end of a line, put hard spaces between the words. To get a hard space, press Home and then the space bar. You can use this with dates, like February 16, 1993, so "1993" won't show up on the next line—or so the beginning of the next line won't read "16, 1993." Do this with names, too, like W. C. Fields, so that "W. C." won't end one line and "Fields" begin the next.

THE SPELLER

Aha, the most basic editing tool of all: the Speller. I'm a terrible typist (I use three fingers), and so I just bang away and then let the Speller correct all my mistakes. It's much faster than trying to correct as you go. WordPerfect's Speller, in my opinion, is the best on the market. It always seems to know what I really meant to type.

Save after a spell check. The most important of all Speller tricks is to save your document after you've spell-checked it. If you don't, all your changes will be for naught.

The Speller works a little differently than the one in WordPerfect DOS. If you're upgrading from DOS Word-Perfect, you'll have to get used to the new Speller shortcuts. Teach your fingers to double-click on a suggested word to replace a misspelled word. To retype a word "manually," double-click on the word that's suggested, if it's not right; then type the new word and press Enter. To avoid reaching for the mouse, press Alt+W to move to the Word text box; then type the word. You don't have to delete the word that's already there, as long as it's highlighted.

Drag the Speller window to reposition it. If the Speller window gets in your way, drag it by its title bar to a new position. You can choose Move to Bottom from its Options menu to put it at the bottom of the screen, but it's often in the way there, too.

Minimize the Speller. Because the Speller is a stand-alone program, you can just click on its Minimize icon to keep it in memory while you edit your document. Just choose Speller from the Tools menu or click on the Speller icon to start it rolling again when you're ready. It's a bit faster than starting it from scratch.

To see the Speller icon, click WordPerfect's Restore icon to make WordPerfect slightly smaller than full-screen size.

You can also go to the Speller by bringing up the Task List with Ctrl+Esc and clicking on the Speller.

If there's a word you habitually mistype, here's a neat trick. If your fingers insist on always mistyping a word, and that mistyping isn't in WordPerfect's spelling dictionary, manually correcting that word every time it appears can drive you crazy. In my line of work, for example, I have to type the word *document* a lot. Somehow it always comes out *docuemt*, which WordPerfect insists must be a misspelling of *decimate*—it doesn't suggest *document* as a choice. For months I tediously corrected it manually. Now I've caught on to the trick: I let the Speller replace *docuemt* with *decimate*, and I just search-and-replace *decimate* with *document* when the Speller's done. It's really much faster than correcting it every time.

Adding new words to the Speller. Unfortunately, there's no way to tell the Speller what your usual mistakes are and what to suggest in place of them. But you can add words to the Speller with the Speller Utility, as you'll see later.

Shortcuts for starting the Speller. Press Ctrl+F1 to start the Speller. On the DOS-style keyboard, it's Ctrl+F2.

 You can start the Speller from anywhere in a document. To check an entire document, choose To End of Document from the pop-up box next to Check in the Speller window (see Figure 4-4). You can be anywhere in your document; you don't have to go to the top before starting the Speller.

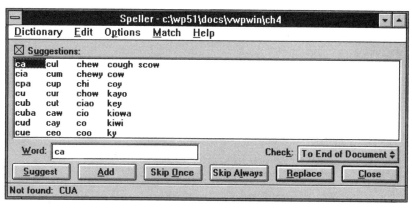

Figure 4-4: The Speller window.

 You don't have to check the whole document. If you just want to check the page the cursor's on, where you've made a few changes, choose Page or To End of Page in the Speller window so you don't go through the whole document again.

To check only a paragraph or two you've added, select the text and then run the Speller.

 Ignoring misspelled or unique words. If you want to leave a word the way it is, click Skip Always or Skip Once when the Speller presents it. Skip Always skips the word if it's anywhere else in the document; Skip Once just skips that instance of the word.

Skip Always doesn't add a word to the spelling dictionary, as you might think. It simply ignores the word until you close the Speller. Click Add to add a word to the dictionary.

Make sure any words you add are spelled correctly.
There's not much point in adding misspelled words to the Speller's dictionary. Double-check a word before you click Add. Later, you'll see how to edit the dictionary to correct mistakes.

Stopping spell-checking. To exit from the Speller before it's finished, press Esc or click Close in the Speller window. Then save your document so the spelling corrections made up to then will be saved.

You can look up word patterns, too. This is a wicked trick to pull if you're playing Scrabble and you can sneak out to your computer.
The wildcard ? stands for any one character and * stands for any combination of characters or no character at all. To get these wildcard characters, choose 1 Character (for a ?) or Multiple Characters (for an *) from the Speller's Match menu. Say you want to check the spelling of relieve because you don't know whether it's *ie* or *ei*. Enter **rel*ve** and click Suggest to get a list of words like *relative*, *relieve* and *relive*. Remember to choose the wildcard characters from the Match menu—don't type a question mark or an asterisk from the keyboard. That's the trick.

Checking alphanumeric words. To make the Speller skip letter and number combinations like F5, uncheck Words with Numbers in the Options menu. Otherwise it stops for each one. Major time-waster.

Checking capitalization. The Speller normally checks for irregular capitalization, like *tHe* and *RePlace*. If your document contains a lot of acronyms (such as *ReDo Industries*) or words with odd capitalization that you want to retain, uncheck Irregular Capitalization on the Options menu or the Speller will stop at every oddly capitalized word.

Otherwise, if the Speller finds oddly capitalized words like *TOday* or *tHe*, it will stop at them. Choose Replace to change the capitalization to normal, like *Today* and *the*.

The Speller checks for double words, too. The Speller will also ask you about double words, like *the the*, which are really easy to overlook, even by experienced proofreaders. I'd leave this option on if I were you.

Speeding up the Speller. To speed up the Speller, uncheck the Suggestions box in the Speller window. Then it won't take the time to bring up a list of suggested words, and you can just retype a misspelled word to correct it.

Paid by the word? Get a word count. Choose Word Count from the Tools menu (on the WordPerfect DOS Speller menu) to get a count of how many words are in your document.

Numbers don't count! Numbers aren't counted as words unless they have a hyphen in them, as phone numbers do. A date like October 28, 1951 is considered one word.

You can add words to the spelling dictionary. To add words to your spelling dictionary, just retrieve the file named WP{WP}US.SUP and edit it like any other WordPerfect document. It's your supplementary dictionary—the one that holds all the words you add during spell-checking. Figure 4-5 shows what mine looked like once.

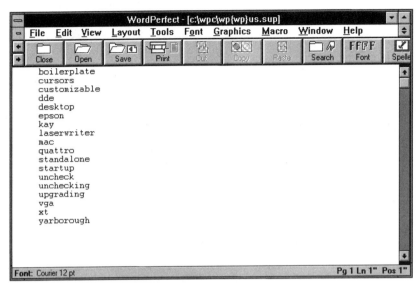

Figure 4-5: You can edit your supplementary dictionary
(WP{WP}US.SUP) just like any other document.

Delete misspelled words from your supplemental dictionary.
It's awfully easy to add misspelled words to your supplemental
dictionary if you click Add before you think while you're spell-
checking. All sorts of garbage can get in there. Do yourself a favor
and delete it.

**If you use WordPerfect for Windows and WordPerfect
DOS, use the same spelling dictionaries.** If you use both
programs, use the same spelling dictionaries. (You'll see how below.)
It doesn't matter which, although the main dictionary in your
C:\WPC directory (WP{WP}US.LEX) is probably more up-to-date,
while the supplementary dictionary (WP{WP}US.SUP) in your
C:\WP51 directory has all the words you've added.

Copy your supplemental dictionary into the directory that has the
WordPerfect for Windows main dictionary. Then use the Location of
Files feature on the Preferences menu to specify that directory as the
location of your dictionary files. In WordPerfect DOS, use the Setup
menu to specify where the dictionaries are.

You can see what's in WordPerfect's main dictionary and add words to it. A stand-alone program called the Speller Utility (SPELL.EXE) lets you look at what's in WordPerfect's main spelling dictionary (WP{WP}US.LEX) and edit it to add new words to it. It's a character-based program like WordPerfect DOS, so don't expect it to look like a graphical Windows program like WordPerfect for Windows. In fact, it's the same Speller Utility used with Word-Perfect DOS.

You can't view the Speller Utility by clicking on an icon. There's no icon for the Speller Utility (unless you created one). To run the Speller Utility, choose Run from the Program Manager's File menu and enter C:\WPC\SPELL. The Installation program normally puts the Speller Utility in C:\WPC, but use a different path name if it's stored in a different directory.

Just edit a supplemental dictionary. You can use the Speller Utility's menu to edit the main dictionary, but it's sort of cumbersome and it takes about 20 minutes for the program to run through the whole thing and update it with your changes. Instead, just edit your supplemental dictionary.

Adding or deleting words in the main dictionary. If you really want to edit the main dictionary anyway, create a file that contains all the words you want to add or delete, separated by hard returns. This beats adding or deleting one word at a time. Then choose Add Words to Dictionary (option 2) or Delete Words from Dictionary (option 3) from the Speller Utility menu (see Figure 4-6).

```
Spell — WordPerfect Speller Utility          WP{WP}US.LEX

0 - Exit
1 - Change/Create Dictionary
2 - Add Words to Dictionary
3 - Delete Words from Dictionary
4 - Optimize Dictionary
5 - Display Common Word List
6 - Check Location of a Word
7 - Look Up
8 - Phonetic Look Up
9 - Convert 4.2 Dictionary to 5.1
A - Combine Other 5.0 or 5.1 Dictionary
B - Compress/Expand Supplemental Dictionary
C - Extract Added Words from Wordlist-based Dictionary

Selection:
```

Figure 4-6: The Speller Utility's menu lets you edit the main dictionary.

Use options 2 or 4 on the next menu (see Figure 4-7) to add or delete all the words in your file at the same time. Option 2 is Add to (or Delete from) Common Word List (from a file), and option 4 is Add to (or Delete from) Main Word List (from a file).

```
Spell — Add Words                            WP{WP}US.LEX

0 - Cancel - do not add words
1 - Add to common word list (from keyboard)
2 - Add to common word list (from a file)
3 - Add to main word list (from keyboard)
4 - Add to main word list (from a file)
5 - Exit

Selection:
```

Figure 4-7: Use options 2 or 4 to add (or delete) a list of words from a file.

The common word list is checked first. WordPerfect checks the common word list and then the main word list. So if you're adding words you use often, put them in the common word list. They'll be checked faster.

Choose option 5 (Display Common Word List) on the Speller Utility's main menu to see what's already in the common word list.

You can enter hyphens in your word list to specify how you want them to be hyphenated. If you want to specify where your new words should be hyphenated instead of letting the program do it, put hyphens in the words. For example, if you have to type names such as *neophosphosteroid* that drug companies or ad agencies often concoct out of thin air (I made that one up; pharmacies of America, excuse me if it's already taken), enter it as *neo-phospho-steroid* to specify how it ought to be hyphenated.

Any word list can be a supplemental dictionary. Any list of words separated by hard returns can be used as a supplemental dictionary. Just save the list with a name that helps you remember that it's a dictionary, like MEDICAL.SUP. (The standard supplemental dictionary is named WP{WP}US.SUP.) Then, when you run the Speller, select Dictionary and Supplementary Dictionary from the Speller menu and click on the name of the supplementary dictionary you want to use.

You might want to make supplemental dictionaries of lists of technical terms or client names that are specific to your work.

Don't put misspelled words in the dictionary or a supplemental word list. Double-check your word lists before using them as supplemental dictionaries or putting them in the spelling dictionary (WP{WP}US.LEX). You can't use the Speller to check them because they're not already there. Perhaps this tip is obvious; but then, perhaps it's not.

Updating the Speller.   If you want the words you add to be displayed as replacement words when you spell-check your documents, use the Speller Utility and compress your supplemental dictionary (option B). Your normal supplementary dictionary, the one that all the words you add goes to, is named WP{WP}US.SUP.

In the Speller Utility, choose option 1—Change/Create Dictionary. Then Choose option 2—Change/Create Supplemental Dictionary. Choose option B—Compress/Expand Supplemental Dictionary, and then select option 1—Compress Supplemental Dictionary. Choose option 0 to exit.

This is a great way to get words like *dialog*, which normally isn't displayed as a replacement, into the list of suggested replacements.

THE THESAURUS

If you can't think of the right word to use, try the Thesaurus. Put the cursor on the word you want to find a substitute for and choose Thesaurus from the Tools menu. If WordPerfect has alternate words in its dictionaries, it suggests them. If you see one you like, click on it; then click Replace.

 The Thesaurus keyboard shortcut is Alt+F1.   To start the Thesaurus from the keyboard, just press Alt+F1.

 You can look up more words than are displayed.   You can look up alternate words for any word in the Thesaurus that has a dot next to it. Just click on it. To look up a word that's not related to the words the Thesaurus is displaying, type the word in the Word box and choose Look Up.

 To insert a replacement, just double-click.   Don't bother highlighting a replacement word. Just double-click on your choice to put it in the document. It's faster.

Add endings like *s, ing* and *ed* to words. The Thesaurus often presents choices for a root word instead of the word you highlighted. For example, if you highlight *indexing*, it shows choices for *index.* So sometimes you'll need to add endings such as *s* or *es* for plurals, or *ed* and *ing.*

The Thesaurus also shows antonyms. An (*ant*) next to a word means that it's an antonym, or the opposite, of the word you looked up.

To see more words, maximize the Thesaurus window. Click on the upward-pointing Maximize icon in the top right of the Thesaurus window to see more words. Or scroll vertically with the scroll bar. If you look up a lot of alternate words, your screen will get cluttered with columns of words. Click on the arrow buttons to the left of the Word box to scroll horizontally through the columns.

There's a History command in the Thesaurus like the Back command in Help. Click on History to see a list of words you've already looked up. If you saw a good word a couple of steps back and think you want to use it, the History command gets you back to it.

You can use the Thesaurus with other programs. The trick to using the Thesaurus with programs other than Word-Perfect is to copy the word from the other program and paste it in the Thesaurus's Word box (you can type it there, but copying and pasting are a lot faster). Then choose Look Up. Copy and Paste your replacement choice back into the other program.

The Copy and Paste commands are on the Thesaurus's Edit menu. You can also use the Windows keyboard shortcuts Ctrl+Ins for Copy, Shift+Del for Cut or Shift+Ins for Paste.

You can use the Thesaurus in other languages. If you've purchased WordPerfect for Windows in languages other than U.S. English, you can switch to that language's thesaurus (and spelling dictionary) by choosing Dictionary and then switching to the Thesaurus for that language. This works in the Speller, too: just select Dictionary and choose Main to switch to a different main dictionary.

Go back to your document by clicking in it. To go back into your document to get a sense of the context to help you choose a word, just click back in the document. You can scroll through your document and edit it, too. Highlight a word and press Alt+F1 to look up another word.

MOVING ON

You've seen all sorts of tricks for editing documents here. In fact, you may never have thought some of these features were designed for editing documents. Well, that's the voodoo.

Now for some formatting magic in the next chapter, "Formatting Secrets." Formatting is another very basic part of word processing. WordPerfect for Windows has lots of neat shortcuts for formatting, and some of them are completely hidden—they're not even in the program's documentation.

CHAPTER FIVE

Formatting Secrets

Pssst! . . . want to hear the most basic formatting secret? A lot of people find it easier to type a document and then go back and format it—especially with graphical word processing programs like WordPerfect for Windows, which let you see the effects of your formatting right on the screen. Of course, it all depends on how you want to work. Formatting has indeed become magic in WordPerfect for Windows, because it's so easy to do and you can see what you're doing. The only things you don't automatically see are page numbers, headers and footers, line numbers and footnotes, but you can use Print Preview to see them.

THE RULER

Most of the formatting you do in WordPerfect for Windows can be done with the Ruler (see Figure 5-1). Here's the Ruler's secret: if you click on the Ruler's icons or buttons, you do one thing, like dragging a margin marker to reset a right or left margin; but if you *double-click*, you do something else (usually you'll get a dialog box).

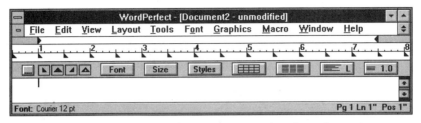

Figure 5-1: Most everyday formatting can be done by using the Ruler.

Press Alt+Shift+F3 to see or hide the Ruler. If the Ruler isn't visible, Alt+Shift+F3 is the key combination that displays it; if it's already displayed, that same shortcut hides the Ruler. On the DOS keyboard, this shortcut is Shift+F11.

Set the Ruler so you always see it. Select Environment from the Preferences menu. Then choose Automatic Ruler Display (see Figure 5-2) from the Environment Settings dialog box. The Ruler then automatically appears in all of your documents.

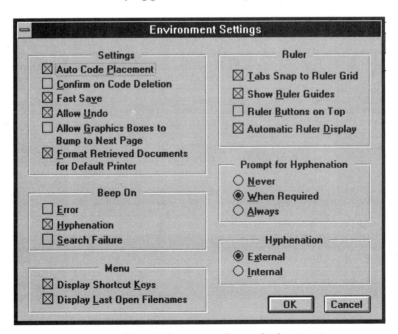

Figure 5-2: Set Ruler preferences through the Environment Settings dialog box.

Switch the Ruler's buttons to the bottom of the screen.
Normally the Ruler's buttons are displayed underneath the Ruler. If you want to see the Ruler right above the text, without any intervening buttons, go to the Environment Settings dialog box and uncheck Ruler Buttons on Top.

Other preferences you can set for the Ruler. If you don't like the way the program is set for tabs to appear at the nearest sixteenth of an inch from where you put them, uncheck the Tabs Snap to Ruler Grid box. Also, if you don't want right and left margins to show up as dotted lines when you drag them to set them, turn off Show Ruler Guides.

TRICKS WITH TABS

It's easy to set tabs with the Ruler, but the Ruler must be displayed before you can use it. You can hide the Ruler while you're typing and display it again when you're ready to do some formatting.

Drag tabs to set them. The little icons across the Ruler in half-inch increments represent tabs. Just drag a tab to reset it at a different location. To select several tabs, drag underneath them. Press Ctrl and drag to add the tabs to the new location; press Shift and drag to replace tabs in the new location. To remove a tab, just drag it off the Ruler.

Tab changes affect the whole paragraph. When you reset tabs, the changes take effect at the beginning of the paragraph the insertion point is in (unless you have Auto Code Placement off, as explained in Chapter 3, "Customizing WordPerfect"). This isn't the way WordPerfect DOS works, so be warned.

Different kinds of tabs. There are four different kinds of tabs—right, left, center and decimal—and each kind of tab can have dot leaders. Here are examples:

Tabs	
Left-aligned tabs:	Right-aligned tabs:
One	One
Two	Two
Three	Three
Center-aligned tabs:	Decimal tabs:
One	89.23
Two	883.22
Three	1.98

 Quickly setting a center-aligned tab. Press Alt+F7 to set a center-aligned tab. On the DOS keyboard, the shortcut is Shift+F6.

 Quickly setting a decimal tab. Press Alt+Shift+F7 to set a decimal tab. On the DOS keyboard, this shortcut is Ctrl+F6.

 Setting dot-leader tabs. To set a tab with a dot leader, click on the Dot Leader button (the one with the four dots on it) on the Ruler and drag it.

Dot-leader tab:

Chapter 1 1

 Setting right-aligned tabs with dot leaders. Press Alt+F7 twice to set a right-aligned tab with dot leaders at the insertion point. (Press Tab to move the insertion point; then press Alt+F7 twice.) On the DOS keyboard, press Alt+F6 twice.

Centered tabs with dot leaders? Why not? Here's how to do it. Put the insertion point before the word you want to have the dot leader appear next to; then press Shift+F7 twice. You'll get an effect like this:

....Centered Text

You can do this with text that has already been centered by putting the insertion point before the text and pressing Shift+F7 again.

Centered text with lots of dot leaders! To get this effect in your document, press Shift+F7 twice for the dot leader to the left; type the text to be centered; then press Alt+F7 twice for the dot leader to the right.

....Centered Text ....

Double-click on any tab marker to set evenly spaced tabs. If you double-click on a tab marker, the Tab Set dialog box appears (see Figure 5-3). It lets you set tabs at evenly spaced intervals so you don't have to figure out the spacing. Click Evenly Spaced and enter the amount by which you want tabs to be evenly spaced.

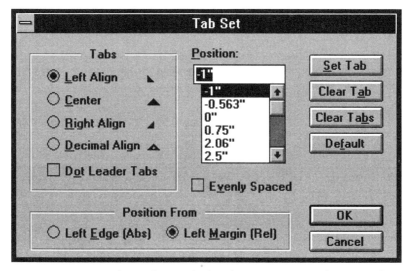

Figure 5-3: Use the Tab Set dialog box to set evenly spaced tabs and to clear tabs off the Ruler.

Clearing tabs off the Ruler. To clear *all* the tabs off the Ruler so you can reset them, don't bother dragging each tab off. Just choose Clear Tabs in the Tab Set dialog box.

Use a hard tab to set a tab on just one line. When you reset tabs, the new tab settings take effect from the beginning of the paragraph you're in through the rest of the document, until you change tab settings again. If you only want to set different tabs for *one line* and then go back to your regular tabs, don't use the Ruler. Use a hard tab instead.

To set a hard tab, choose Line from the Layout menu; then choose Special Codes and select a hard tab. (Or use the Alt+Shift+F8 shortcut to the Special Codes dialog box.)

Press Shift to set tabs exactly. Normally tabs "snap" to an invisible ruler grid in sixteenth-of-an-inch increments. This is the program's default, but you can use the Environment Settings dialog box to change it.

To turn the feature off temporarily just to set a few tabs, press Shift while you set the tabs. This applies to setting right and left margins, too.

INDENTING

All the indenting commands are on the Layout menu (you see them after you choose Paragraph), but they also have shortcuts, as you'll see in the following tricks.

To indent the first line of a paragraph, use the Tab key. The Indent command indents *every* line in a paragraph, including and following the line the insertion point is in. For a tab indent only at the beginning of a paragraph, use the Tab key, not Indent or its shortcut, F7. See Figure 5-4.

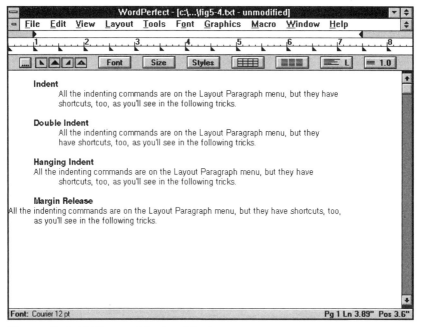

Figure 5-4: Different kinds of indents.

Don't use the space bar for indents! It may look OK on the screen to indent text by pressing the space bar, but if you switch to a different font or use the document in another program, your indents will get messed up. That's because a space is a relative measure: it depends on the font you're using and its size. For indents, use the Tab key or one of the indent commands, not that space bar.

Double indents? Press Ctrl+Shift+F7. To indent a paragraph equally from the right and left margins, use a double indent. This is called a Left/Right indent in WordPerfect DOS.

Double indents are often used for displayed quotes.

Hanging indents? Use Ctrl+F7. Hanging indents are those in which all the lines of a paragraph are indented except for the first line. You'll see these often in lists like bibliographies.

An easy way to remember indent shortcuts. Indent short-cuts all use some combination of the F7 key:

To Select:	Shortcut
Indent	F7
Double indent	Ctrl+Shift+F7
Hanging indent	Ctrl+F7

Remove indents by deleting their codes. The sure-fire way to remove an indent you don't like is to open the Reveal Codes window (Alt+F3) and delete the offending code or codes.

The insertion point doesn't move in codes like it did in WordPerfect DOS. WordPerfect for Windows is preset for Confirm on Code Deletion (choose Preferences from the File menu, then choose Environment) to be switched off. When it's off, the insertion point appears to ignore the invisible formatting codes as it moves through them. If old habits die hard and you want Word-Perfect for Windows to work like WordPerfect DOS (each time you pressed a Right or Left Arrow key, the cursor moved to format codes one by one), turn on Confirm on Code Deletion. This setting also prompts you each time you try to delete a format code.

Reset tabs to change the size of indents. When you indent text, WordPerfect uses the tab settings that are in effect. If you want to indent by 0.25-inch increments instead of 0.5-inch increments (which is the default), reset tabs on the Ruler. Use the Tab Set dialog box to reset tabs in equal increments, as explained earlier in this chapter.

Keep tabs the same by putting them in styles. If you change tabs several times in a document and also indent text, you may wind up with different sizes of tabs and different indents in various places in the document. To avoid this, put tab settings in your styles and apply the style to the text.

Use the Tab Set dialog box to change the alignment character.
You've often seen memos that start out like this:
Memo to:

    From:

  Subject:

Have you ever wondered how to align text this way? Change the alignment character.

To do this, press Alt+Shift+F8 to bring up the Insert Special Codes dialog box. Then, in the Decimal Align Character box, type the character you want text to be aligned on (see Figure 5-5). Then close the dialog box.

```
┌──────────────────────────────────────────────────────────────┐
│ ▭              Insert Special Codes                            │
│                                                                │
│ Hard Tab Codes:                Hard Tab Codes with Dot Leaders:│
│                                                                │
│   ○ Left [HdTab]                 ○ Left [HdTab]                │
│   ○ Center [HdCntrTab]            ○ Center [HdCntrTab]          │
│   ○ Right [HdRgtTab]             ○ Right [HdRgtTab]            │
│   ○ Decimal [HdDecTab]           ○ Decimal [HdDecTab]          │
│                                                                │
│ Hyphenation Codes:             Other Codes:                    │
│                                                                │
│   ○ Hyphen [-]                   ○ Hard Space [HdSpc]          │
│   ○ Dash Character               ○ End Centering/Alignment [End C/A] │
│   ○ Soft Hyphen -                                              │
│   ○ Hyphenation Soft Return [HyphSRt]   ○ Decimal Align Character: [ ]│
│   ○ Hyphenation Ignore Word [Hyph Ign Wrd]  Thousands Separator: [ ]│
│                                                                │
│                                       [ Insert ]  [ Cancel ]   │
└──────────────────────────────────────────────────────────────┘
```

Figure 5-5: To change the alignment character, first use the Insert Special Codes dialog box.

Whenever you want text to align on that character as you're typing, press Alt+Shift+F7. The message "Align char," along with the alignment character you've chosen, appears on the status bar. Go ahead and type; whenever you type that character, text will align around it.

Normally the decimal point is the alignment character.

Any of WordPerfect's special characters can be the alignment character. To use a special symbol as the alignment character, open the Insert Special Codes dialog box and click Decimal Align Character. Double-click on the character in the box. Then press Ctrl+W and select the symbol you want to use.

MARGIN MAGIC

WordPerfect's default margin settings are for 1-inch margins all around, but you can change them whenever you want to. To change the margins for an entire document, move to the top of the document first (Ctrl+Home). If you're changing the margins for only part of a document, be aware that the change will take place at the beginning of the paragraph you're in (if you have Auto Code Placement on). It's probably easiest to set margins by using the Ruler, but you can also use the Layout menu or the Ctrl+F8 keyboard shortcut.

You can't drag to set top and bottom margins. You just drag the right and left margin markers on the Ruler to set them, but where's the marker to drag to set top and bottom margins? Nowhere. To set top and bottom margins, double-click on a margin marker to display the Margins dialog box (see Figure 5-6) or press Ctrl+F8.

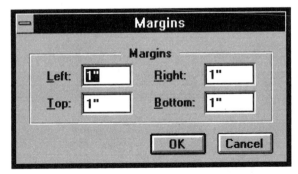

Figure 5-6: Set top and bottom margins in the Margins dialog box.

Use Margin Release to put text outside the left margin. The Margin Release command (choose Layout; then Paragraph) moves the insertion point to the previous tab setting. If the insertion point is at the left margin, Margin Release moves it outside the left margin. Shift+Tab is the shortcut for Margin Release—you don't have to use the menu system.

What's that good for? Well, you might want to number a paragraph or two out in the left margin. To do this, press Home to move to the beginning of the line, press Shift+Tab and type your paragraph number. Press Tab; then type the paragraph.

If you want WordPerfect to number paragraphs automatically, don't use Margin Release. Use the Paragraph Numbering feature instead (see Chapter 7, "Spells for Your Special Problems").

Sometimes text disappears when you use Margin Release. If you use the Margin Release command when the insertion point isn't at the left margin but is somewhere in a line of typed text, the next thing you type will overwrite text already on the line.

SEEING WHAT'S ON THE SCREEN

Sometimes you can't see everything on the screen while you're formatting text. You'll see several ways to get around screen problems in the following tips, but the easiest is to reset the right margin until you can see everything on the screen at once. Switch back to a 1-inch right margin when you're through typing.

Switch to Draft mode or change the display pitch to see more text on a line. If your document has been formatted in a PostScript font or a small-sized font, the lines of text may extend beyond what the screen can show. Switching to Draft mode will sometimes let you see the lines on the screen.

If you switch to Draft mode and still can't see the entire line, here's another trick. Choose Document from the Layout menu; then choose Display Pitch. Click Manual and increase the number in the box by clicking on the arrow. Click OK. Experiment until you can get the whole line on the screen.

Use a horizontal scroll bar to see text that won't fit on the screen. There's another scroll bar to use if you choose Display from the Preferences menu and click Display Horizontal Scroll Bar. Normally you won't need it, but it's handy if your text is wider than the screen (if you have a big spreadsheet or a lot of columns, for example).

PAGE MAKEUP MARVELS

Most documents are longer than one page, so here's some sorcery for formatting pages with headers and footers, changing page sizes, using page numbers, keeping text from being split between pages and more.

Shortcut to the Page menu: Alt+F9. The shortcut to the Page menu, which has a lot of important page-layout features, and which you can get to from the Layout menu, is Alt+F9. On the DOS keyboard, the shortcut is Shift+F8 P.

To break a page, press Ctrl+Enter. This is a very easy tip, but some folks don't know about it. And some books don't cover it until about page 300. So here it is: to force a page break at the insertion point (make a hard page break), press Ctrl+Enter.

Deleting a hard page break. This is another easy one, but it can cause trouble if you don't know about it. To delete a hard page break, put the insertion point just below the line that represents the page break; then press Backspace or Del.

You can also locate and delete the [HPg] code that represents the hard page break.

Soft page breaks are harder to change.   Soft page breaks are harder to change. WordPerfect puts them in as you type. Their code is [SPg]. If you don't like the way the program is breaking pages, there are only a few things you can do:

- Add extra hard returns to a page by pressing Enter.
- Change the top and bottom margins of the page.
- If you're using a different size of paper, switch to a different page size (see the next tip).

See the tip about changing line height ("Adjust the leading to control space between lines"), later in this chapter, for one last sneaky thing you can do.

WordPerfect lets you switch paper sizes within a document.   If you're printing with a WordPerfect printer driver, you can switch paper sizes within a document. (If you're printing with a Windows printer driver, you're stuck with one paper size for the whole document. See Chapter 8, "Spinning Straw into Gold: Printing," for an explanation of why you can print two different ways in WordPerfect for Windows.)

To change paper sizes, choose Paper Size from the Layout/Page menu; then pick a size.

Don't do this unless you're really going to put that size paper in your printer, or you'll get what's euphemistically called "unexpected results."

Formatting headers and footers.   When I first learned WordPerfect, it was a mystery to me how other people got the date and the page number and all that into their headers and footers and got text to center or appear flush left. It's no big secret: you can format headers and footers just like regular text. You can change their font, too, and WordPerfect will automatically switch back to your text font when you return to your document.

All the keyboard shortcuts work in the Header or Footer editing window. You can use the menu system instead of shortcuts, if you'd rather. But just to show off, here's how to set up the following footer with keyboard shortcuts:

Chapter 7   October 28, 1993   Page 7-1

    Press Alt+F9 and choose Headers or Footers. This brings you to the Headers or Footers dialog box. Click Create. Type **Chapter 7**, press Shift+F7 (Center), press Ctrl+F5 (Date Text), press Alt+F7 (Flush Right), type **Page 7-** and click Page Number. Click Close when you're finished.

You can have several headers or footers in a document, each saying something different. To change the text in your header or footer, set up a new one. You don't have to discontinue the old one, as you might think. WordPerfect will just use the new one from that point on in your document.

    This is a great tip for those of you who work on classified documents in which the footer has to say "Confidential" or "Top Secret" or "Shred After Reading" or some such on different pages.

Header (Footer) A is for left pages and Header (Footer) B is for right pages. This may be obvious to you, but it wasn't immediately obvious to me. I think of the first page as being a right-hand page, and so of course it would be Header A. It isn't. But using Header (or Footer) A is just fine if you're putting it on every page anyway.

Suppress a header or footer when you don't want it on a page. Stop a header or footer from being printed on a particular page by choosing Suppress from the Layout/Page menu. You'll see the Suppress dialog box, which lets you suppress any or all headers, footers or page numbers (see Figure 5-7).

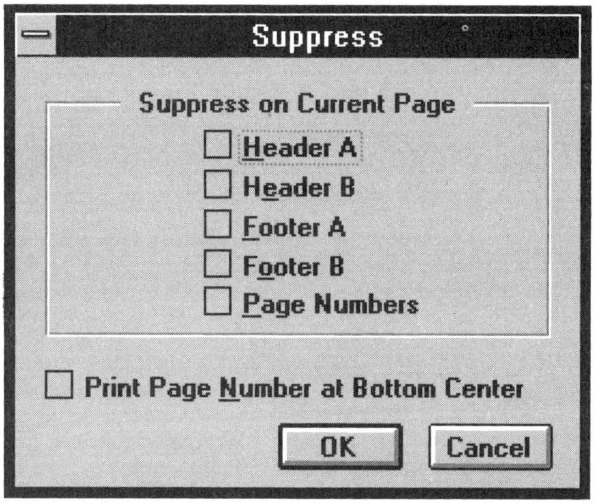

```
                    Suppress
         ┌─ Suppress on Current Page ─┐
              ☐ Header A
              ☐ Header B
              ☐ Footer A
              ☐ Footer B
              ☐ Page Numbers

      ☐ Print Page Number at Bottom Center
              [  OK  ]  [ Cancel ]
```

Figure 5-7: You can suppress headers,
footers and page numbering, too.

It's a sophisticated touch to have no footer or page number on
the first page of a business letter but to begin one on the second
page. Just create the footer at the beginning of the letter and suppress it on that first page. If your letter is longer than one page,
you'll have a footer on the following pages without having to remember to create one.

Set up a standard format for your business letters, or create a
style, so you only have to do this once.

**When Auto Code Placement is on, a header appears on the
page you create it on.**   If Auto Code Placement is on, your
header will appear on the page you create it on. If you don't want
the header to appear on the page you create it on, be sure to suppress it. With WordPerfect DOS, you wouldn't get that header until
the next page anyway (unless you set it up at the very beginning of
the page). But with WordPerfect for Windows, you'll get the header
on the same page.

Getting your header in the right place, no matter where it's created. Sometimes things go awry and you get headers where you don't want them—sometimes even in the middle of a page. To get around that problem, set up a header or footer anywhere in your document. Then delete the header code, move to the beginning of your document (press Ctrl+Home) and undelete the header code.

A delete-undelete trick to move codes. WordPerfect for Windows doesn't let you copy and paste codes without text. Here's the voodoo way through the back door: delete the codes, then move to the place where you want them and undelete them.

You can put graphics in headers and footers. For a nice touch, put your company's logo in your headers and footers, if it's available in a graphic format WordPerfect can accept (see Chapter 9, "Desktop Publishing Sorcery").

You can also use a horizontal rule in headers or footers to separate them from the text.

You can use special symbols, too. Here's a nice footer for business stationery:

Kay Nelson · **Computer Books** · **5751 Pescadero Creek Road** · **Pescadero, CA 94060**

Don't use page numbering *and* a header or footer. If you turn on page numbering and set up a header or footer in the same place, text may overlap when your document is printed. There are two ways to get around this.

- Put page numbers in the header or footer, as you saw in a previous tip. It's much more elegant to put your page number in the header or footer, anyway.
- Add a hard return as the *first* line in the header or as the *last* line in the footer, so the page number will print on a line by itself. It always prints on the first or last line of the page.

Header and footer margins don't automatically change.
If you change left and right margins in your document, you have
to change them in your headers and footers, too, if you want them to
have the same margin settings as the text. See the next tip.

Set up a header and footer style. If you're using several
different headers or footers in a document and you change
margins, you'll have to change each header and footer margin individually. To get around that, set up a style for your headers and footers.
Then just change the margins in the style. All your header and footer
margins automatically change when you edit the style. Magic.

You can search for headers and footers. If you have to look
for your headers and footers, remember that you can search
for their codes. Choose Search from the Edit menu, click Codes and
then select Header or Footer A or B.

WordPerfect doesn't automatically number pages. Word-
Perfect is preset not to number pages, so you have to remember to do this every time you want numbered pages. And if you're
writing documents that are longer than one page, you probably want
page numbering. So take this tip: go to the Preferences menu,
choose Initial Codes and turn on page numbering. To do this,
choose Page Numbering from the Layout/Page menu; then pick a
position for your page numbers and click OK. That way, all your
documents will have numbered pages.

If you don't want all your documents to have page numbers,
record a macro that turns on page numbering and assign it to a button so you can just click on it to turn it on in any document you want.

You can use text with page numbers. If you want page
numbers to have text with them, such as *Chapter* or *Section*,
click in the Accompanying Text box in the Page Numbering dialog
box (see Figure 5-8) and type the text you want to appear with every
page number. The [^B] stands for the page number itself.

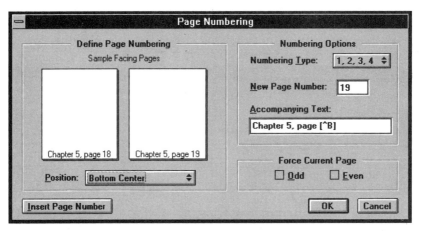

Figure 5-8: You can include text with page numbers by using the Page Numbering dialog box.

For example, if you want page numbers to appear as *Chapter 4, Page n* (where *n* is the page number), enter **Chapter 4, Page** and type a space. Make sure that [^B] is there.

Text added to page numbers appears every time the page number is used.   If you're generating a table of contents or an index, don't use text with your page numbers. You'll get things like *Chapter 4, Page 45* in your table of contents, which is obviously not what you want.

Use the New Page Number box to number documents sequentially.   If you've created documents that have chapters or sections and you want to number their pages in sequence, go to the Page Numbering dialog box at the beginning of each chapter or section and fill out the New Page Number box with the number that it starts on.

If you're printing two-sided pages, remember that odd-numbered pages are always on the right and even-numbered pages are always on the left. If a chapter or section starts on a right-hand page, it should have an odd number (the previous left-hand page may be blank).

Keeping text together. WordPerfect has three different commands for keeping text together. They're all on the Layout/Page menu, but they're a little complicated. Here they are in plain English in the following tips.

Avoid stray lines at the tops and bottoms of pages with Widow/Orphan. To prevent single lines of paragraphs from being printed at the tops or bottoms of pages, you can check the Widow/Orphan option on the Layout/Page menu.

Avoid breaking tables and charts with Block Protect. To keep a table or list from being split between two pages, use the Block Protect feature. As long as the table takes up one page or less, it will be kept on one page. To use this feature, select the whole table, list or chart and use the Block Protect command.

Keep headings with their text by using Conditional End of Page. To be sure that a heading stays with at least a line or two of its accompanying text (so you don't get headings by themselves at the bottom of a page), use Conditional End of Page. Put the insertion point above the heading; then, without moving the insertion point, count down to the last line you want to keep with the heading. If you're using double spacing, each line counts as two lines. Then choose Conditional End of Page and enter the number of lines to keep together.

Check page breaks just before you print. Reviewing page breaks (if that's important to your document) should be the last thing you do before you print. Do it after you've run the Speller, and after you've made any editing changes that could change page breaks.

FONT SECRETS

There are several different ways to change fonts in your documents.
Knowing about them can keep you from going crazy later, when you
aren't getting the results you expect.

- Change the Printer Initial Font to change the base font in all
  the documents you create from now on. To do this, choose
  Select Printer from the File menu; then click Setup and Initial
  Font.
- Change the Document Initial Font to change the base font in
  the current document only. To do this, select Document from
  the Layout menu; then choose Initial Font. (But don't say I
  didn't warn you about not using Document Initial Fonts back
  in Chapter 3, "Customizing WordPerfect.")
- Change the font "locally" by using the Ruler's Font button or
  the Font dialog box. Press F9 for a quick keyboard shortcut. If
  you change the font at the beginning of the document, it's
  changed for the whole document until you pick another font.

Auto Code Placement doesn't apply to fonts.   Font changes
take effect at the insertion point, not at the beginning of the
paragraph or the beginning of the page, like some format changes do
when Auto Code Placement is on (see Chapter 3).

Shortcuts for changing font styles.   Use the following shortcuts instead of bringing up the Font dialog box every time
you need bold or italic type or an underline. You can remove any of
these styles by switching to Normal.

Font	Shortcut
Bold	Ctrl+B
Italics	Ctrl+I
Underline	Ctrl+U
Normal	Ctrl+N

Use these shortcuts to change font size if you're not using a PostScript printer. Ctrl+S displays the Size menu, where you can change font size. Or you can double-click on the Size button to display the Font dialog box, where you can choose a different point size. But see the next tricks if you have a PostScript printer.

If your printer can handle scalable fonts, you can use odd point sizes. Normally, you're restricted to the list of point sizes WordPerfect shows. But if you're using TrueType fonts or if you have a PostScript printer or an H-P LaserJet III, for example, you can use scalable fonts to specify any weird point size you want, like 7 pt. or 11.5 pt. type. Enter it in the Point Size part of the Font dialog box.

PostScript printer? Don't use the Size commands, except for superscripts and subscripts. The Size boxes in the Font dialog box and the commands on the Size menu let you change type to Small, Large, Extra Large and so forth, but these are all relative sizes. To specify an exact point size, choose a size in the Point Size box (see the previous tip).

Assign fonts to the Ruler. Keep the fonts you use most often on the Ruler so you can switch to them quickly. To add a font to the Ruler, double-click on the Ruler's Font button. Then choose Assign to Ruler from the Font dialog box. Double-click on a font to put it on the Ruler.

Delete unused fonts from the Ruler. To delete from the Ruler a font you aren't using any more, double-click on its name in the Fonts on Ruler list in the Font dialog box.

STYLES SECRETS

A *style* is any combination of formatting codes you apply to text without having to type all the commands for the codes one by one. Once you've set up a style, you can use it over and over again. For example, to change all the secondary headings in a document to a different font and point size and also to switch them to italics, you could set up a style and apply it instead of changing each individual second-level heading.

To set up a style of your own, double-click on the Styles button on the Ruler and choose Create. This brings you to the Style Properties dialog box.

Enter a descriptive name in the Name box of the Style Properties dialog box (see Figure 5-9). In the Description box, explain what the style will be applied to, such as second-level headings. Then pick a Type (see the following tips).

Figure 5-9: Describe what your styles are for so you can keep track of them.

Use paired styles to turn an effect on and off. A paired style is used to format a certain element of text that appears at various points in your document, like a heading or a displayed quote. The formatting codes are turned on at the beginning and off at the end of the text you apply them to.

Use an open style to turn an effect on and leave it on. If you click on the arrowheads next to Paired in the Style Properties dialog box, you'll see other types of styles. Choose Open only for formatting that should affect an entire document—like line spacing, justification and so forth. Open styles are good for formats you use regularly, such as reports, newsletters and forms.

Use the Enter key to turn a style off. Usually you press Enter to insert a hard return for a new paragraph or a blank line. But you can make the Enter key work in a sneaky way: it can turn a style off. You'd do this, for instance, if you were formatting a heading and wanted to return to regular text. To set up the Enter key for this job, choose Style Off from the pop-up list that appears when you click on the arrowheads under Enter Key Inserts.

If you're using the Enter key to turn a style off, you might want to end the style with a hard return so you don't have to press Enter twice (once to turn the style off and once to move to the next line).

Make the Enter key turn a style on and off in a list. Choose Style On/Off for the Enter key (click on the arrowheads under Enter Key Inserts) to define a style for creating bulleted list items or numbered paragraphs. The style will be turned off and then on again when you press Enter to create the next bullet list item or paragraph.

What's that "comment" box in the Style Editor window? When you click OK to start putting in formatting codes for your style, you'll see the Style Editor screen, shown in Figure 5-10. If you create a paired style, the comment box is displayed; if you create an open style, there is no comment box. The comment box represents the text that the paired style will be applied to. Think of it as a placeholder. Put the style codes *above* the comment box.

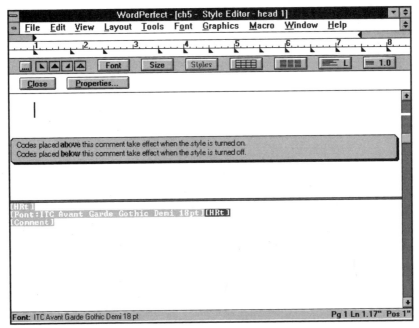

Figure 5-10: The Style Editor window lets you insert formatting codes for a style.

And how do you get the formatting codes to appear? Easy. Just do whatever you'd normally do to produce them. To set up a paired heading style for 18-pt. ITC Avant Garde Demi with a blank line above and below it, for instance, you'd press Enter to generate a [HRt] code, double-click on the Font button on the Ruler, and choose ITC Avant Garde Demi and 18 pts. from the Font dialog box. Click after the Comment box and press Enter again for the final hard return.

The quickest way to create a style. The absolutely quickest way to create a style from existing text is to copy the formatting codes from your document and paste them into the Style Editor window.

Edit a style to reformat a document. When you edit a style, all the text it's applied to reformats automatically when you return to your document. To edit a style, double-click on the Ruler's Styles button to bring up the Styles dialog box, select the style you want to change, click Edit and change the formatting codes.

There's no "normal" style unless you create one. Unlike some other word processing programs, WordPerfect doesn't have a Normal style. Instead, you can use an open style that's in effect for the whole document.

The Styles dialog box shortcut: Alt+F8. To bring up the Styles dialog box, just press Alt+F8 or double-click on the Ruler's Styles button.

Put styles on the Ruler. To see any styles that are available for a document, click on the Styles button on the Ruler. See the following tips for how to make more styles available.

Save styles to use in other documents. If you don't save a style, you can only use it in the current document. In a different document, you'll have to define it all over again. Save in a style file the styles you've created for a particular document so you can use them again in other documents.

To save the styles you've used in a document, choose Save As from the Styles dialog box. Use a name that helps you remember what the styles are for, such as NEWSLTTR.STY. That .STY extension isn't required, but it helps you identify the file as a style file. WordPerfect automatically displays all the files that have the .STY extension when you click Retrieve in the Styles dialog box.

Create a style library. Set up a "style library" of all the styles you'd like to have available so you can see them in the Styles dialog box. To do this, use the File/Preferences menu and choose Location of Files. Under Styles, enter the path name of the directory where you want to store your style files. Then, to specify which style file you want to have available when you use the Styles dialog box, choose Filename and enter the style file's name. If you don't remember the exact name, click on the tiny folder icon (see Figure 5-11) to see your files.

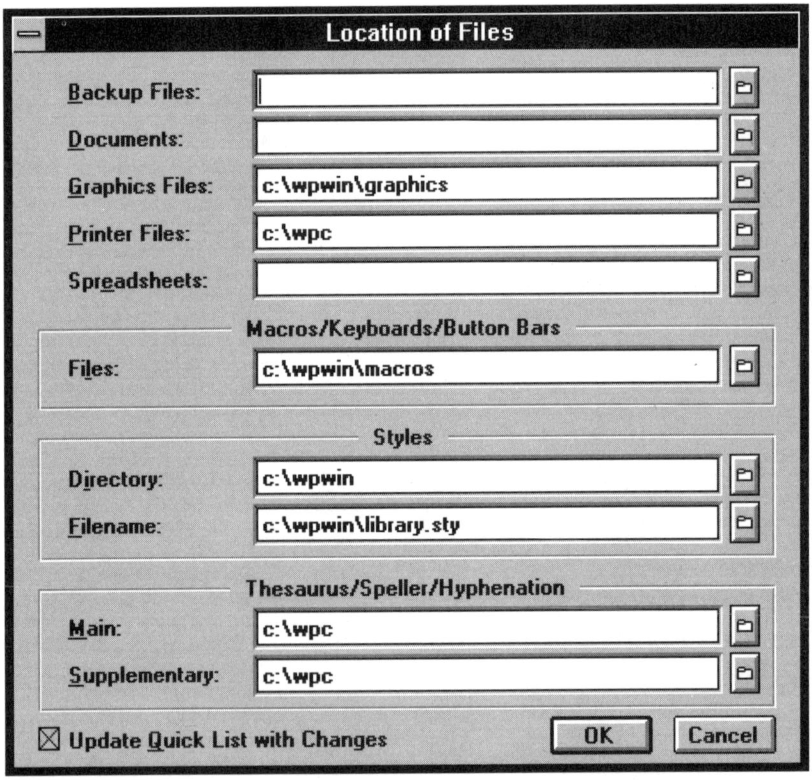

Location of Files		
Backup Files:		
Documents:		
Graphics Files:	c:\wpwin\graphics	
Printer Files:	c:\wpc	
Spr**e**adsheets:		
Macros/Keyboards/Button Bars		
Fi**l**es:	c:\wpwin\macros	
Styles		
D**i**rectory:	c:\wpwin	
Filename:	c:\wpwin\library.sty	
Thesaurus/Speller/Hyphenation		
Main:	c:\wpc	
Supplementary:	c:\wpc	
☒ Update **Q**uick List with Changes	OK	Cancel

Figure 5-11: Use the Preferences menu and choose Location of Files to specify where your style files are located.

Keep your style files in a separate subdirectory. If you keep all your style files (.STY files) in a subdirectory of their own, you won't run the risk of overwriting an existing style by giving a new style its name.

Be sure to tell WordPerfect which directory this is. Use the Location of Files dialog box on the Preferences menu.

Forgot to save a style? Here's a sneaky trick. It's not absolutely necessary to save a style in order to use it in another document. There's a back door.

Assuming that you've saved the *document* that has the styles you want to use again, start a new document—the one you want to use those styles in. Double-click on the Ruler's Styles button (or press Alt+F8). Click on Retrieve and enter the name of the document that has the styles in it. It doesn't have to have a .STY extension; in fact, it *won't* have a .STY extension because you didn't save the styles. But you'll retrieve the styles in that document instead of the document itself. Voodoo.

Use the Properties button to change a style's name, type and description. It's not immediately obvious how to change a style's name. The secret is to click on the Properties button in the Style Editor (see Figure 5-12). Then you can edit a style's description and type, too.

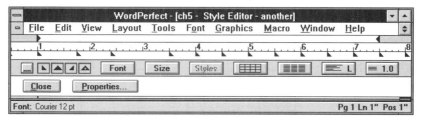

Figure 5-12: Use the Properties button in the Style Editor to edit a style's name, type and description.

To delete a style, use the Styles dialog box. Although you can delete a style from a document by searching for the [Style On] codes and deleting them, there's a faster way. Just use the Styles dialog box. Highlight the style you want to delete and click Delete.

When you copy text, styles come with it. If you copy a block of text from one document to another, all the styles come with it. You can wind up with a very big document that has a lot of styles in it. You might want to delete a few you're not using.

Leave the format codes in place when you delete a style if you're planning to use the document in another program. Not all word processing programs recognize WordPerfect's styles. So if you've applied styles to a document and then want to use the document in another word processing program, this trick deletes the styles but leaves the formatting codes in place: click Leave Format Codes when you choose Delete.

Applying styles to existing text. To apply a style, highlight the text you want to apply it to; then pick the style from the Styles list. It's fastest to use the Ruler's Styles button. If you use the Styles dialog box (or its shortcut, Alt+F8), you'll have to click the On button, too.

There's a hidden Name Search feature in the Styles list. To select a style from the list in the Styles dialog box, just type the first letters of its name. This is the secret to setting up a macro that will select a style (see Chapter 10, "The Magic of Macros," for more about macros).

Applying styles as you type. You can also apply styles as you type, but it's a bit more cumbersome. WordPerfect puts a [Style On] and [Style Off] code in your document when you apply a style. To turn off the style, you need to move the insertion point to the right of that [Style Off] code—but you won't see that code unless you have the Reveal Codes window open.

A sure-fire way to delete the effects of a style change.
Sometimes you can't turn off a style you've turned on somewhere. It can drive you nuts. To turn off the effects of a style, locate
and delete either its [Style On] or [Style Off] code. That will do it.

Voodoo for turning styles off. Here's a trick you may have
missed for turning a style off (it was buried in an earlier tip):
press the Right Arrow key at the point where you want to turn the
style off. This moves the insertion point over the (invisible) [Style
Off] code. Or click anywhere else outside the area in which the style
is on. That moves the insertion point outside the [Style Off] code, too.

Tired of changing fonts? Make a style. If you find that
you're switching fonts often in a document, make a style for
the change. Create a paired style that turns the new font on and off.
Then drag to highlight the text that's in a different font and choose
the style from the button on the Ruler. You won't have to switch
back to your regular font; the program does it for you.

How to see what the codes are in a style. Put the insertion
point on the [Style On] code while the Reveal Codes window
is open. The code expands to show you the codes that make up that
style. Neat.

Use WordPerfect's built-in styles. WordPerfect comes with
several predefined styles. Use them. There's a Bullet List style
already set up, as well as one for bibliographies. The style called *Tech
Init* can be used for numbered headings in a document; it turns on
Outline mode and numbers paragraphs. Use the previous tip to see
what codes are in these styles, or select them one by one in the Styles
dialog box and choose Edit to see exactly which codes they use.

TABLES TRICKS

With WordPerfect for Windows, the chore of creating tables becomes remarkably easy. In the following tricks you'll see tips not only for creating and editing tables but also for using tables for organization charts and parallel columns.

Use the Ruler to set up tables. It's magic. Click on the Tables button on the Ruler. It looks like a tiny spreadsheet with cells in it. A grid will appear. Just drag the mouse across it to highlight the structure you want your table to have (rows and columns, for instance).

Or double-click on the Tables button to get the Create Table dialog box, where you can specify the number of rows and columns you want, if you'd rather do it that way (see Figure 5-13).

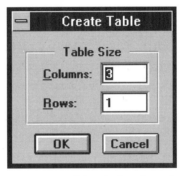

Figure 5-13: The Create Table dialog box is another way to create tables.

To create a b-i-g table, use the Create Table dialog box. You can create a table that has 32 columns and (gasp) 32,767 rows if you use the Create Table dialog box instead of dragging on the grid. Hope you've got enough paper.

The status bar shows where the insertion point is in a table. When you create a table, the insertion point is in cell A1, so you can begin typing. Look at the status bar to see which cell you're in if you lose your place.

Use the Tab key to move between cells in a table. Press Tab to go from cell to cell, or Shift+Tab to go backward.

 Tabs in tables? Of course. To put a tab in a table, press Ctrl+Tab.

More keyboard shortcuts for moving in tables. Actually, the easiest "keyboard" shortcut is to use the mouse and just click in the cell you want to go to. But if you're furiously typing away, here are some shortcuts for moving the insertion point:

- To go to the last cell in a row, press End twice.
- To go to the first cell in a row, press Home twice.
- To go to the beginning of the cell to the right or left, press Alt+Right Arrow or Alt+Left Arrow.
- To go to the beginning of the cell above or below, press Alt+Up Arrow or Alt+Down Arrow.

Selecting cells. The trick here is to move the mouse pointer until you see it change to an arrowhead. At the top border of a cell, it changes to an upward-pointing arrowhead. At the left edge of a cell, the mouse pointer changes to a left-pointing arrowhead.

To select a single cell, click when you see the arrowhead. To select a row, click when you see the Left Arrow. To select a column, double-click when you see the Up Arrow.

Selecting an entire table. Point to a cell border. When the insertion point becomes an arrowhead, click three times and your table is selected. You can change its font or do whatever you want with it without selecting row by row.

 Selecting a block of cells. To select a block of cells, just drag over them with the mouse.

Selecting text instead of cells.   If you drag over cells with the mouse, you'll select the cells, not the text. You *can* select text only if you carefully drag so you don't hit a cell border—but it's tedious. Here's where you can use WordPerfect's "hidden" Select mode. Press F8 and you'll select text only, even if you drag across cell borders.

You can delete text quickly without deleting your table's structure.   Don't bother deleting text in columns and rows one cell at a time if you're deleting an entire column or row, or several columns or rows. Highlight the column or row; then press Delete or Backspace. You'll see a dialog box that gives you a chance to choose whether you want to delete text only or the row or column itself.

You can delete all the text in a table this way, too. Select the whole thing (see a previous tip) and press Del.

A hidden shortcut for deleting text.   To delete from the insertion point to the end of the cell, use the Ctrl+Del shortcut. It's not on any menu.

Save your table before you edit it!   The fastest way to create a table is to get the information in the cells and then go back and pretty it up. But save it first, just in case something goes wrong while you're editing it.

The keyboard shortcut for the Tables menu: Ctrl+F9.   Pressing Ctrl+F9 brings up the Tables menu so you can edit your table. You can also get to the Tables menu by choosing Tables from the Layout menu.

To add a row, press Alt+Ins.   This is a quick way to add a row without bringing up the Table Options dialog box. An added row is inserted *above* the row that has the insertion point in it.

To append a row, press Alt+Shift+Ins.   Press Alt+Shift+Ins to append a row to a table. A row that you append is inserted *below* the current row.

Deleting rows.   To quickly delete one row, use the Alt+Del shortcut. To delete several rows, select them first and then press Delete or Backspace.

To change column widths, just drag a column marker.   If you have a table on the screen, the Ruler changes to show column markers above it (see Figure 5-14). Just drag them to change column widths.

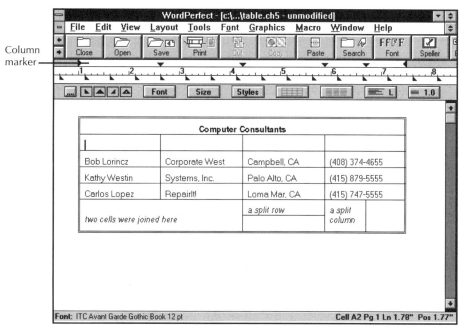

Figure 5-14: Dragging a column marker changes the width of the column.

Dragging to reset column widths makes other columns move. Press Shift and drag to change one column's width without moving the other columns.

Press Ctrl and drag to change the whole table's size as you resize the columns.

To change the number of cells in a row, join them or split them. It's not immediately obvious how to get unequal numbers of cells in rows. The secret is to join them (to make fewer cells) or split them (to make more cells).

For example, you'll quite often want to have headings in tables, like the one in Figure 5-14, where all the cells in the first row have been joined to make one cell, and cells in the bottom part of the table have been split and joined to make unequal numbers of both cells.

To join cells, highlight them and choose Join from the Tables menu (remember that Ctrl+F9 shortcut to get to the Tables menu).

To split a cell, put the insertion point in it and choose Split from the Tables menu. You can split it into rows or columns.

Text entries in the cells you join will be separated by tabs. WordPerfect doesn't delete text already entered in cells that you join. Instead, it separates each entry with a hard tab. You can delete what you don't want, or reformat the text.

Set equal columns with the Format Columns dialog box. To specify an exact width for columns, choose Columns and Define from the Tables menu and enter an exact column width in the Format Column dialog box (see Figure 5-15).

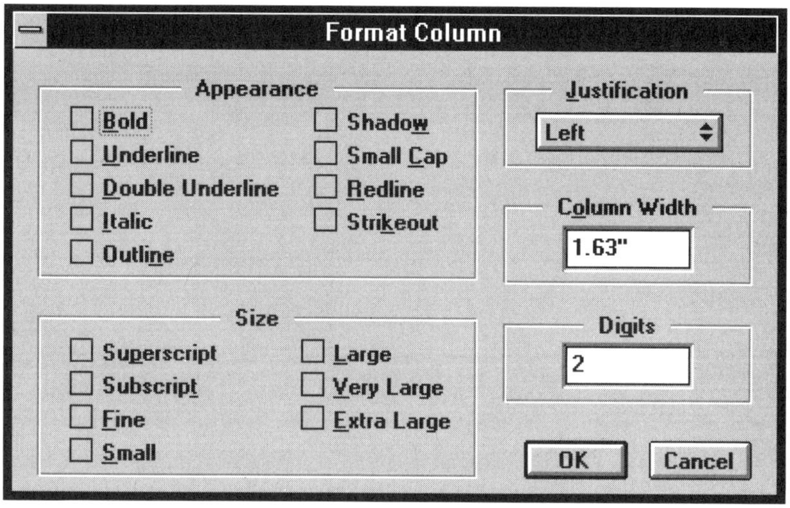

Figure 5-15: Use the Format Column dialog box to specify equal columns.

Set attributes for an entire column, including justification, with the Format Column dialog box. You also set the justification for text within a column, as well as the column's appearance and size, in the Format Column dialog box. It's often a lot faster to set column and text attributes here than to change these things as you type text in cells.

Set several attributes at once for a cell with the Format Cell dialog box. To change several things about a cell—such as typeface, justification and so forth—use the Format Cell dialog box (see Figure 5-16). Instead of highlighting the text in the cell, pressing Ctrl+B (for Bold), and then changing the justification and whatever else, choose Cell from the Layout/Tables menu to get the Format Cell dialog box.

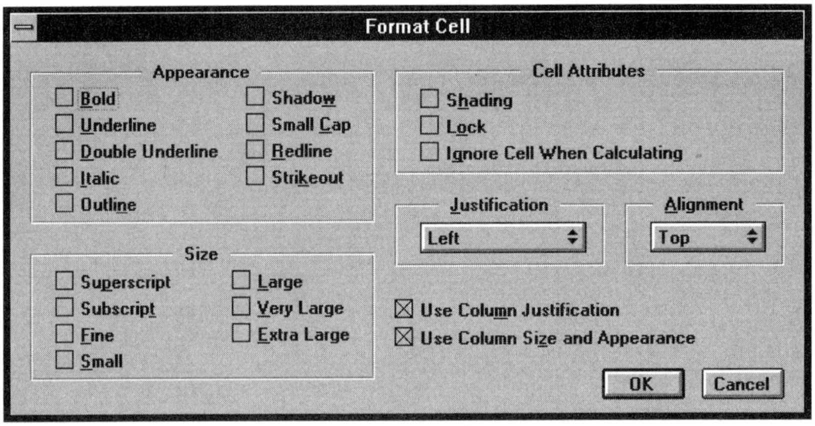

Format Cell

Appearance

☐ Bold ☐ Shado̲w
☐ U̲nderline ☐ Small C̲ap
☐ D̲ouble Underline ☐ R̲edline
☐ I̲talic ☐ Stri̲keout
☐ Outli̲ne

Size

☐ S̲uperscript ☐ La̲rge
☐ Subscri̲pt ☐ V̲ery Large
☐ F̲ine ☐ E̲xtra Large
☐ S̲mall

Cell Attributes

☐ S̲hading
☐ L̲ock
☐ I̲gnore Cell When Calculating

Justification

| Left ↕ |

Alignment

| Top ↕ |

☒ Use Colu̲mn Justification
☒ Use Column Size and Appearance

OK   Cancel

Figure 5-16: To change more than one format in a cell, use the Format Cell dialog box.

Don't bother to highlight a column before formatting it.
Just click to put the insertion point in the column you want to format; then choose Column from the Tables menu.

If you're formatting more than one column, just select a cell in each one. Don't bother to highlight the entire column.

Reformat individual cells to override a column's justification. If you've got a few cells in a right-justified column that you want to have aligned on the decimal point, override the column's justification by selecting the cells and picking Decimal Align in the Format Cell dialog box. This is often useful in columns in which cells with text and cells with numbers are mixed.

Don't try to format rows like you format columns. To reformat cells in tables, format the cells themselves or format the columns. The Format Row dialog box just lets you set the height of the row and choose whether you want more than one line of text per cell in the row (see the next tips). You can't change justification, set widths or do anything else that the Format Cell and Format Column dialog boxes let you do.

You can set a fixed row height.   Normally the height of a row adjusts to fit the text that you type in it. If one cell has more text in it than another, the row expands to accommodate the largest cell. You can turn this feature off. Choose Row from the Tables menu, click Fixed and enter in the Format Row dialog box the fixed row height you want to use (see Figure 5-17).

Figure 5-17: Use the Format Row dialog box to set row heights.

Entering a big table of numbers? Check Single Line.   You can also turn off the feature that allows you to enter more than one line of text in a cell. Click Single Line in the Format Row dialog box, and from then on each time you press the Enter key you'll move to the next cell. This is a neat trick for using the numeric keypad to enter numbers in tables.

Lock cells whose contents you don't want changed.   If you're setting up a form for other folks to use, there may be some areas you don't want to change. You can lock those cells by selecting them and choosing Cell and Lock from the Tables menu. From then on, nobody will be able to even put the insertion point in those cells—unless they unlock them, of course.

To unlock a locked cell, select it with the mouse and choose Cell and Lock again, or use the Table Options dialog box and click Disable Cell Locks.

Changing fonts in tables. You can change the font in tables just as you do in regular documents. Select the text you want to change; then double-click on the Font button on the Ruler and choose your font.

To change the font for all the text in a table, switch fonts just outside the table, before it begins. You can't select all the text in a table and change fonts; the Font button is dimmed.

Unfortunate zooming in tables. Sometimes, when you scroll tables, the Ruler zooms so that table columns become very wide on the screen. If this happens, press Ctrl+F3 to refresh the screen.

Making columns with tabs into a table. This is a lot easier than retyping a table! Just select the text and choose Tables from the Layout menu; then choose Create and fill out the Convert Table dialog box (see Figure 5-18). You may have to do a little formatting, but it sure beats retyping the whole table.

Don't forget that you can cut or copy and paste text into table cells, too. This simple hint can be a real timesaver.

Figure 5-18: Don't forget that you can convert typed text to tables with this dialog box.

Double-click on any column marker to get the Table Options dialog box. This is a really hidden mouse shortcut. You have to display the Ruler to do it. Just double-click on a column marker above the Ruler to get the Table Options dialog box (see Figure 5-19). It lets you put shading in cells and position the table on the page.

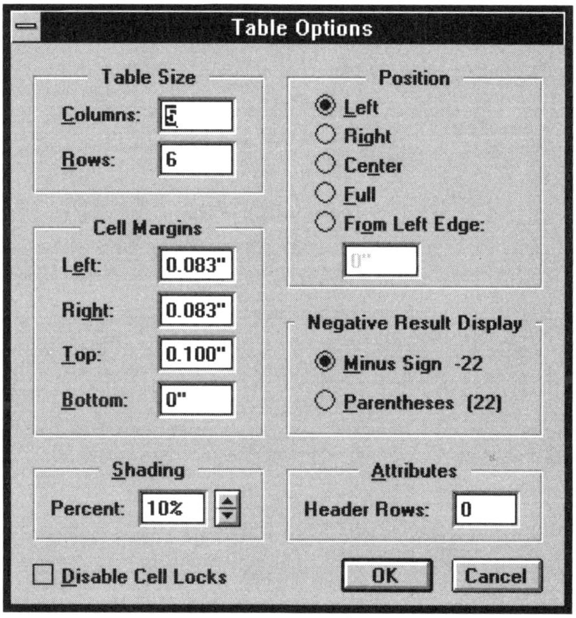

Figure 5-19: The Table Options dialog box lets you adjust a table's appearance.

To position a table on the page, use the Table Options dialog box. Normally tables fill the space between the left and right margins, but if you delete a column your table suddenly aligns on the left margin. To change this, use the Table Options dialog box to pick a new Position (Left, Right, Center, Full or From Left Edge).

Use the Lines command to delete rules in tables. If you want a table to appear without rules, or with rules above and below it only, or with a different pattern of rules, choose Lines from the Tables menu. This brings you to the Table Lines dialog box, where you can pick a different pattern for your lines (see Figure 5-20).

If you choose None for all of the lines, your table keeps its formatting and only the rules disappear.

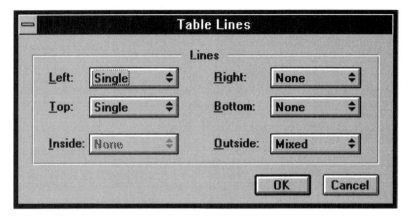

Figure 5-20: Use the Table Lines dialog box to get rules out of your tables or to pick a different pattern of rules.

Want to repeat column headings in tables longer than one page? If a table is too big to fit on one page, you may want to repeat its column titles on the following pages. You can do this without retyping and reformatting the column headings.

Here's the trick: take a good look at your table and count down from the top row to the row that has the column headings you want to repeat. Then choose Header Rows from the Table Options dialog box and enter *that row number* as the row to be used as the header.

Don't use shading of more than 10% if you want to read text in tables. If you're planning to put text in shaded cells, go light on the shading or you won't be able to read the text. Heavier shading is OK in rows or columns that aren't meant to be read but are used to separate areas of the table.

You can have only one shading setting per table (but there's always voodoo). WordPerfect lets you choose only one percentage of shading per table, but there's a sneaky way around this (see Figure 5-21, which is actually three tables stacked on top of each other). Just create one table immediately below the other and pick different shadings for each one.

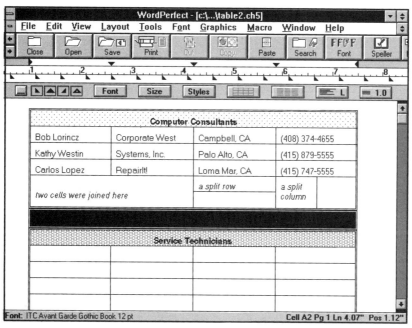

Figure 5-21: Stack tables on top of each other to produce the effect of different percentages of shading within one table.

You can't put a table in a column unless it's in a Graphics box. The easy way around this restriction is to select the whole table, copy it and then paste it in a Graphics box. See Chapter 9, "Desktop Publishing Sorcery," for more about these magic boxes.

Use tables as organization charts. The easy way to create an organization chart like the one in Figure 5-22 is to enter the text in table cells and to delete the unwanted cell borders.

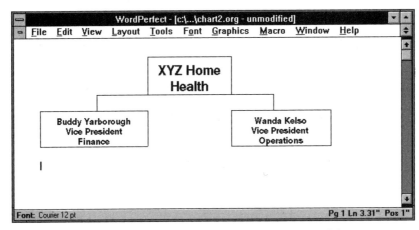

Figure 5-22: Create an organization chart from a table.

Use tables instead of Parallel columns. It's much easier to type text in table cells than to set up and use Parallel columns. It's a lot easier to format text in table cells, too. If the text entries you want to put in Parallel columns are relatively short, save yourself some trouble and make a table instead. If you don't want any rules in it, just delete all of them.

You can create tables that make calculations like spread-sheets. If you need to create an invoice form that automatically calculates totals and subtotals, figures out the tax to be added and so forth, don't bother firing up your spreadsheet program. You can do the same thing in WordPerfect's tables.

To enter a formula in a cell, choose Formula from the Tables menu. In the Tables Formula dialog box (see Figure 5-23), use the normal notations + for Add, - for Subtract, * for Multiply and / for Divide. To calculate a 7.5% sales tax on a total in cell D5, for example, enter **D5*.075**.

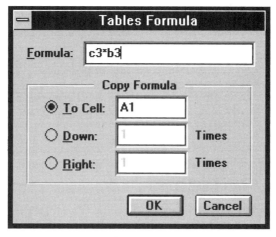

Figure 5-23: Put formulas in table cells
with the Tables Formula dialog box.

Calculating totals, subtotals and grand totals. Here's a
shortcut for calculating subtotals, totals (the results of all
subtotals) and grand totals (the results of all totals). Instead of setting up a formula that uses cell references, just use these symbols in
the cells of the column in which you want to calculate the totals:

- Use + for a subtotal—the results of adding all the numbers in
  the cells directly above that cell.
- Use = for a total—the results of adding all the numbers in the
  cells with + (the subtotals) directly above.
- Use * for a grand total—the results of adding all the numbers
  in the total cells (those with =) directly above.

WordPerfect doesn't automatically recalculate. If you
change the numbers in your table after you've set it up with
formulas, choose Calculate from the Tables menu to recalculate it.
WordPerfect doesn't do this automatically, like some spreadsheet
programs do.

Copy formulas instead of retyping them. This a real time-
saving trick. Very often you'll want similar formulas in other
parts of your table. Just copy a formula to another cell instead of

retyping it. If you choose Down or Right from the Tables Formula dialog box, WordPerfect copies the formula with cell addresses that are relative to the original formula. So if the formula in the current cell is E5*F5, it becomes E6*F6 when you copy it to the right.

If you choose To Cell, WordPerfect copies the formula exactly as you entered it, with the same cell references.

Tabbed tables are a thing of the past.   Don't fool around with using tabs to set up multiple columns or tables unless you're doing a really simple chart or list. Use WordPerfect's Table or Column features instead. Columns of tabbed data are notoriously difficult to edit in WordPerfect, so why use them when there are much easier ways of accomplishing the same thing?

COLUMNS TIPS

WordPerfect has two types of columns: Newspaper columns and Parallel columns. Newspaper columns flow from the bottom of one column to the top of the other. Text in Parallel columns stays next to the entries on either side of it (see Figure 5-24).

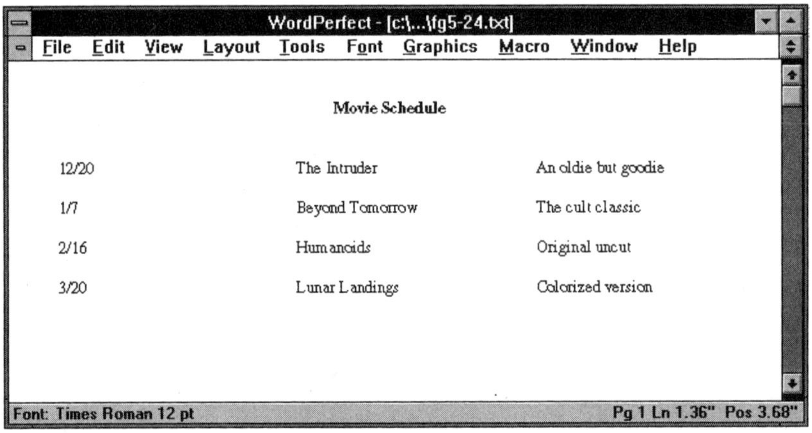

Figure 5-24: Use Parallel columns for such things as schedules and scripts, or for any text you want in side-by-side columns.

Type text first; then format it for Newspaper columns. This is much more efficient than typing text in columns. For one thing, displaying a large number of columns on the screen can slow down your system, especially if you're using lots of graphics and making font changes. Type text first; then make it into columns.

This doesn't apply to Parallel columns, which keep text side-by-side with its fellow entries.

Converting typed text to columns. To convert text into columns, put the insertion point where you want the first column to appear and define the columns (see the following tips for how to do this). Then go to the end of the text and turn columns off (click on the Ruler's Column button and choose Columns Off).

You can convert text to either Newspaper or Parallel columns, but it's usually easier to do for Newspaper columns. If you convert text to Parallel columns, you'll need to go through the text and press Ctrl+Enter at each point where you want a column break.

Use the Ruler's Column button to create text in columns. Click on the Column button on the Ruler to choose how many columns you want. You can choose from two to five columns.

For more than five columns, double-click on the Column button. If you want more than five columns, *double-click* on the Column button. That brings up the Define Columns dialog box (see Figure 5-25).

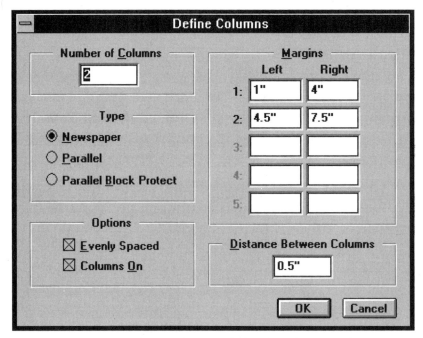

Figure 5-25: The Define Columns dialog box lets you format columns in a variety of ways.

Use the Define Columns dialog box to make sure columns are evenly spaced. It's easy to "eyeball" a couple of columns on the screen to make sure they're equally spaced, but it's tedious to figure out the exact spacing for larger numbers of columns. The trick is to use the Define Columns dialog box and click Evenly Spaced.

It's easy to change the number of columns. To change the number of columns you want on a page, just put the insertion point anywhere in a column and pick a different number of columns from the Column button on the Ruler. You don't have to search for codes or select all the columns.

Fast trick for removing columns. To remove columns, just drag the shaded margin marker that's between the columns up above the Ruler. Drag it down off the Ruler.

You can resize columns easily this way, too. As you drag the margin marker, the columns will resize.

Mixing the number of columns on a page. What if you have three columns on a page and want to create two columns on the same page? The trick is to turn the three columns off (click on the Column button on the Ruler and choose Columns Off). Then put the insertion point where you want the new columns to be, choose Columns On and choose 2 Columns.

Shortcut for turning columns on and off. When you're ready to resume regular text, go to the Columns menu from the Layout menu and choose Columns Off. If you're interested in doing things the easy way, use the unlisted shortcut Alt+Shift+F9.

Make a Columns button. If you find that you're turning columns on and off a lot, make a button for it. Choose Button Bar Setup from the View menu; then choose Edit. Then choose Columns On from the Layout/Columns menu. Repeat the process for making a Columns Off button.

You only have to set up columns once. Once you've defined your column style, you can use it for subsequent columns by choosing Columns On from the Columns menu or using the keyboard shortcut Alt+Shift+F9.

You can't turn columns on and off unless you've set them up earlier in your document. If you try to turn columns on and you haven't actually defined a column format somewhere earlier in your document, the Columns On choice will be dimmed. That's because WordPerfect needs to locate a [Col Def:] code that tells it what kind of columns to turn on.

To break a column, press Ctrl+Enter.   It's just like making a page break: pressing Ctrl+Enter breaks the column and starts a new column.

Check the status bar to see where you are.   If you get lost in a large number of columns, check the status bar to see where the insertion point is.

Use a mouse for columns.   It's so easy to click with the mouse to move from column to column that I wouldn't even try to put text in columns or edit columns without one. But you can also use keyboard shortcuts to move from column to column. To move to the column to the right, press Alt+Right Arrow. To move to the column to the left, press Alt+Left Arrow.

You have to set Parallel columns through the Define Columns dialog box.   You can create Newspaper columns by choosing the number of columns from the Ruler's Column button, but you have to use the Define Columns dialog box (double-click on the Column button) to set Parallel columns.

Shortcut for moving through Parallel columns.   Press Alt+Up Arrow and Alt+Down Arrow to move the insertion point to the beginning of the text in the area immediately above or below the insertion point. This trick works only in Parallel columns.

Sometimes it's easier to use tables than Parallel columns.   If your entries are short, put them in a table instead of in Parallel columns. Tables are much easier to edit. To achieve the same effect as Parallel columns, just use the Table Options dialog box and delete all the rules.

Parallel columns are not easy to edit. WordPerfect inserts codes in Parallel columns that basically tell the program to treat each column entry as a mini-page. If you're not aware of the exact position of these [HPg] codes, you can run into trouble when you edit text in Parallel columns.

To make things easier on yourself, open the Reveal Codes window while you edit text in Parallel columns so you can see where the codes are. (Or use the previous trick.)

To stop Parallel columns from breaking between pages, choose Parallel Block Protect. If you want your columns *not* to be split between pages but to remain always on the same page, choose Parallel Block Protect from the Define Columns dialog box.

Don't choose this unless you know that your columns are going to be shorter than one page.

Turn off the display of side-by-side columns for major editing jobs. To do major editing in several columns, choose Preferences from the File menu and then choose Display. Uncheck Display Columns Side by Side in the Display Settings dialog box. It's easier and faster to edit the text in just one column at a time. Turn the display back on when you're done.

JUSTIFICATION TRICKS

Justification and alignment are two very similar things. *Center*, *left*, *right* and *full justification* all refer to how text is *aligned* on a page in relation to the left and right margins. But WordPerfect calls it *justification* when you align several or more lines of text, and *alignment* when you align only one or two lines of text. So if you want to justify a paragraph and all the text that follows it, you'd use the Justification button on the Ruler. To justify only one line, you'd use the Layout/ Line menu or press Alt+F7, its keyboard shortcut.

To change justification for one or two paragraphs only, select them first. To change the justification of only one or two paragraphs in a document, select them and then click the Justification button. The rest of your document won't change.

Shortcuts for changing justification. Instead of clicking on the Ruler's Justification button, use these shortcuts to change justification in a document:

To Select:	Shortcut
Center justification	Ctrl+C (for Center)
Full justification	Ctrl+J (for Justification)
Left justification	Ctrl+L (for Left)
Right Justification	Ctrl+R (for Right)

Full justification can cause weird word spacing. With Full justification, space is added between words to stretch text equally between left and right margins. This can add as much as four times the usual amount of space between words, and sometimes you won't like the results.

The easiest way to fix this is to turn on hyphenation to give the program more flexibility in calculating line breaks. (Choose Hyphenation from the Layout/Line menu.) You can also go into the Typesetting dialog box and change the justification limits there (choose Typesetting from the long Layout menu).

If you choose Center or Right justification for a paragraph that's already typed, you may lose some formatting. You'll lose any tabs and indents you've set as well as any codes for Flush Right or Center if you apply Center or Right justification to a paragraph that already contains these codes. Remember it as the Undo WiZard (Ctrl+Z)!

If you use Flush Right within a line of typed text, it can overwrite text. If this happens, locate the [Flsh Rgt] code and delete it. Then try again in a blank line.

To center text in columns, move away from the left margin. WordPerfect centers text around the insertion point if it isn't at the left margin when you choose Center. So to center text in columns, use the space bar or the Tab key to put the insertion point at the center of the column; then choose Center from the Layout/ Line menu (or press Ctrl+J), and type the heading for the column. The text stops being centered as soon as you press Enter. In my opinion, this is the fastest way to do it.

You can also set a center tab at the correct location and then press the Tab key to place the insertion point at that tab.

If there are tabs on a line, WordPerfect won't center text between the right and left margins. If text isn't centering between the right and left margins, open the Reveal Codes window (Alt+F3) and see if you've pressed the Tab key by mistake and put invisible [Tab] codes in the line.

The wizard's way to center text on a page. Have you ever tried to figure out how many blank lines to put above and below text to center it exactly in the middle of a page, such as on a one-page letter or cover sheet? WordPerfect can do it for you.

Choose Center Page from the Layout/Page menu. Then type the text you want centered. (If the text is already typed and you're centering the first page of the document, press Ctrl+Home to move to the beginning of the document before you choose Center Page.)

The trick is to have the insertion point at the beginning of the page and to make sure there's nothing else on the page when you choose Center Page. To make sure you're on an absolutely blank page, you can insert a page break with Ctrl+Enter; then choose Center Page.

This centers text vertically on the page. If you want text centered both vertically *and* horizontally, as in a cover sheet, use Center justification on it, too.

LINE SPACING

Changing line spacing in WordPerfect is simply a matter of clicking on a button. You can mix line spacing within a document and even use odd spacing like 1.25 (one-and-one-quarter) lines. This section shows you some tricks to use for line spacing and discusses the mysterious topics of line height and leading, too.

Use the Ruler's Line Spacing button to set line spacing quickly.   Instead of going to the Layout menu, choosing Line and then choosing Spacing, click on the Ruler's Line Spacing button.

Double-click on it to get the Line Spacing dialog box, where you can pick a spacing other than 1, 1.5 or 2.0. If your printer can handle it, you can enter weird spacing such as 2.1 or 3.75 (most dot-matrix printers can't do this).

You can change line spacing in the current paragraph only.   When you click on the Ruler's Line Spacing button and pick a different line spacing, the spacing in your document from the insertion point to the end is changed. To change spacing in just one part of a document, select the text before you click the Line Spacing button.

Line spacing depends on line height.   What's the difference between line spacing and line height, which is another choice on the Layout/Line menu? Well, the actual amount of line spacing is determined by the line height. The distance from the baseline of one line of text to the baseline of the next line of text is one line height, so with single spacing there's one line height between baselines of text. Double spacing is two line heights between baselines.

WordPerfect calculates line height automatically. If you switch to a different-sized font in a line of text, the line height changes to accommodate the largest font in that line. If you select a fixed line height in the Typesetting dialog box, it can cause trouble if you mix font sizes on a line. For a better way to take control of line heights, see the following tips.

Adjust the leading to control space between lines. The space between lines of text is called *leading*. Normally Word-Perfect adds two points of leading between lines of text in proportionally spaced fonts. (Monospaced fonts, like Courier, have leading built into them.) Those extra two points are counted in the line height.

So instead of setting a fixed line height, which may cause problems if you mix font sizes in a line, adjust the leading. Choose Typesetting from the long Layout menu, and you'll see the Typesetting dialog box, shown in Figure 5-26. The part you'll use is Line Height (Leading) Adjustment. (Tip: If you don't see the Typesetting choice on the Layout menu, you've turned on Short Menus. Use the View menu and select Short Menus to remove the check mark next to it.)

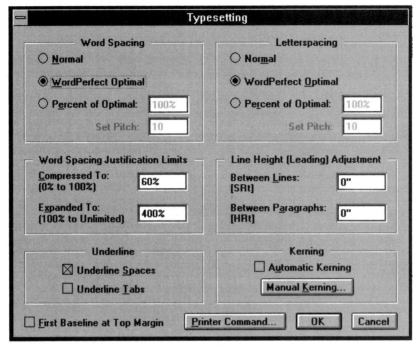

Figure 5-26: Use the Typesetting dialog box to get sophisticated formatting in your documents.

Select Between Lines or, for a very sophisticated effect, Between Paragraphs to add extra space between lines or paragraphs.

Sneaky trick for fitting text on a page. If you just need to fit one or two extra lines on a page, use this trick: delete just a tiny bit of space between lines. To delete two points of space, enter a measurement such as **-2p** in the Between Lines box of the Typesetting dialog box. Use points, because fonts are usually measured in points. Remember that entering an abbreviation with a measurement causes WordPerfect to automatically convert the measurement to inches, so use **p** for points instead of trying to figure out how many inches that is!

Use Print Preview (Shift+F5) to see the effects of your changes. If you don't want the change you made to be in effect to the end of your document, change back to regular leading on the next page.

SPECIAL CHARACTERS

Some formatting chores call for special characters. You saw a couple of these—for em and en dashes—in Chapter 4, "Editing Alchemy." Here are a few more.

Smart quotes. A lot of word processing programs have "smart quotes" built into them, but WordPerfect doesn't. Smart quotes are curly quotes that open and close a quotation. If you look closely, you'll see that opening quotes curl in a different direction than closing quotes. The quotes in this book are smart quotes. The other kind of quotes are just straight up and down, and they make your documents look like they're typed on a typewriter instead of a computer that probably costs thousands.

Using smart quotes gives a professional touch to your documents. To get them easily, record a macro that inserts the opening quotes and another macro that inserts the closing quotes. Then make the macros into buttons and click on the buttons when you need smart quotes.

Here's how to do that. The macro gets assigned a key combination, too, so you'll be able to insert the quotes either via the keyboard or via the buttons.

Choose Record from the Macro menu, or press Ctrl+F10, the keyboard shortcut. Press Ctrl+Shift+O (for "open quotes"). Word-Perfect names the macro CTRLSFTO.WCM. You could use a name here, like *open*, if you'd rather.

Enter **open quotes** as the descriptive name; then click Record. Press Ctrl+W and choose the Typographic symbols set. Click on the open quotes (look at the ones in this book to see which they are) and then click Insert and Close. Choose Stop from the Macro menu or press Ctrl+Shift+F10, the keyboard shortcut.

Now you can insert open quotes into a document by pressing Ctrl+Shift+O. But go ahead and make it into a button for your Button Bar.

Choose Button Bar Setup from the View menu; then choose Edit. Select Assign Macro to Button and highlight CTRLSFTO.WCM. That's it. Now you've got an opening-quote button, too.

Repeat the process for closing quotes. You might want to name that one Ctrl+Shift+C (for Close).

A slightly more sophisticated macro that you could apply to a document once it's typed could search for all double quotes preceded by a blank space and replace them with opening quotes; then it would return to the top of the document and search for all the remaining double quotes (which at that point would be closing quotes), and replace them with closing quotes. See Chapter 10, "The Magic of Macros."

Bullet lists? Easy.   There's a built-in bullet list style on the Ruler's Styles button. *Use it*. Once you turn that style on, you'll get a nicely formatted bullet each time you press Enter. Then you can just type the text for that item.

To turn off the bullet list effect, press Alt+F3 to open the Reveal Codes window. Then move the insertion point beyond (to the right of) the [Style Off] code.

MOVING ON

Although this chapter seems to have gone on forever, it hasn't covered all the possible formatting tricks. In Chapter 7, "Spells for Your Special Problems," you'll see tricks for formatting tables of contents and indexes, using paragraph numbering and outlining, and formatting such widely different things as mailing labels and equations. Chapter 9, "Desktop Publishing Sorcery," will give you lots more sophisticated formatting tips for creating pull-quotes, reversing out text, creating columns separated by rules and placing borders around pages. But in the next chapter we're going to take a look at ways to manage your documents with WordPerfect's File Manager.

Tricks for Managing Your Documents

Keeping track of the documents you create in WordPerfect is a chore that can be done in WordPerfect itself or in its very handy stand-alone File Manager. The File Manager has features that let you do things you can't do within WordPerfect, such as create new directories and select several files at once to rename, copy or delete. In addition, it has very sophisticated search features that let you locate files by name or by content. You can also use it to print documents, start other application programs and get information about your system.

In this chapter, we'll first look at tricks you can use to manage your documents within WordPerfect for Windows, and then we'll see some File Manager magic.

Before you use WordPerfect's file management capabilities very much, it's important to understand directories, subdirectories, paths and wildcards. So let's begin with a brief review. If you know all this stuff already, skip this section.

Files are organized into a system of directories on your computer's hard disk, just as paper files are stuffed into file folders in a filing cabinet. A directory can hold different kinds of files such as programs (like WordPerfect for Windows), the documents you create, spreadsheets and graphics. It can also contain other directories, called subdirectories, just like stuffing a file folder inside another file folder.

If you stuff very many folders inside folders (in other words, if you have a lot of subdirectories within directories), you can easily get lost when you want to find something in a particular subdirectory. Your computer can get lost, too, so it lets you use a command called PATH (in your AUTOEXEC.BAT file) that tells it where to look for programs. WordPerfect for Windows, when you installed it, set up your path to tell your computer where your WordPerfect files are (unless you told it not to), so you don't have to worry about that. You do need to know the rather cryptic way you have to write out your path: each subdirectory is separated from the next-higher level subdirectory by a backslash, and your hard disk drive letter is followed by a colon. So the path to your WordPerfect for Windows directory probably looks like this (assuming that drive C is your hard drive):

`c:\wpwin`

If you store documents in a subdirectory named DOCS under C:\WPWIN, its path looks like this:

`c:\wpwin\docs`

You'll see this type of path notation in Open, Retrieve and Save As dialog boxes as well as in the File Manager, so it's good to understand how it works.

As for wildcards, they're special characters, just as in poker, that can stand for other characters. The asterisk (*) represents any number of letters (or none at all), and the question mark (?) represents any one character (or none at all). So *.* stands for "everything" (any or all of the eight characters in a file name plus any three-character extension) and ?LTTR.DOC stands for files that begin with one character and are followed by LTTR.DOC, such as 1LTTR.DOC, ALTTR.DOC and so forth. You can use wildcards to speed up operations on files with similar name patterns, so you can manipulate several files at a time.

Those are the basics. Now you're ready to begin.

MANAGING DOCUMENTS IN WORDPERFECT

There are often-overlooked options in Open, Retrieve and Save As dialog boxes (called *directory dialog boxes*) that you can use to do a lot of your document housekeeping within WordPerfect, without going out to the File Manager. In addition, WordPerfect has a Document Summary feature that can be used to organize your documents. And if security is a problem, you can even lock your documents with a password so nobody (including you) can see what's in them without supplying the password.

Keyboard shortcuts for opening and closing documents.
WordPerfect has shortcuts for the basic commands that manage your documents. Here they are:

Operation	CUA	DOS
Save	Shift+F3	F10
Save As	F3	F10
Clear document	Ctrl+Shift+F4	Ctrl+Shift+F7
New	Shift+F4	
Close application	Alt+F4	Alt+F4
Close document	Ctrl+F4	
Next application	Alt+Esc or Alt+Tab	Alt+Esc or Alt+Tab
Previous application	Alt+Shift+Esc	Alt+Shift+Esc

Don't use these extensions when you save files. The extensions .DLL, .PRS, .WWK, .INI and .WCM have special meanings in WordPerfect for Windows. Don't use them in your file names! Also, don't use the extensions that have special meanings to DOS: .BAT, .EXE, .COM and so forth.

The hidden Name Search feature in directory dialog boxes. If you know the first few letters in the name of the document you're looking for, click anywhere in the Files box in an Open, Retrieve or Save As dialog box. Then just type those characters to go directly to the file's name.

Use Home or End to go to the beginning or end of a list. These two keyboard shortcuts save you from having to scroll all the way to the top or bottom of a long list.

What's that weird [..]? At the beginning of the Directories list in a directory dialog box, there's a mysterious notation: [..] (see Figure 6-1). It's shorthand for the parent directory, or the directory just above the directory you're looking into, in the hierarchy of directories. Double-click on this symbol to move up one level in your directory system, where you can switch to another branch.

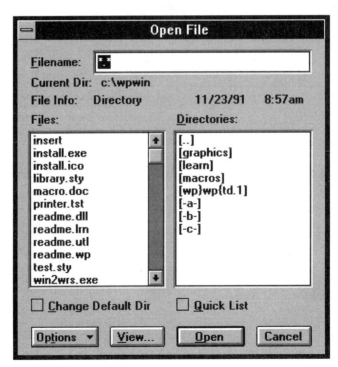

Figure 6-1: Clicking on [..] lets you switch to another branch of your directory tree.

Say you're looking in C:\WPWIN\DOCS but you want to see what's in C:\QPRO. The C:\QPRO directory won't be listed because it's in a different branch. To move up the directory tree and cross over to that branch, click on [..], which puts you at C:\WPWIN, and then click on [..] again to get to C:\ (the root directory). Then you'll see C:\QPRO, and you can double-click on it to see what's in it.

You can view what's in a file without actually opening it.
After you've highlighted a file name in an Open dialog box, you can click the View button to see what's in it without actually taking the time to open it (see Figure 6-2). You can view graphics files this way, too, which is really convenient.

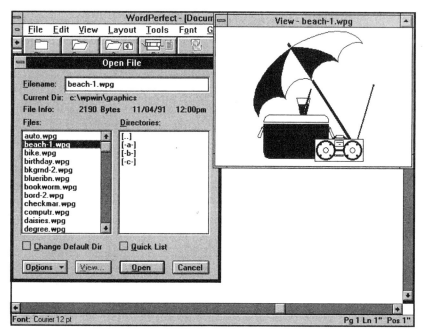

Figure 6-2: The View window shows you the contents of files without actually opening them.

Press the Down Arrow to see what's in the next file.   When you're in an Open dialog box, you can use the View feature to review what's in a directory by just pressing the Down Arrow until you've gone through as many files as you like. You don't have to highlight each file name one by one.

Resize the View window to see more.   Remember the window secret: you can move (and usually resize) any window that has a title bar. The View window has a title bar, so you can move and resize it. Make it bigger to see more of it. Just click in the title bar to make it full-screen size.

Use keyboard shortcuts to move through View windows. You can use the usual keyboard shortcuts Ctrl+End to go to the end of a document in a View window, or Ctrl+Home to go to the beginning. PgUp and PgDn work, too.

Don't check Change Default Directory in a directory dialog box unless you really want to do that.   The default directory is the one that WordPerfect automatically opens when you choose Open, Retrieve or Save As. If you check the Change Default Directory box in any of those dialog boxes, you'll make each directory you look at the default directory. Even if you click Cancel to leave the dialog box without selecting any files, the last directory you looked into will be the default directory when you choose Open, Retrieve or Save As again. If you're just looking through directories to find a certain document, you may not want to do this.

On the other hand, if you're changing directories, keeping the Change Default Directory box checked gives you the ability to easily switch the default directory—even to another drive.

The default directory isn't always the same as the directory that's current when you start WordPerfect. WordPerfect uses as the default the directory you choose on the Preferences menu for storing your documents when you start the program. If you've checked the Change Default Directory box in a directory dialog box, the default directory changes as you open directories, but the directory you chose on the Preferences menu will still be the default directory the next time you start WordPerfect.

Just type a path in the Filename box and press Enter to change directories. The brute-force way to change directories is to just type a path in the Filename box in a directory dialog box. For example, if you want to switch to a directory that's named C:\WP51\DOCS\VOODOO, just type that in the box and press Enter. If you're switching to a directory that's a few levels down (or up) in your filing system, this is often faster than double-clicking on a series of directory names to get there. The catch is that you have to know the path to the directory you're going to.

Use numbers to put a directory at the top of the Directories list. It's nice to have directories that you use a lot appear at the beginning of the Directories list in directory dialog boxes. Start its descriptive name with a letter near the top of the alphabet or a numeral, like *1 Voodoo WordPerfect*. Then you won't have to spend a lot of time looking for the directories you use most often.

What if you don't see the directory list? If you don't see the directory list, you're looking at a Quick List (see Figure 6-3). This is a neat feature in WordPerfect for Windows that lets you specify which files and directories you work with most often, so you don't have to go hunting through your whole directory system.

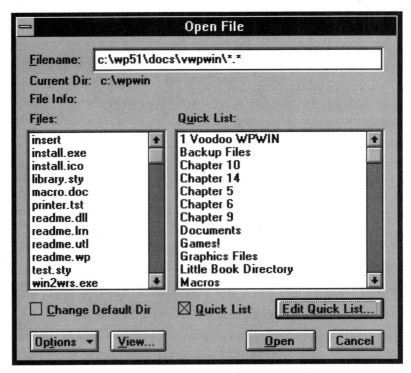

Figure 6-3. Set up a Quick List of the files and directories
you work with frequently.

If you're looking at your Quick List and want to see into other
directories, *uncheck* the Quick List box. You'll see a regular directory
list. This may be obvious, but I kept forgetting it when I first started
working with WordPerfect for Windows.

**Press Alt+Q to switch between the Quick List and the
Directories list.** This is a handy little hidden shortcut that
saves you from having to reach for the mouse to uncheck the Quick
List box when you want to look in directories that aren't on your
Quick List. Remember, once a list is active, you can use the also-
hidden Name Search feature to go directly to a directory by typing
the first few characters of its name.

Setting up a Quick List. To set up your own Quick List, open a directory dialog box (an Open, Retrieve or Save As dialog box). Check the Quick List box and choose Edit Quick List and Add. You'll see the dialog box shown in Figure 6-4.

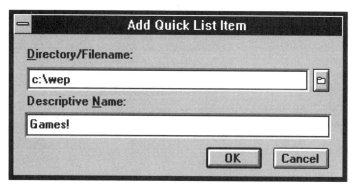

Figure 6-4: Use this dialog box to pick what's going into your Quick List.

Click on the tiny folder icon to see all your directories; then just double-click on a directory to put it in the top box. Click OK. You could also type the path to the directory you want to add.

Use descriptive names in your Quick List. WordPerfect automatically puts the path name in the Descriptive Name box, but why not use a descriptive name? Delete the path name in the box and type in the name you want to appear in your Quick List.

You can use uppercase and lowercase letters as well as spaces in Quick List names. Be descriptive so you can find things easily. If you're used to WordPerfect DOS's long document names feature, this is how to get the same effect in WordPerfect for Windows. (Yes, you can still use long document names in the File Manager if you use document summaries, as you'll see later.)

Put frequently used documents in your Quick List, too. You aren't restricted to putting directories in your Quick List; put documents you use often there, too. In fact, you can use wildcards to put *patterns* of document names in your Quick List.

Say you'd like to create a Quick List item that stands for all the tables of contents for a book's chapters. I used the extension .TOC for all the tables of contents for the chapters in this book. So I enter C:\WPWIN\DOCS*.TOC in the Directory/Filename box and enter Chapter Tables of Contents in the Descriptive Name box (see Figure 6-5). So now, to find a table of contents for a particular chapter quickly, all I need to do is double-click on the Chapter Tables of Contents entry to see all those file names at once.

An aside: if you're used to WordPerfect DOS, you may not have assigned extensions to your document names. With WordPerfect for Windows, you can get lots of mileage out of using extensions, as you see here, so perhaps it's time to start thinking about assigning extensions to your documents to classify them into types. You could use .LTR for letters, .RPT for reports, or an abbreviation of a project's name for documents pertaining to that project. If you do this, you can quickly put those documents in your Quick List by category.

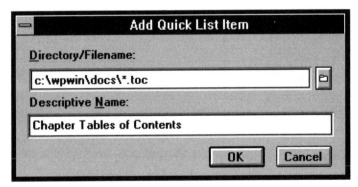

Figure 6-5: You can use wildcards to set up Quick List items.

Your Quick List stays the same in the File Manager. The Quick List you set up in WordPerfect appears in WordPerfect's File Manager, too. You can edit it from WordPerfect or from the File Manager.

There are lots of things hidden under a directory dialog box's Options button. The Options button in a directory dialog box acts as a mini-File Manager. It has options that let you delete, copy, move or rename files as well as find files by name or content.

You can delete several files at the same time. It's not immediately obvious, and you can't do it with the Copy or Move/Rename options, but you can use wildcards with the Delete option to delete several files at once. Enter ***.*** in the File to Delete box (see Figure 6-6) to delete everything in the directory. Enter ***.rpt** to delete all files ending in .RPT.

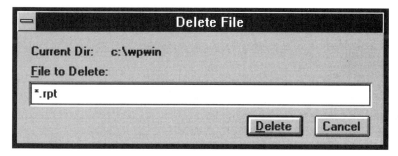

Figure 6-6: You can use wildcards to delete files, but you can't use them to copy or rename files.

You can copy a file and rename it at the same time. The trick to making a copy of a file under a new name is to edit the path name and enter the new name of the file in the To box of the Copy File dialog box (see Figure 6-7). You'll wind up with two copies of the file—one with the original name in the original location, and the other with the new name in the new location.

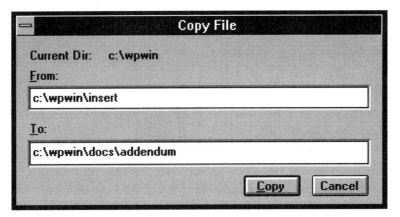

Figure 6-7: Copying and renaming a file.

Don't type the file name twice if you're not changing it.
You don't have to type the file name in the Copy File dialog box's To box if you want it to have the same name in the new location. Just edit the path to the directory you want the copy to appear in. The same applies if you're moving a file and not changing its name.

You can move a file and rename it at the same time, too.
In the To part of the Copy File dialog box, just edit what's there by typing the new name at the end of the path. WordPerfect erases the file in its original location and moves it to the new location, giving it the new name.

You can use Save As instead of Rename. To make a copy of a file in a new location or under a different name, use the File menu's Save As command instead of using Rename. It's a little faster if you already have on the screen the document you want to make a copy of.

Don't move files that WordPerfect needs to find. If you move files that WordPerfect often needs to locate, such as macros or graphics files, it may not be able to find them unless you go to the Preferences menu and indicate which directory you moved them to.

If you can remember part of a document's name, you can find it. The Find command in the Options pop-up list lets you search your whole hard disk (and floppy disks, too) for a file. You only need to remember all or part of its name. If you remember the whole name, enter it in the File Pattern box (see Figure 6-8). If not, use wildcards for the parts you can't remember. If you know a file starts with AUG but you can't remember how it ends, for example, enter **aug*** to search for files beginning with AUG and ending in anything.

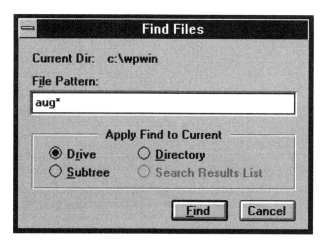

Figure 6-8: Use wildcards if you can't remember a file's whole name.

Click Subtree to search the current directory and any directories that may be underneath it. Click Drive if you really have no idea where the file is.

WordPerfect finds all the files that match your pattern and displays them in a Search Results list (see Figure 6-9). You can then click View to see what's in the files and figure out which one you want. To open the file in a WordPerfect editing window, double-click on its name in the Search Results window.

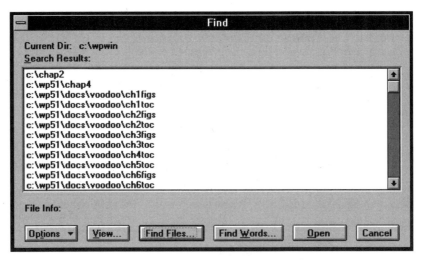

Figure 6-9: Search results are displayed in a special window.

If you don't know all or part of a file's name, try searching for words in it. Click the Find Words button to find a file if you know that a certain word or phrase is in the file you're looking for. Just remember that WordPerfect searches only for whole words unless you use wildcards to specify a word pattern (see Figure 6-10). If you know, for example, that the document you're looking for mentions a company named something like *Western Industry*, but you're not sure whether it's *Western Industrial*, *Western Industries* or maybe even *Western Independent*, enter **"western ind*"**. (You have to use quotes because you're searching for a phrase.)

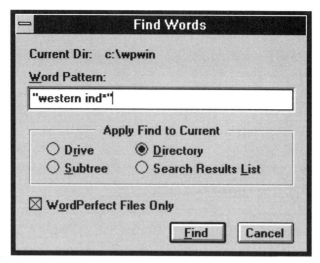

Figure 6-10: Use the Find Words dialog box to locate words within documents.

Once you locate the file that has the words in it, use the View feature to look in it.

You can do very complex word searches. You can do a few types of complex word searches to locate documents. To find documents that contain two word patterns, enter the words separated by a semicolon or a space. To look for both *Western* and *Eastern*, enter **western;eastern** or **western eastern**. (Use lowercase letters to find all occurrences of a word, no matter how it's capitalized.)

To find documents that contain either one word pattern or the other, separate them with a comma or a vertical slash (I). Entering **western,eastern** or **westernIeastern** locates documents that contain either *Western* or *Eastern*.

And to find documents that *don't* contain a word pattern, use a dash (this is the AND NOT operator). For example, to find files that contain *Western* and not *Eastern*, enter **western;-eastern**.

Use quotation marks to find phrases. To search for a phrase, be sure to put quotation marks around it. If you want to find the phrase *net 30 days*, you'd enter it as **"net 30 days"**. Otherwise WordPerfect searches for documents that contain the words *net* and *30* and *days*.

Don't do word searches on your whole hard disk unless you've got time to spare. Your computer can search file names relatively quickly, but choosing Find Words and then choosing to search the entire hard disk can take a while. Try to use one of the other options in the Find Words dialog box—Directory or Subtree, for instance.

Press Ctrl+W to search for special characters. Yes, you can search for special symbols by pressing Ctrl+W to bring up the WordPerfect Characters dialog box when the Find Words dialog box is open. This is a neat trick to use if you know the document you're looking for has a special symbol in it, like a copyright (©) or foreign-language character.

You can refine searches by combining Find Files with Find Words. Once you think you've found the right documents, you can search them for specific words or phrases to narrow down your choice. Just click the Apply Find to Current Search Results List (in the Find Words dialog box) when you do the word search.

If you use a password, better not forget it. WordPerfect encrypts the password you enter and stores it in the file's header prefix, which you normally can't see. (The password isn't stored in the WPWP.INI file, so don't bother looking there.) All the backup files, undelete files and so forth associated with the file are locked, too. There are code-breaking packages that you can purchase, but they're really difficult to use. Just use the *same password* for all your documents, and you'll stand less chance of forgetting it.

Capitalization doesn't count in WordPerfect passwords.
Although it does matter to some programs whether you use capital or lowercase letters in a password, WordPerfect doesn't care. It recognizes KITTY or kitty or kiTTY as your password.

Assigning a password to a file doesn't stop others from moving or deleting it. Other people can delete or move your locked file to another directory even if they don't know the password. So you *can* lose locked files. Assigning a password, however, prevents others from looking at or printing a file.

There are a couple of other much sneakier things to do to protect files. You can make them read-only files so they can't be changed, or make them hidden so they don't show up in any directory listing. See the File Manager tips in the last half of this chapter for this.

If you retrieve a locked document into an unlocked document, the composite document isn't automatically locked.
It's possible to reveal the contents of a password-protected file if you use the Retrieve command to retrieve it into an existing document and then forget to password-protect that document. To avoid this, always open a locked document into a blank editing window.

Use document summaries to manage your files. You can use WordPerfect's Document Summary feature with the File Manager to locate documents by keywords, subjects or types that you assign to them, the author and typist of the document, or the date of creation or revision.

To assign a document summary, open the document first. You can't create a document summary for a document that's not on the screen. Choose Document from the Layout menu; then choose Summary and fill out the dialog box (see Figure 6-11) with as much or as little information as you want to keep track of. Be sure to save your document with its new summary.

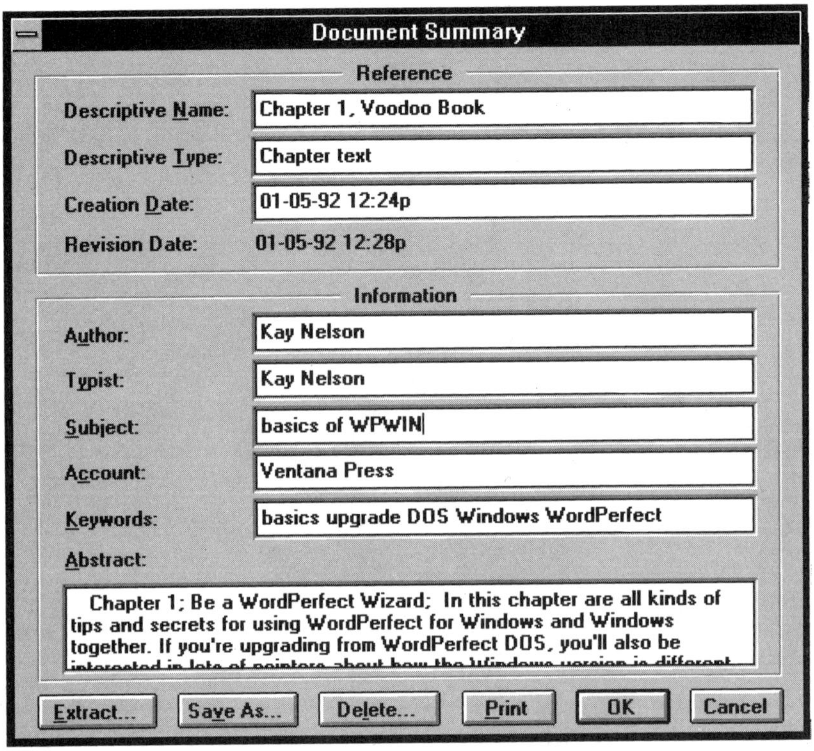

Figure 6-11: The Document Summary dialog box lets you keep track of several different types of information about documents.

Save As saves only the document summary, not the document. Some people like to save their document summaries as separate files. That's what the Save As command in the Document Summary dialog box is for. It doesn't save the document. Save the document in the usual way (click the Button Bar's Save button).

The Creation Date is the date the summary, not the document, was created. This can drive you nuts if you're not aware of it. If you want the Creation Date to reflect the date *the document* was created, change the date in the Creation Date box.

The Revision Date also shows when the document summary, not the document, was last revised. But you can't change it.

You can locate documents quickly with document summaries. It's much faster to search for a subject or a specific word than to scan an entire document, so using document summaries can speed up searches in the File Manager. See the tips on searching in the File Manager later in this chapter.

You can print document summaries. If you manage a large amount of word processing, you may want to print out your document summaries and keep them in a loose-leaf binder for easy reference. You can print a document summary from the Document Summary dialog box, or from the Print menu (choose Multiple Pages; then click Print and check the Document Summary box).

Extract the first 400 characters of a document and put them in your document summary. Instead of typing an abstract, which is usually a summary of what a document contains, use the Extract option on the Document Summary dialog box to retrieve the first 400 characters of a document into the Abstract box.

You can also extract the subject of a document without retyping it. Most legal memos have a subject line that begins with *RE:*. You can use the Document Summary dialog box's Extract option to retrieve the first 150 characters that follow the *RE:* (or up to the first hard return) into your document summary.

If you use something like *Subject:* or *Topic:* instead of *RE:*, use the Preferences menu to insert whatever you use.

If you use the Extract option, you'll get both Subject and Abstract text. You'll also get an Author and a Typist, if you've saved a document summary before. You may need to change these, if they aren't the same for the current document.

If you use document summaries routinely, check the Create Summary on Save/Exit box in the Preferences menu. The Preferences menu has settings you can change for document summaries, too. If you check the Create Summary on Save/Exit box, you'll be prompted to fill out the Document Summary dialog box when you first save a document. That way you won't forget to do it.

Assign types to documents so you can sort them by type in the File Manager. If you'd like to sort your documents by type—such as by client, project, as memos or letters and so forth—in File List windows in the File Manager, assign them a type in the Document Summary dialog box, and you'll be able to sort them that way in the File Manager.

Use document summaries for long document names in the File Manager. Even if you don't want to manage your documents with the Document Summary system, you can use document summaries to assign long, descriptive document names that show up in the File Manager's File List (see Figure 6-12). These are really neat for helping you keep track of what a document is.

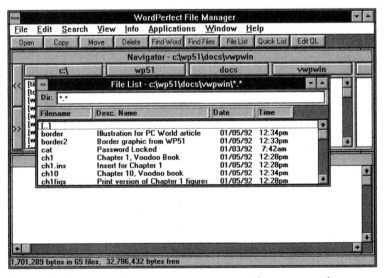

Figure 6-12: Use document summaries if you want long document names that show up in the File Manager.

To have them appear in the File Manager, click anywhere in the blank part of a File List window's Button Bar and choose Descriptive Name from the pop-up list that appears.

To have them reappear the next time you use the File Manager, go to the File Menu, choose Preferences, choose Environment and then click Save Current Layout on Exit.

Document summaries slow down the File Manager. Once you've started creating document summaries and using descriptive names, the File Manager has to scan each directory for document summaries, so it will be a bit slower to open File List windows.

FILE MANAGER TRICKS

WordPerfect for Windows has a File Manager that's superior to Windows's File Manager. It has its own Button Bar and preferences you can set, and it comes with a built-in set of keyboard shortcuts. Use the File Manager for all file "housekeeping" duties—copying, renaming and deleting groups of files and directories, locating files with its Advanced Find features, starting other programs and so forth.

The File Manager is a stand-alone program, so you can go back and forth to it from WordPerfect without closing it. The fastest way to return to the File Manager is to choose it from the Task List (Ctrl+Esc brings up the Task List).

CUSTOMIZING THE FILE MANAGER

Make a button for the File Manager. If you use the File Manager a lot, make a button for it and put it on your Button Bar, or use the keyboard shortcut Alt+F F.

You can make Button Bars in the File Manager, too. You can create specialized Button Bars and make macros into buttons in the File Manager just as you do in WordPerfect (see Chapter 3, "Customizing WordPerfect," for tips about creating Button Bars). Choose Button Bar Setup from the File Manager's View menu. You might want to make a button for Select All or Search Next, for example. Button Bars created in the File Manager have the extension .FMB instead of .WWB, which is the extension for WordPerfect Button Bars.

You can also choose whether you want the File Manager's Button Bar displayed, whether it's to be text only and where it's to be on the screen. From the View menu, choose Button Bar Setup; then choose Options.

The File Manager has its own set of preferences. Choose Preferences from the File menu and then choose Environment to get to the Environment dialog box, where you can set preferences about how the File Manager should work (see Figure 6-13). Most of the things you can change have to do with whether you get dialog boxes when you perform certain operations—such as copying, moving or deleting files, replacing files that have the same names, and opening or printing files created by another application program.

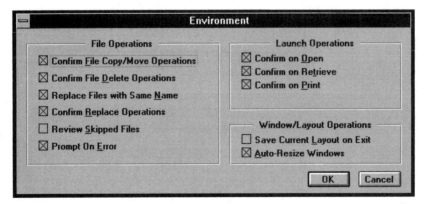

Figure 6-13: Set preferences for the File Manager in its Environment dialog box.

STARTING PROGRAMS FROM THE FILE MANAGER

You can start WordPerfect from the File Manager. Instead of double-clicking on the WordPerfect icon to start it from its Windows group, you can start it from the File Manager (if the File Manager is already running). Just double-click on WPWIN.EXE.

Open a document and start WordPerfect at the same time. To open a WordPerfect document and start WordPerfect for Windows at the same time from the File Manager, just double-click on a document's name. That's it.

Start programs from the File Manager. When you install WordPerfect, your WordPerfect for Windows programs such as the Speller and the Thesaurus are automatically put on the File Manager's Applications menu, and you can start them from there. You can have 15 applications listed there, so feel free to add your most-used programs. (See the next tip for how to do this.)

Put DOS in your Applications menu. It's nice to be able to go out to DOS from the File Manager to run the MEM command, for example, to see how you're using memory, or to format a floppy disk. To add DOS to your Applications menu, choose Applications from the File Manager menu; then choose Assign to Menu. Type **DOS Prompt** in the Descriptive Name box. In the Command Line box, type **command.com**. You shouldn't have to type the full path to where COMMAND.COM is stored, as it's undoubtedly already in your path.

Type *exit* to return to the File Manager from DOS. There's no prompt on the screen about this, but to get back to the File Manager from DOS, you need to type **exit** at the DOS prompt and press Enter.

You can Run programs from the File menu.   To start a program by using the File menu's Run command, just enter the command used to start it in the Run box. For example, you'd enter **winword** to start Word for Windows.

USING FILE MANAGER WINDOWS

The File Manager has different kinds of windows.   In the File Manager, Navigator windows let you move through directories. They show a little hand that points to the next level of directories until you get to the last subdirectory in the branch, which lists files because there are no more directories to show. Directory names are in brackets.

Viewer windows show you the contents of files. Normally you'll see a Navigator window and a Viewer window when you first open the File Manager (see Figure 6-14), unless you check Save Current Layout on Exit in the File Manager's Preferences Environment dialog box. You can easily change the layout, as you'll see shortly.

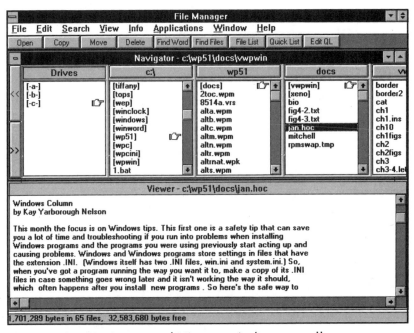

Figure 6-14: Navigator and Viewer windows usually appear when you first open the File Manager.

File List windows provide more details about files, such as the last date you used them, and Quick List windows show the Quick List you set up in WordPerfect—the files and documents you use most frequently (see Figure 6-15). You can edit your Quick List here, too.

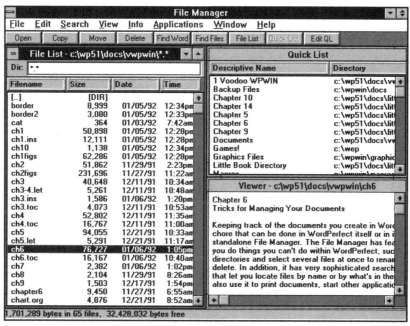

Figure 6-15: The File Manager also has File List windows and Quick List windows.

Just click to move through the Navigator. To change to a different directory and see what's in it when you're in a Navigator window, double-click on the directory name. To view the contents of a file in a Viewer window, click on the file name once. If you double-click on the name of a WordPerfect document, the File Manager assumes you want to open it.

You can open more directories in the File Manager than it can display on the screen. To see in other directories, click on the Navigator's arrow buttons (they're on the left side of the window) or press the Left Arrow or Right Arrow keys.

The secret for opening these Navigator, Viewer, File List and Quick List windows: use keyboard shortcuts.　Ctrl+N opens a Navigator window; Ctrl+Q opens a Quick List window; Ctrl+F opens a File List window; and Ctrl+V opens the Viewer window.

Ctrl+F6 moves you to the next window.　This keyboard shortcut isn't listed on the File Manager's menus, but you can use it to move between File Manager windows, too.

The layouts you use in the File Manager depend on what you want to do.　If you're reorganizing your directories—deleting and renaming them, for example—you may want to open a Navigator and Viewer window. If you're looking for different documents or moving files from one directory to another, a File List window and a Viewer window are more appropriate. Choose Layout from the View menu to pick different layouts of windows, or use the above keyboard shortcuts to open File Manager windows one by one.

You can open more than one Navigator and File List window. If you need to see two different drives at once, or look into separate branches of your directory system, open two Navigator windows. For instance, you'll often need to copy files from your hard disk (drive C) onto floppy disks. If you're looking at a Navigator window showing what's on drive C and you've put a floppy disk in drive B, you can open another Navigator window to see what's on drive B.

Move, tile and close File Manager windows to keep your screen clear.　Your screen can get cluttered very quickly in the File Manager. Drag File Manager windows by their title bars to move them out of the way. To resize a File Manager window, move the mouse pointer to a border; when it becomes a double arrowhead, drag inward or outward to make the window smaller or larger.

If your screen is really cluttered, just moving a few windows won't do the trick. Try choosing Tile from the Window menu

(Shift+F4 is the shortcut) to get just a peek into each window. You could also try cascading windows with Shift+F5.

If tiling windows doesn't help, you've opened a lot of windows! Close them all at once and start over from scratch by choosing Close All from the Window menu. Then choose a different layout, and you'll be looking into the directory you looked at last.

The Window menu lists all the open windows.   You can make a window active (or bring it to the top of the stack, if it's tiled) by choosing it from the Window menu, but you need to know which window you're looking for. All the windows you have open are listed at the bottom of the menu.

You can minimize File List windows, too.   Don't forget this neat trick. If you're looking in a File List window that you know you'll need to return to later, minimize it by clicking its Minimize icon. It stays handily out of the way until you're ready to use it again—you won't have to go hunting for it.

Use wildcards in a File List window's Dir: box to see selected files.   If you only want to see files that have a certain extension or a certain pattern to their names, use wildcards in the File List window's Dir: box. For example, entering ***.wpg** lists only WordPerfect graphics files, and entering **oct??** lists files with names like OCT21, OCTBB and so forth.

Press Home and End to go to the top and bottom of long file lists.   You saw this trick for directory dialog boxes in WordPerfect. It works in the File Manager, too; so do PgUp and PgDn.

Use the Viewer window to review graphics files.   Graphics files, because of DOS's file-naming conventions, have short, nasty cryptic names that don't tell you much about what's in them.

(What's CNTRCT-2.WPG, anyway?) Use the Viewer window to review your graphics files, including any clip art collections you buy, so you know what these graphics look like.

The Viewer window only shows text in a file that has both text and graphics. If a file has text and graphics, the Viewer shows you only the text. Too bad.

Very Important Tip: You can search in the Viewer window. Although it's not listed on any menu, WordPerfect's Search feature is available in the Viewer. Just press F2 to start a search. This is a really handy way to locate the exact document you're looking for.

If you're looking for a document that has the phrase *1993 royalties* in it and you're pretty sure that it has *Budget* in its name, for example, click on the first file named *Budget*, press F2, and enter **1993 royalties**. If the program doesn't find it, highlight the next document with *Budget* in its name and repeat the search by pressing F2 and Enter. Press the Down Arrow key to go to the next document in the list.

Shift+F2 lets you search for the next occurrence of what you're looking for; Alt+F2 is the shortcut for Previous.

SELECTING, COPYING, MOVING, RENAMING & DELETING FILES

Shift-click to select adjacent files in the File Manager. To select several files listed next to each other, click on the first one; then hold the Shift key down and click on the last one.

Ctrl-click to select nonadjacent files. Press Ctrl and hold it down while clicking on the files you want, if they aren't next to each other.

Ctrl-click to deselect files, too.   To deselect a file, press Ctrl and click on the file name. To deselect *all of the selected files in that window except one file,* just click on that one file.

Selecting files in different directories.   To select files in different directories, open a File List window for each directory. (You may need to tile the windows.) Then Shift-click to select adjacent files or Ctrl-click to select nonadjacent files.

Sometimes it's faster to Select All files and then to deselect a few.   To select almost all the files in a directory except a few, use this trick: choose Select All from the Edit menu (Ctrl+S) to select all of them; then deselect the ones you don't want.

There's an Unselect All command, too.   The Edit menu has an Unselect All command (Ctrl+U) that instantly unselects all the files you've selected.

And you can skip files.   You can drag to select a bunch of files that are next to each other and then just choose Skip to skip copying or deleting those that you don't want. There's a Skip button in the Copy and Delete dialog box. This is a neat timesaving trick.

Instead of typing path names, click on the tiny folder icon when you copy files.   Just click on the folder icon next to the To box when you copy (or move) a file from one location to another (see Figure 6-16) so you can choose a directory by clicking on its name. You can avoid having to type complicated file names this way.

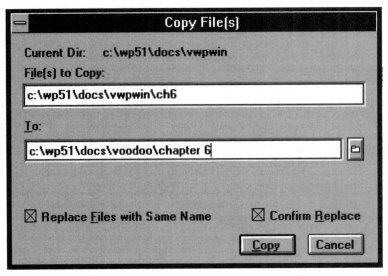

Figure 6-16: When you copy a file, you get this dialog box.

The File Manager's dialog boxes will differ, depending on whether you've selected files first. It's not your imagination. If you've selected more than one file, the dialog boxes you see when you copy, delete or move/rename files will be different. The difference is that if you've selected more than one file, you get a Skip option and a thermometer bar that indicates how the operation is progressing. Figure 6-17 shows the Copy File(s) dialog box you get when you've selected several files first.

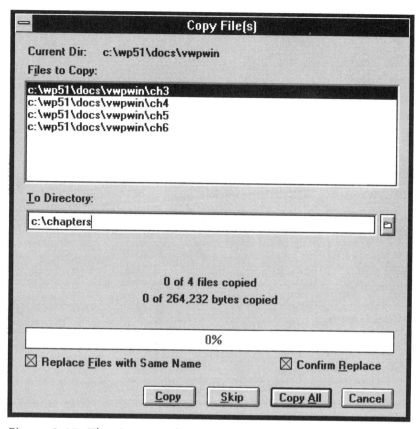

Figure 6-17: The Copy, Delete and Move/Rename dialog boxes have more options if you select files first.

Drag to move files. Once you've selected a file (or files) you can drag them from one File List window to another. You'll need to open the window the files are going to, and you'll need to drag sideways so you don't select more files as you drag across them. Try tiling (Shift+F4) if your windows are too cluttered.

To move files from one disk to a different disk, press Alt while you drag. This is a safeguard against moving files from your hard disk to a floppy disk by mistake.

Press Ctrl and drag to copy files on the same disk. To copy a file from one directory to another on the same disk, press Ctrl as you drag.

To copy a file onto a different disk, you can just drag without pressing Ctrl.

If you selected several files, you can just drag the last file you selected to drag them all.

For large housekeeping jobs, turn off the confirming dialog boxes. You can use the File Manager's Environment dialog box (choose Preferences to see it) to turn off all the dialog boxes you see that ask you to confirm if you really want to move or copy files and directories. If you're doing mass moving, you can save time by turning these dialog boxes off; then you don't have to respond to them and can just drag files to their new locations.

Ctrl+C is the shortcut for Copy, and it lets you use wild-cards. This one's easy to remember, and it's neat to use even if you've temporarily turned off the confirmation dialog boxes so you can quickly move and copy files by dragging them. The advantage to using Ctrl+C is that it brings up the Copy File(s) dialog box (see Figure 6-18), where you can use wildcards to specify file name patterns. In a big directory, it's much faster to enter ***.doc** to copy all the files ending in .DOC than to select each one of them.

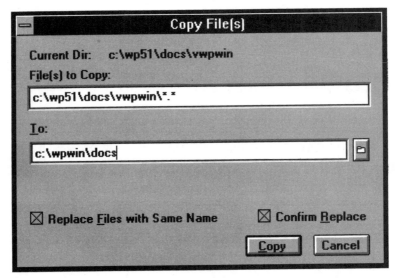

Figure 6-18: Use the Copy File(s) dialog box if you want to use wildcards.

You can copy entire directories and their subdirectories.
You can copy a directory and all its associated subdirectories if you choose Files in Directory and Subdirectories in the Copy Directory/File(s) dialog box (see Figure 6-19).

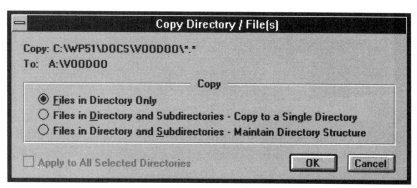

Figure 6-19: When you highlight a directory, you'll get this Copy Directory/File(s) dialog box.

You can copy several files and directories into different locations. Here's how to speed up your copying chores. If you're copying a bunch of files in the same directory, select them all first. Then choose Copy (or press Ctrl+C). Click on the tiny folder icon in the Copy File(s) dialog box to select the name of the directory to copy them to, and put it in the To box. To skip the files you don't want to copy, select them and click Skip.

Copying all the files in a directory. Easy. First, choose Select All from the Edit menu, or press Ctrl+S when the cursor is anywhere in the directory. All the files will be selected, and you can copy them into another directory or onto a floppy disk.

If the directory you want to copy to doesn't exist, the File Manager creates it for you. Don't bother creating a new directory first. Let the File Manager do it for you. Just type the path name to the new directory in the To part of the Copy File(s) dialog box, and you'll be asked if you want the directory to be created if it doesn't exist.

Ctrl+T is the shortcut for Create Directory.   To create a new directory instead of letting the File Manager create it for you as the need arises, just press Ctrl+T and type the full path name for the new directory. Be sure not to type a backslash at the end of the directory name. Also, be aware that the File Manager assumes you want to create the directory in the current directory. Use a full path name if this isn't the case.

You can delete files with Ctrl+D or Del.   Either Ctrl+D or Del deletes a selected file or files. If you've selected more than one file, you can either pick Delete All from the Delete dialog box that appears (to delete all the selected files), or you can select files you don't want to delete and choose Skip.

The speedy way to delete directories.   If you're used to DOS, you probably remember that you painstakingly had to delete everything in a directory and all its subdirectories before you could delete the directory. WordPerfect for Windows lets you speed up this process. If you've highlighted a directory (or several directories) and you choose Delete, you'll see a Delete Directory/File(s) dialog box asking what you want to delete. To delete the selected directory and all its subdirectories, including all the files in them, choose Files in Directory and Subdirectory – Delete Directory Structure. Choose Apply to All Selected Directories if you've selected several directories to delete. You'll be asked to go through this process again for the other directories you've highlighted, but you can choose Skip to skip any you don't want to delete.

You can't delete hidden files when you delete directories.   If the File Manager refuses to delete a directory, there may be hidden files in it. Tips later in this chapter will show you how to make hidden files appear so that you can delete them.

Ctrl+R is the shortcut for Move/Rename.   You can move files to different directories or rename files by pressing Ctrl+R or choosing Move/Rename from the File menu. If you use the asterisk wildcard character (*) in the Move/Rename dialog box, you'll get the Move Directory/File(s) dialog box (see Figure 6-20) because WordPerfect knows that you want to move a bunch of files.

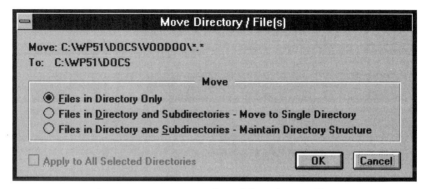

Figure 6-20: If you use an asterisk wildcard, you'll get this Move Directory/File(s) dialog box.

You can move entire directories and maintain their structure by clicking Files in Directory and Subdirectories – Maintain Directory Structure. If you have a laptop computer and you're constantly transferring files and directories back and forth from it to your office computer, this can really speed up your work.

But be warned that if you move WordPerfect for Windows to a different drive, you'll need to edit several .INI files that tell Windows where certain files are. There's a trap about this back in Chapter 1.

To rename a directory, don't type a path name in the To box.   Just type the directory's new name in the To box of the Move/Rename dialog box, not the path name. If you type a backslash, WordPerfect assumes you want to create a new directory.

You can copy or move a file and rename it at the same time.
You saw this trick earlier, and it applies to the File Manager,
too. In the To part of the Move/Rename dialog box, just edit the
path and type the new name at the end. WordPerfect erases the file
in its original location (if it's a move) and copies or moves it to the
new location, giving it the new name.

**The File Manager can create new directories for you with
Move/Rename.** As with the Copy command, the File Man-
ager will create a new directory for you when you use the Move/
Rename dialog box and type a nonexistent directory in the To box.

MORE FILE MANAGER MAGIC

**There's a hidden Column Manager in File List, Quick List
and Search Results windows.** Click in the shaded part of the
header, where the text buttons are, to use the hidden Column Manager in File List, Quick List and Search Results windows. In a File
List window, a hidden pop-up menu will appear. Choose Attributes
to see a file's attributes, Full Path to see the full path name leading to
where the file is stored, or Descriptive Name and Descriptive Type to
have the File Manager search your document summaries and list the
names and types you used there.
This is how you get to see what WordPerfect DOS called long
document names.

**You can rearrange the buttons in File Lists, Quick Lists and
Search Results windows.** Just drag them to where you want
them. For example, you might like to see a file's Date before its Size
(size has never meant much to me). To remove a button (and the
information that goes with it), drag it out of the window. You can
get it back by clicking in the header and choosing that category
again.

Edit your Quick List in the File Manager, and the changes will be reflected in WordPerfect. While you're in the File Manager, take the time to edit your Quick List and bring it up-to-date. All your files will be much more accessible to you than in WordPerfect, and you can easily choose the ones you want to put in your Quick List. Refer back to the tips about editing your Quick List in WordPerfect earlier in this chapter.

Customize your File Lists. Choose Options from the View menu to customize your File Lists. You'll see the View Options dialog box (see Figure 6-21), where you can choose what information you want to see, and in what order.

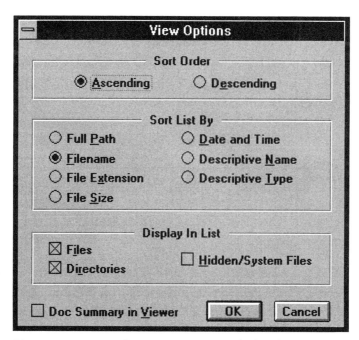

Figure 6-21: Use the View Options dialog box to set up File Lists the way you want to see them.

Choosing Date and Time as the sort order. If you want to view at the tops of File Lists the documents you most recently worked with, choose Date and Time as the sort order. This is a handy trick to use if you'd like to review your most recent work at a glance.

Change the display font in the File Manager. If you choose Font from the View menu or press F9, you can pick a different font and point size for type in File Manager windows. It's just one more trick you can use to customize the File Manager. You may want a smaller font to display more information than usual in a window, for example.

Choose Apply Font To in the Font dialog box to tell Word-Perfect which File Manager windows to apply the new font to.

FINDING THINGS IN THE FILE MANAGER

If you're doing a word search, enter as much text as you can. If you click the File Manager's Find Word button to locate text in documents, try to enter as much text as you can to uniquely identify what you're looking for. Although you can use wildcards, it's better to use complete words and phrases so Word-Perfect will find only the documents you're looking for.

If you're searching by file name, use wildcards. If you're searching for file names, though, the opposite is true. It's good to use wildcards in the Find Files dialog box because of DOS's restrictions on file names (only eight characters plus a three-character extension). For example, you can find all the files that end in .DOC just by entering ***.doc**.

This is another good reason to use extensions for the documents you create. It makes them easier to find.

Don't search for *.* (everything). When you choose Find Files or Advanced Find from the Search menu or by clicking a button, the Search Text box has *.* in it, standing for "everything."

Don't search for that. The results would be meaningless. (Think about it.)

Use the Viewer after the File Manager finds files. You can use the Viewer to review files the File Manager has found for you. They'll be listed in a Search Results window, so just highlight the first file and press Ctrl+V for View.

Use Advanced Find to search by date. The Advanced Find feature on the Search menu is useful if you want to search for files by date—when you know that you worked on a document sometime since last Wednesday, for example, but you can't remember what you named it.

Choose Advanced Find from the Search menu (Ctrl+F2 is its shortcut) and enter the earliest and latest dates that you want to search through in the File Date Range boxes (see Figure 6-22).

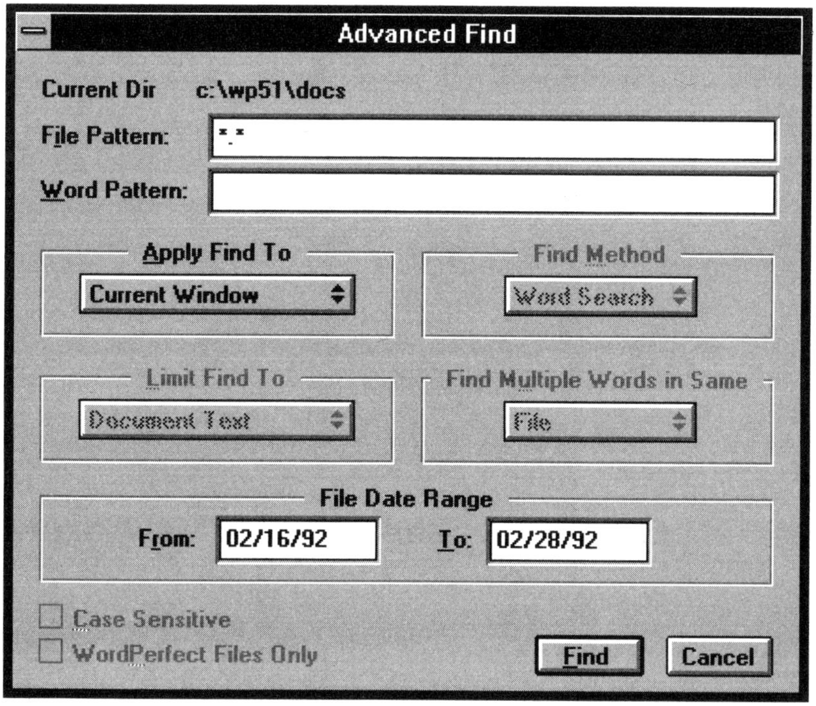

Figure 6-22: Use the Advanced Find dialog box to search by date.

To search your whole hard disk, check Current Drive. The Advanced Find dialog box normally searches only through the files listed in the active window. To search your whole hard disk, the current directory, or the current directory and all of its subdirectories (the "Current Subtree"), choose one of the other options in the hidden pop-up list under Apply Find To.

The shortcut for Advanced Find is Ctrl+F2.

Check String Search to search for nonalphabetic characters. Normally the File Manager searches only for words, not for punctuation marks such as commas and quotation marks. To search for a phrase that has punctuation in it, use Advanced Find and do a String Search instead of a Word Search.

You can search for more than one word, too. You can type two or more words in the Advanced Find dialog box's Word Pattern box and choose from a pop-up list how you want those words to be located. You can specify that WordPerfect find the words, for example, if they occur on the same line, in the same sentence, in the same paragraph and so forth. Just click next to Find Multiple Words in Same and you'll see the pop-up list. This can really refine your searches.

Keep WordPerfect Files Only checked to speed up searches. If you're searching only through the documents you've created in WordPerfect, keep that WordPerfect Files Only box in the Advanced Find dialog box checked to speed up your searches. WordPerfect for Windows can search WordPerfect 5.1 for DOS files, too.

You can search for words in the File Manager using logical operators, too. The comma, space, semicolon, vertical bar and dash can be used to indicate the logical operators AND, NOT, and AND NOT in word searches. (See the tips earlier in this chapter, starting with "You can do very complex word searches.") Logical operators work the same way in the File Manager as they do in WordPerfect.

Advanced Find lets you search through document summaries.
Here's where those keywords you used in your document summaries come in handy. Click under Limit Find To to see a long pop-up list of things Advanced Find can search for you. Select Keywords, Account, Subject or any of the other document summary categories to search through them.

You can narrow your searches step by step. Once you've searched for a file, you can click on the File Manager's Find Files or Find Words button again and apply another set of criteria to the files that have been located. The File Manager opens another Search Results window. This makes it easy to narrow your searches until you locate the exact file you're looking for.

Just press F2 to search the active window. This is a neat trick to know about. You can search through File List and Viewer windows in the File Manager just by pressing F2. This makes it easy to search through descriptive names in a File List window, for example, or to search through all the text in a document displayed in a Viewer window.

You can search for WordPerfect characters, too. Press Ctrl+W to get the WordPerfect Characters dialog box; then pick your character set and your character.

TRICKS FOR FILE ATTRIBUTES

Don't change archive or system attributes. In DOS, every file has four attributes, which are special characteristics that tell DOS exactly what type of file it is and how it's being used. All these attributes are toggles: they're either on or off. The four attributes, when they're on, are:

- the *archive* attribute, which means that a file has been used lately.

◆ the *hidden* attribute, which means the file won't appear in a directory listing.

◆ the *read-only* attribute, which indicates that the file can't be changed.

◆ the s*ystem* attribute, which means that the file is a DOS system file.

You can choose Change Attributes from the File menu to change a file's attributes in the File Manager. Normally you'll almost never change the archive attribute. (Check out *Voodoo DOS* if you're curious about when you might.) Don't ever change the system attribute.

Make files read-only to protect them. If there are files you don't want to change, make their attribute read-only. You might do this for document templates, if you use them for boilerplate, or for last year's budgets you want to keep a record of, or for anything else you don't want to be changed.

Hide a file to make it really invisible. You can hide a file that you don't want other people poking into by giving it the hidden attribute. But remember that you did it, because the file won't show up in a regular directory listing. (You can use Windows's File Manager to see it, though. Choose By File Type from its View menu and click Show Hidden/System files.)

When you copy directories, hidden and system files aren't copied. If you have hidden files in a directory to protect them from prying eyes (see the tips about hiding files by changing their attributes earlier in this chapter), they won't get copied unless you copy them individually. To see a file you've hidden, use the Attributes command to turn its hidden attribute off. Highlight the directory name that the hidden file is in and press Ctrl+A (the shortcut for Change Attributes). Enter the name of the hidden file; then make sure that the Hidden box is unchecked and click Change. (Better remember what those hidden file names are, or sneak out to Windows's File Manager and check.) Then you can copy them.

MISCELLANEOUS FILE MANAGER TRICKS

Choose Info to get information about your system. Selecting Info from the File Manager's menu lets you get information about your system, Windows, your hard disk and floppy disks, your printer and so forth. Choosing Disk Info is a good way to see how much space is left on a floppy disk that you're planning to copy files onto (see Figure 6-23).

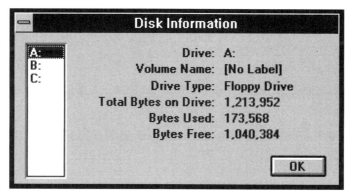

Figure 6-23: Use the Disk Information dialog box to check out a floppy disk quickly.

You can print from the File Manager, too. Instead of going back to WordPerfect to print files, print them from the File Manager. You can select several files at once, choose an application to print them, and send them all to the printer (Ctrl+P is the shortcut), which is much faster than displaying each document on the screen and sending it to the printer individually.

Choose Printer Setup from the File menu if you need to change the printer that's currently selected.

Need disk labels? Print File Manager windows. It's often useful to print out the contents of a floppy disk to use as a label on the disk itself. You can print entire File Lists, or you can print a list of selected files.

Choose Print Window from the File menu; then choose whether you want to print a list of all the files or just the files you've selected.

You can do this with Search Results windows and Quick Lists, too.

You can copy File Manager windows to the Clipboard, too. If you need to use a File List window or a Navigator window as a graphic in a document, just copy it and paste it in the document. Use Ctrl+Ins or choose Copy to Clipboard from the Edit menu, because Ctrl+C is for copying files. This is a handy way of getting long, complicated lists of technical information about your files (date revised, size in bytes and so forth) into your documents.

You can copy or append selected text from the Viewer window to the Clipboard. This is a neat trick for getting text into a document without retyping it. Just select it in the Viewer window, copy it and paste it into your document.

You can associate files with programs that can open them. If you've used Windows before, you may be familiar with this technique. After you've "associated" a file with a program that can open it, all you have to do is double-click on the file's name to start the program.

To use the File Manager to associate files, choose Preferences from the File menu; then choose Associate. You'll see the Associate dialog box (see Figure 6-24), where you can pick the file type you want to associate with a program and pick the program you want to associate it with (under Associated Application).

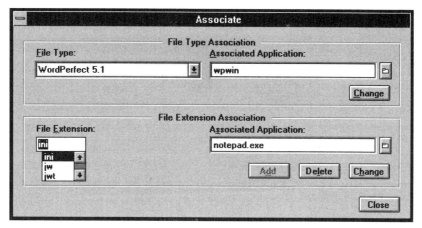

Figure 6-24: Use the Associate dialog box to associate files with programs that can open them.

To see how this works, click .INI under File Extension. You'll see that extension is already associated with the Windows Notepad. Double-clicking on any file with the extension .INI automatically starts the Notepad and opens the file.

You can set up a system of extensions of your own, too. If you've used a three-character extension to identify file types, type the extension in the File Extension box. Then click Add, choose Associated Application and click on the tiny folder icon to see into your directories, where you can click on the name of the program you want to associate with that type of file. You can just type the command used to run the program (if you know it) in the box instead of hunting through your directories. For example, you'd type **wpwin.exe** to set up WordPerfect for Windows as the associated application. Then click Change to actually create the association.

You can open files from other programs in the File Manager.
If the File Manager hasn't been started from WordPerfect, you can highlight a file and choose Open (or double-click on its name), and the File Manager starts the program associated with that document and opens the document at the same time. You'll see a

dialog box (see Figure 6-25), where you can choose Open to start
the program WordPerfect is recommending or click on pop-up lists
to choose a different file type or another application to open the file.

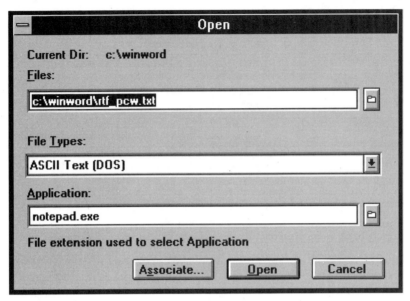

Figure 6-25: The File Manager asks you to confirm which
program you want to use if you're opening a document
created by another application.

If you've already started WordPerfect and you use the File Manager to open a document created in another program, it assumes that
you want to convert that document into a format WordPerfect can
use, and you'll see a dialog box where you can click Open and then
choose from a list of file conversion formats to convert the file.

Here are all the File Manager's shortcuts. You've seen them throughout the chapter; now here they are for easy reference:

Shortcut	Operation
Ctrl+A	Attributes (change)
Ctrl+C	Copy
Ctrl+D	Delete
Ctrl+F	View File List
Ctrl+G	Change Directory
Ctrl+N	View Navigator
Ctrl+P	Print
Ctrl+Q	Quick List
Ctrl+R	Rename
Ctrl+S	Select All
Ctrl+T	Create Directory
Ctrl+U	Unselect All
Alt+F4	Exit
Ctrl+Ins	Copy to Clipboard
Alt+Ins	Append to Clipboard
Ctrl+F2	Advanced Find
F2	Search Active Window
Shift+F2	Search Next (in Viewer windows)
Alt+F2	Search Previous (in Viewer windows)
F9	Font
Shift+F4	Tile Windows
Shift+F5	Cascade Windows
F1	Help
Shift+F1	What-Is Help

MISCELLANEOUS FILE MANAGEMENT VOODOO

Documents have a way of enlarging: here's how to cut them down to size. WordPerfect keeps a document's styles (and various other things about it) in a prefix at the beginning of the file. Sometimes your files can get much larger than they really are because of this invisible prefix. If that happens, and you wind up with a 3-Mb document that you know isn't really that big, use this voodoo trick.

Open a new document (Shift+F4 is the shortcut), type one character and then retrieve your overweight document. Then delete the character that you typed. Your document should shrink back to its original size. Hey, it works. Don't ask me why; it's voodoo.

Can't open a Word for Windows document? WordPerfect for Windows can't convert a Word for Windows document that was saved with Fast Save in Word for Windows. Go back into Word for Windows, open the document and choose Save As from its File menu; then deselect the Fast Save option. You should be able to open it in WordPerfect for Windows then.

Absolute voodoo for updating your documents. If you've decided to use a different set of initial codes than the ones you used previously, your old documents (when you open them) will still be formatted the old way; WordPerfect doesn't go back and retrofit old documents with new codes.

Here's the voodoo way to do that. Open a new document window and, without putting anything in it, save it under some name. Then Retrieve into it your old document that you want formatted with new initial codes. Save it under its old name.

Want to use a Windows Write document in WordPerfect? Convert it to a Word document first, in Windows Write. Then you can open it in WordPerfect for Windows.

Use Save As to save a document in another format. In the Save As dialog box, there's a pop-up list next to the Format box that lists all the different formats WordPerfect for Windows can save documents in. Most of the popular word processing, spreadsheet and database programs are listed there. If you don't see the one you want (such as DeScribe or JustWrite, for example, which aren't there as of this writing), use Rich Text Format (RTF).

Be sure to give the document a different name when you save it in another format, so the new version doesn't overwrite the Word-Perfect version. Use an extension to help you identify the file's format, such as .WSD (for WordStar) or .RTF.

If you open a document from another program, Word-Perfect saves it in the same format. WordPerfect identifies a document's program (or asks you to) the first time you open it. Thereafter it saves it in that same format when you choose Save. If you want to make a WordPerfect version of the document, use the Save As command and save it as a WordPerfect document.

ASCII or ANSI? There are two basic text-only formats, ANSI and ASCII, and their variations. Windows programs use the ANSI standard, and DOS programs use the ASCII standard. The one you choose depends on how you want to use the document—with DOS programs or with Windows programs.

If the word processing program you're converting the Word-Perfect document for accepts RTF, use it instead of a text-only option so more formatting is preserved in the converted document.

By the way, if you're used to WordPerfect DOS, ASCII Text (DOS) is what you remember as DOS Text.

Importing spreadsheets via the back door. WordPerfect for Windows lets you import data from the most popular spread-sheet programs. Here's the sneaky way around getting a spreadsheet from a different program into your WordPerfect document: save it in a format that WordPerfect recognizes. Even the most obscure spreadsheet programs usually have an option for saving in one of the "biggie" formats, such as Lotus 1-2-3 or Microsoft Excel. Use that; then you can bring in your spreadsheet just as though it were created by the more popular program.

When to import spreadsheet data as a table and when as text?   If you're importing spreadsheet data you're planning to format in WordPerfect (changing fonts, adding italics and boldface, adding explanatory text and so forth), it's better to bring it in as a table so you can use the neat table editing tricks available through the Ruler (see Chapter 5, "Formatting Secrets").

If you bring the spreadsheet in as text, its data appears in columns separated by tabs and rows separated by hard returns. Any headings formatted in the spreadsheet program will be left-aligned.

Also, WordPerfect lets you bring in as many as 32 columns if you choose Table, but only 20 columns if you choose Text.

Spreadsheets are usually bigger than your page.   Most spreadsheet programs nowadays let you create really giant spreadsheets. If you try to bring in spreadsheet data that's wider than your WordPerfect page, you'll get a warning message that the data extends beyond your margins. Here are a few voodoo tricks for avoiding this problem.

◆ Check to see how much data you're planning to bring in. Then create a table structure in WordPerfect big enough to hold it, if you can. (You can have 32 columns and 32,767 rows, but you can't have very much data in such narrow columns on a regular 8.5-by-11-inch page.)

◆ Import sections of data as smaller tables instead of using the whole spreadsheet.

◆ Format your WordPerfect page with tiny right and left margins and a small font.

◆ Go into the spreadsheet program and narrow the columns, or delete unneeded columns of data.

◆ Do the table in Landscape mode (sideways). Choose the Page menu from the Layout menu and choose Paper Size. Pick a different paper orientation before you set up your table.

Use named ranges in your spreadsheet program. Word-Perfect lets you specify a named range when you import or link a spreadsheet. It's much easier to remember that you want a range named *febsales* than a range of cells D55 through F77. Get in the habit of using named ranges and make things easier on yourself.

If you haven't used named ranges, you can indicate a range of cells either by a colon (:), a period (.) or two periods (..). For example, A20:H40, A20.H40 or A20..H40 indicates cells in column A, row 20 through column H, row 40.

The voodoo way for quickly reformatting spreadsheet data. Bring the data in as a table; then double-click on a table column marker above the Ruler. You'll immediately get the Table Options dialog box, where you can specify shading and rules for your table.

Link spreadsheet data instead of importing it. You can have WordPerfect update the data from your spreadsheet program as you change it in that program if you link the data instead of importing it. Choose Create Link instead of Import from the Spreadsheet menu.

If your spreadsheet program supports Dynamic Data Exchange, you can create a special kind of link called a DDE link. The difference between it and a regular link is that as you change the data in your spreadsheet program, it's automatically changed in your Word-Perfect document; you don't have to save the spreadsheet first, as you do with a regular link. This is really voodoo: you can change the data in a spreadsheet window and see it change in your document!

The trick to creating a DDE link is to start the spreadsheet program and then switch to WordPerfect for Windows. Then choose Link and Create from the Edit menu, not from the Tools menu. If the spreadsheet program supports DDE links, you'll see a list of the files you can link to.

You can lose formatting if you don't create your table first.
When you link spreadsheet data, formatting changes you
make to it will be lost the next time you update it to reflect the
changes in the spreadsheet. Try this sneaky trick around that trap:
create a table to hold the data and format it the way you want; then
put the insertion point in cell A1 and create the link.

If there are other formatting changes you want to make, such as
switching to a different font and point size, put the formatting codes
for them before the [Link] or [DDE Link Begin] codes so they'll be
in effect on the data.

There's a Paste Link feature, too. A Paste Link pastes the
contents of the Clipboard and sets up a link at the same time.
This is a quick way to link data, because all you have to do is copy it
instead of specifying its range and storage type and all the other
things you have to do when you set up a DDE link. This type of link
isn't possible with all Windows programs, though, and its choice (on
the Edit Link menu) will be dimmed if you can't do it.

MOVING ON

This chapter has looked at all sorts of strategies for managing your
documents, both in WordPerfect for Windows and in its stand-alone
File Manager. The next chapter, "Spells for Your Special Problems,"
explores ways to use WordPerfect's more specialized features—such
as creating tables of contents and indexes, doing mail merges, using
footnotes and endnotes, sorting and alphabetizing lists and so forth.

Spells for Your Special Problems

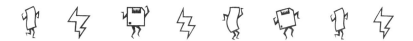

Get ready for a mixed bag of tricks in this chapter. You'll find everything that doesn't fit anywhere else. From merging mailing lists to indexing—there's a tip about it here for you.

Most of these techniques are for things you'll probably *not* do every day, such as creating a table of contents or alphabetizing a list. You won't see much "how-to," but remember that you can use Help to look up the steps for doing a complex procedure.

The most basic trick of all is this: record a macro for a specialized procedure while you've got it in your mind. If you've done something once, record a macro that will do it again—so you don't have to remember it or look it all up one more time. Then when you need to use a specialized technique again, just play your macro.

LIST MAGIC

You can use WordPerfect to keep track of a list of items in a document as well as the pages they're on. You can create lists of figure captions, equation numbers, maps, charts or tables; you can bring up a list of key words or vocabulary terms, too.

Which goes in what list? WordPerfect automatically keeps track of all Graphics box numbers and any captions you've entered for them. Figure boxes are kept in list 6, Table boxes in list 7, Text boxes in list 8, User-defined boxes in list 9 and Equations boxes in list 10. If you've used any of these types of Graphics boxes in a document, you can get one of these lists just by defining the list, entering a number (6–10) and generating the list. WordPerfect will go through your document and create a list of your Graphics boxes, their captions (if any) and their page numbers.

Lists 1 through 5 are for lists you create yourself, for things such as maps, illustrations or vocabulary terms—and their page numbers.

The standard method for creating lists. The basic way to create a list is the same for all types of lists. First, *mark* the text to be referenced—a heading for a table of contents or an entry for an index. Then *define* the list, which means that you pick a preset style for its format and indicate exactly where in your document the list should appear. As the final step, *generate* the list, which tells the program to run through your document and pull out the list entries and their page numbers. It doesn't really matter whether you mark the text or define the list first, but you do need to generate it last, or you won't get the list at all.

Press F12 for Mark Text. This handy keyboard shortcut brings up the Mark Text menu, where you can choose which list your selected item will belong to.

An item can belong to only one list. WordPerfect can't put one item into two different lists automatically. Any one item can belong to only one list.

Shift+F12 is the shortcut to the Define menus.   To start defining any type of list, press Shift+F12. The list will appear on the page where the code for its definition is.

Where should you put reference lists?   Reference lists usually come after the table of contents but before the first page of a document. You'll probably want to create a new page for the list (press Ctrl+Enter) and then define it.

   If you want your document to start on page 1 and you're putting your reference lists after the table of contents, be sure to go to the beginning of the first document page and choose Page from the Layout menu; then pick Numbering, choose a page number and a position and enter **1** as the new page number.

Don't forget to generate your lists.   If you forget to tell WordPerfect to generate your lists, they won't appear in your document. This is the most common mistake you can make. Alt+F12 is the shortcut for Generate.

WordPerfect keeps track of graphics Table boxes, not tables.   WordPerfect automatically keeps track of graphics Table boxes, not tables that you create with the Tables feature or with tabs.

It's easier to do reference lists *after* you've written a document.   Don't drive yourself crazy trying to keep track of lists as you write. Go back and mark the items for the lists after you've written the document.

Preview pages before you generate lists.   If you've got a lot of tables or graphics in a document, check that your pages break as you want them to before you generate your reference lists. Use Print Preview.

TABLES OF CONTENTS

Let WordPerfect create tables of contents for you. A table of contents is just a special kind of list. The program keeps track of as many as five levels of headings (more, if you cheat) for a table of contents.

You can have more than five levels of headings in a table of contents.   To get around the program's limitation of five levels, mark as fifth-level headings all the headings lower than that; then just manually reformat your table of contents after it's generated. The page numbers will all be there, so all you have to do is indent the lower-level headings.

Tables of contents, indexes and tables of authorities are all just different types of lists.   The same basic procedure explained in the earlier tip, "The standard method for creating lists," applies to tables of contents, indexes and tables of authorities (citations in a legal document or bibliography). They're all just lists to WordPerfect.

Don't mark table of contents entries with the mouse: there's a bug in early versions of WordPerfect for Windows.   In WordPerfect DOS, you could mark table of contents or table of authorities entries by blocking the text along with any font attribute codes that accompanied it, such as codes for bold or italic type. But there's a bug in early versions of WordPerfect for Windows that won't let you do this: the insertion point jumps if you try it. If you've got an early release of WordPerfect, play it safe by marking table entries with the keyboard. Open the Reveal Codes window, press Alt+F4 to start the selection and use the arrow keys to complete the selection.

Use the Styles feature on headings if you're going to do a table of contents.   If you use styles for the headings in your document, you can rest assured that all your headings will be styled the same. You can change them all at once, too. And you can easily search for them to mark them for the table of contents.

If you're not using styles for headings, try this trick. As you write, mark the beginning of each heading with a unique character such as @; you can then just search for all the @s (and delete them) to find headings to be marked for inclusion in the table of contents.

Define the table of contents on the page where you want it to appear. A table of contents usually comes after the title page, on a page by itself, so press Ctrl+Home to go to the beginning of the document and then press Ctrl+Enter and the Up Arrow key. Type any title you want the table of contents to have, like *Contents.* Then press Enter until you're at the line you want the first entry to be on. Go ahead and define the table. Then—important step—press Ctrl+Enter again so your document starts on the next page.

Remember to begin page numbering in your document with page 1. To number the first document page as page 1 (not the table of contents page, but the first text page), go to the beginning of the first document page and choose Page from the Layout menu; then pick Numbering, define a page number position and enter **1** as the new page number.

When to use a "wrapped" format. If you've got a big table of contents with lots of lower-level entries, it's a good idea to display the last level of entries in a wrapped format. The last level of entries are "wrapped" all on one line; headings and page numbers are separated by semicolons. Otherwise each entry is on a separate line and your table of contents will go on forever.

Pick a page number style for each heading level if you don't want dot leaders. If you don't choose a different page number style for each level of heading, your entries will all be flush right with dot leaders, as shown in Figure 7-1. The program very helpfully shows you samples of your choices as you select them.

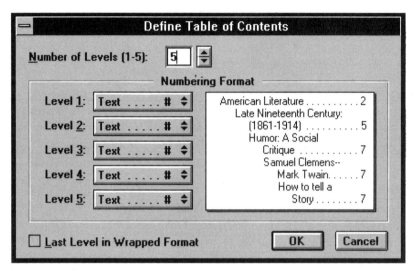

Figure 7-1: The Define Table of Contents dialog box reflects the styles you choose for each level of entry.

Check for blank pages before you print. If you're printing on both sides of a piece of paper, be sure to allow for blank left-hand pages when you figure out your page numbers. You may need to add some blank left-hand pages to your document to make sections and chapters start on right-hand pages. Right-hand pages are always odd-numbered, and left-hand pages are always even-numbered.

Deleting items from tables of contents. Yes, you can edit the text of a table of contents after it's generated. But if you delete items without removing the [Mark] codes around them, they'll appear in your table again whenever you choose Generate from the Mark Text menu. To unmark an item for a table of contents, delete either the [Mark] or [End Mark] codes around it.

When you generate a document, *all* your reference lists, indexes and so on are generated. Here's the scenario. You've edited a few entries in a generated reference list just to save time. Then you realize that page breaks in your document have changed, so you decide to generate the document again so the page numbers will be accurate in all your reference lists. You'll lose the editing you did.

If you're getting two tables of contents, here's why. When you define a different style for a table of contents, be sure to delete the old [Def Mark: ToC] code, or you'll get *two* tables of contents, one for each code.

Be careful about deleting tables of contents. To delete a table of contents, locate and delete both the [Def Mark: ToC] and [End Def] codes. If you only delete one, you'll either get an error message or an extra table of contents.

INDEXING MAGIC

WordPerfect can automatically create indexes for you. Of course, you have to locate and mark the entries to be used in it. There are a few tricks you can use to avoid the perils of "mindless" indexing, which is what the program does if you don't watch out.

Use a concordance file to index a simple list of terms. There are two ways to locate entries you want in your index. The first is to go through your document and search for each one manually; the second is to use a *concordance* file, which is a list of all the words or phrases you want to index.

To make a concordance file, open a new document and type a list of the words or phrases you want in the index, separating each one by a hard return. Be sure to type them just as they're written in your document. Then save the concordance file, giving it a name you can remember. You'll have to supply the name when you define the index.

Sort your concordance file. If you wind up with a very large concordance file (several pages), sort it alphabetically to speed up the index process.

WordPerfect won't locate plurals unless you put them in the concordance file. If you want to index *Disk* and *Disks*, you have to put both entries in your concordance file. Capitalization doesn't matter, so if you enter *Disks*, for example, the program will also index *disks*.

All your index items will be main topics unless you mark subtopics in the concordance file. If all the entries in your concordance file are main topics—fine. But if the concordance file contains subtopics, mark them as such. Here's an example: say that you want the entries *Norton AntiVirus* and *Virex* to be subtopics under *Virus Protection*. You have to select the phrase *Norton Anti-Virus* (because it's more than one word) and choose Index from the Tools menu. You'll see that WordPerfect assumes you want it to be a main topic. Instead, type *Virus Protection* as the main topic and then enter *Norton AntiVirus* a subtopic. Repeat for *Virex*, but this time you don't have to select it first because it's only one word. Just put the insertion point anywhere in it.

A concordance file can't make decisions for you. Be aware that using a concordance file never takes the place of using your head as you mark index entries. See the following trap.

WordPerfect indexes a phrase just as it appears in your document. If you want your entry to be *Jones, John* instead of *John Jones* (which is probably how it is in your document), you'll need to change the wording of the entry when you mark it. If you use a concordance file, you won't have a chance to change it.

You can mark an entry to be indexed under more than one subject. This is sometimes called *double posting*: you mark the same term to be indexed under more than one subject. For example, you could mark the term *floppy disk* to be indexed under *Disks* as well as under *Floppy disks* and *Data storage*.

Be judicious about mixing double posting with *See Also*s, and distinguish between *See* and *See Also*. If you use double posting, use *See Also* sparingly. They're both designed to do the same thing. And remember that *See* means there are *no* page references for that term ("It's not listed here; see another term."); *See Also* means "There are more references for this under the other term."

Keep an index list in a second document window. If you're marking an index manually, keep a list of the phrases you've marked in a second document window so you won't forget how you're indexing a topic.

Defining your index on the page where you want it to appear. When you define an index, be sure to move the insertion point to the place in your document where you want the index to be. This is usually at the very end of the document, so press Ctrl+End. To make the index begin on a new page, press Ctrl+Enter.

Deleting an index item. To delete an item from an index, locate and delete its [Index:] code. If you just delete the item from the generated index, it'll reappear when you generate your document again.

Deleting an index. To delete the entire index from a document, delete the index pages themselves and then locate and delete the [Def Mark:Index] code that's in the page where you defined the index. (You can search for it to find it easily.) Otherwise the index will be generated again when you generate your document.

Generate your index again if you edit your document. If you edit your document so that page breaks change, be sure to generate your index again. This is why it's best to index as the last step in preparing a document.

TABLES OF AUTHORITIES

Tables of authorities, which are used in legal documents, are lists of citations. The first citation is called the *long form*, and it consists of the full citation. Later references to the same authority use the *short form*, which is an abbreviated version of the long form.

You can use the Tables of Authorities feature to create bibliographies. Even if you're not involved in the legal profession, you may have a use for tables of authorities. You can use them as bibliographies at the end of a document, too.

Before you begin, figure out how many sections you'll be using and what each section is for. Tables of authorities are usually divided into *sections*, and WordPerfect keeps track of as many as 16 sections. Each section consists of a specific kind of citation, such as cases or statutes. It's a lot easier to figure out what these sections will be before you define a table of authorities.

Search for citations from the beginning of the document. To begin marking citations in a document, press Ctrl+Home to go to the top of the document. You can then search for specific citations or scroll through the document.

Use Extended Search to pick up all your citations. If your document has citations in footnotes or endnotes, use Extended Search to search through the whole document. A regular search doesn't search notes.

Marking citations. Here's a fairly foolproof system to use for marking citations, to make sure you don't miss one. When you locate the first instance of a citation, select it—the whole thing. Then choose Mark Text from the Tools menu and choose ToA Full Form. Select the section number or type it in the Section Number box in the Mark ToA Full Form dialog box (see Figure 7-2). Then enter the short form or nickname you want to use to identify the citation (since they're usually pretty long). Click OK. You'll be placed in a window where you can edit the full form. You can insert italics, bold, indents and so forth, to make it just as you want it to appear in the table. When you're done, click Close.

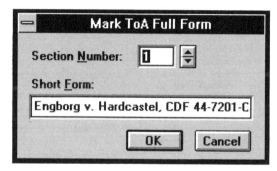

Figure 7-2: Marking a citation for a table of authorities.

Then search for the next instance of the citation. When you find it, mark it with the short form.

Search for all occurrences of that same citation in the document. Then go back to the top of the document and begin the search for the next citation.

You have to use a unique short form for each citation. If you use the same short form with more than one full form, you'll get an error message when you generate the document. Also, if you enter a short form that doesn't correspond to any full form,

WordPerfect won't know where to put it, so you'll see it listed with an asterisk at the beginning of your table of authorities.

Tables of authorities are usually at the beginning of a document; bibliographies are usually at the end. After you've marked all the citations, you'll need to define the style of the table. The page on which you define the style is where the table will appear. You'll probably want to create a new page for it and type a heading for that page. In fact, you may want to have each section begin on a new page.

Be sure to start page numbering with 1 after you define a table of authorities. You'll get an error message when you generate the table if you don't do this. (Of course, if you're setting up a table of authorities to use as a bibliography at the *end* of a document, this step isn't necessary.)

Check page numbering before you generate a table of authorities. Be sure that your document's pages are numbered accurately before you generate a table of authorities (or any reference list that uses page numbers, for that matter). You may need to add blank left-hand pages if you're preparing a document that will be bound.

Editing citations. You've generated your table of authorities (or bibliography). Then you realize you have one or two citations wrong. To edit a citation in a table of authorities, edit the full form and then generate the table again.

Deleting tables of authorities. To delete a table of authorities, locate and delete the [Def Mark: ToA code].

CROSS-REFERENCES

This neat feature lets you mark cross-references to figures, tables, footnotes and so forth (as when you say, "See the table on page 23" or "See Figure 21 on page 119") and automatically keeps track of them even if page numbers change in your document.

When you mark a target, the position of the insertion point is important. After you've marked a reference and you're ready to mark its target, be sure to position the insertion point just *after* the target (to its right). If you look at the status bar, you'll see a message telling you to move to the target and press Enter. This is important! Open the Reveal Codes window to make sure you get the insertion point *after* the target. Then press Enter.

Mark references and targets separately to cross-reference more than one item. To mark more than one target for a reference (like "See the figures on pages 44, 78 and 96"), mark the reference and the targets separately in the Mark Cross-Reference dialog box. You only have to mark the reference once; then mark each target separately.

You can also mark references and targets separately if you haven't finished your document yet, or if you want to cross-reference several pages at a time. A question mark appears after the reference until you've marked its target.

If you've repaginated, regenerate! If you repaginate your document, you'll need to generate your cross-references again so the page numbers will be accurate.

TRICKS WITH NOTES

Footnotes appear at the bottom of a page; *endnotes* usually appear at the end of a document or chapter. A note can be either a footnote or an endnote—but not both. In general, use footnotes to explain something mentioned on that page; use endnotes to cite bibliographic sources or if your notes are many and lengthy. I'll call both footnotes and endnotes "notes" in the tricks that follow.

 You don't normally see notes on the screen. This is one area where WordPerfect for Windows isn't WYSIWYG. Choose Print Preview to see how notes will look.

 Copy and paste note text. Instead of retyping text already in your document into a note, copy and paste text into the note-editing screen. It may not be exactly what you want, but you can edit it faster than retype it. Book or article titles are especially good candidates for copying and pasting.

 You can format notes, too. When you type a note, use formatting niceties like first pressing F4 to indent each line after the first line (or WordPerfect will wrap the second line back to the left margin) and using italics for book titles.

 Number notes starting with something other than 1? Sure. If you want to number notes with a number other than 1, use the New Number option (choose Footnote from the Layout menu; then choose New Number). This is helpful if you're writing notes in sections of text that ultimately become part of a master document.

 A regular search doesn't look in notes. Use Extended Search to search through your notes.

 Create a page for your endnotes. If you're using endnotes, you'll see a choice on the Endnote menu for endnote placement. This lets you specify the page you want the endnotes to appear on. Be sure to create a new page for them by pressing Ctrl+Enter; locate the insertion point at the beginning of this page before you use this option. WordPerfect asks you whether you want to restart endnote numbering or carry on numbering from the last note.

It's hard to delete an endnote placement code. The only way I've been able to delete an endnote placement code is to select it in the document, not in Reveal Codes, and then delete it.

Be careful if you use endnotes and an index. If you have endnotes and an index, the index will come before the endnotes unless you use an endnote placement code before your index.

You need to generate endnotes to see them. The program won't create the endnote text until you generate the document. You'll see a tiny number in your text, but it won't be there when the document is printed. Even after endnotes are generated, you'll need to use Print Preview to see them.

Converting footnotes to endnotes, voodoo style. To convert footnotes to endnotes, press Ctrl+Home to go to the top of the document; define columns; then go to the end of the document (Ctrl+End). To get the original format back, go to the beginning of the document and turn columns off. WordPerfect doesn't allow footnotes in columns.

There's a footend macro that converts footnotes to endnotes in a somewhat safer and more prosaic way (converting your entire document to columns resets any margin changes you may have made), but if you haven't reset margins anyway, why not use voodoo?

To convert endnotes to footnotes, play the endfoot macro supplied with the program.

Moving footnotes? Delete and undelete them. Here's another voodoo trick: highlight a [Note Num] code and delete it; then move to the new location where you want the footnote to appear and undelete it. This beats retyping!

Want to see what's in a note without editing it? To see the beginning of the text in a note, open the Reveal Codes window and put the insertion point on the code for the note so it's selected. You'll see the text in the note without having to edit it.

Change note options at the start of your document. Go to the beginning of your document before you change note options. That way you'll be sure that all of your notes will be in the same style. You'll also be able to find the [Ftn Opt] and [End Opt] codes easily, if you want to change options again (see the next trap).

Changing options more than once can cause trouble. The results of having more than one [Ftn Opt] or [End Opt] code per document can drive you crazy. If your notes aren't all looking the same, a stray option code is probably the culprit. Search for them and delete any extras.

Print *(Continued...)* with long footnotes. If you're using long footnotes, you may want to have WordPerfect print *(Continued...)* at the end of a footnote that's broken across pages. The *(Continued...)* is repeated at the beginning of the note on the next page.

You can change the note numbering style. If you don't want to use the program's preset numbering style (plain superscripts in the same font as your text), choose Style in Text or Style in Note in the Footnote Options dialog box. You'll see a long list of the styles you can change. Remember that this applies to the *note number* only, not to the note text. To change or format the text's style, edit it in the note-editing window.

Use WordPerfect Characters as footnote symbols. If you'd rather "number" footnotes with symbols that aren't on the keyboard, such as daggers, choose Characters from the Numbering Method pop-up list in the Footnote Options dialog box and press Ctrl+W when the insertion point is in the Characters box.

Hint: instead of using just one character (it's repeated twice for the second note, and so on), use different characters.

This trick is often used for footnotes in tables that are basically all numbers; it's easier to read the footnote designator if it's a symbol instead of a number.

Footnotes at Bottom of Page? Note options are fairly self-explanatory, except for Footnotes at Bottom of Page. Of course footnotes will be at the bottom of the page! This option lets you specify that if the page isn't completely filled with text, the footnotes will come after the last line of text instead of at the absolute bottom of the page.

Put your footnotes in a different font. Use this trick to put your footnotes in a different font. Locate the code for footnote or endnote options ([Ftn Opt] or [End Opt]). If you haven't set up any options, go to the top of your document and choose Footnote or Endnote from the Layout menu; then choose Options. Just press F7 if you don't want to use any options.

Open the Reveal Codes window so you can see the code. Put the insertion point just before the [Ftn Opt] code and change to the font you want to use. (You can pick a smaller point size, too.) Then move to just after the code and change the font back to the regular text font. This beats changing the size for every note code!

You can't put footnotes in table headers. If you try to create a footnote in a table header, WordPerfect changes it to an endnote. Table headers are the headings that you specify to have repeated when a table continues on more than one page. You can put footnotes in heading or subheading cells, though, at the beginnings

of columns. But when your table is longer than one page and you
specifically set up a header row, you can't footnote what's in that row.

OUTLINE & PARAGRAPH NUMBERING TRICKS

Outlining in WordPerfect takes some getting used to. Just try it and
see. When Outline mode is on, WordPerfect inserts a paragraph
number each time you press Enter. This makes it easy for you to type
automatically numbered topic paragraphs.

Type the text of your outline first.   It's faster (and certainly
less confusing) to type your outline first (including the outline
numbers) and then indent the outline numbers to the desired level.
Go back and put the insertion point on each number and press Tab
or Shift+Tab to put the outline entries at the level you'd like.

Make a button for outlining if you use it a lot.   If you use
outlining a lot, you can record the steps for turning it on and
off in a couple of macros. Then make buttons for the macros (see
Chapter 3, "Customizing WordPerfect").

Choose Bullet outline style for presentation graphics.   You
can select from six different predefined outline styles. The
program's preset style is a Roman-numeral numbering system. Bullet
style is nice to use for topic lists for presentations. It gives you nicely
formatted outlines without numbers.

Quickly editing outlines.   Associated entries in an outline
(the second- and third-level entries under a first-level entry,
for instance) are called an *outline family*.
    You can move, copy or cut entire outline families by choosing
Outline from the Tools menu and choosing one of those items. This
lets you quickly restructure an outline you've created.

You're getting numbers every time you press Enter! If you keep getting numbers when you press Enter, you've probably turned outlining on and haven't turned it off again.

Using more than one outline in a document. WordPerfect remembers where outlining left off and just keeps on numbering when you turn outlining on again. To use more than one outline in a document, define a new one (Alt+Shift+F5) and set Starting Paragraph Number to begin with 1.

Number alignment in outlining. WordPerfect is absolutely pesky about the way it aligns outline numbers (misaligns them, in my opinion). Look at Figure 7-3. The program aligns them strictly flush left, as in Items I through III. It's standard, however, to align them on the period, as in Items IV through VI: use the Right Par outline style to align numbers on the period.

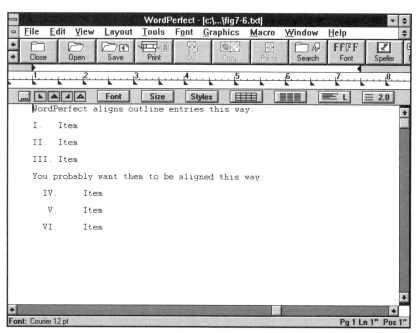

Figure 7-3: You can make WordPerfect align outline numbers on the period.

When should you use paragraph numbering and when should you use outlining? There's also a Paragraph Numbering feature, which is very similar to outlining. Here's the secret: use paragraph numbering when you want to be able to control where the number appears and the level it's at; use outlining if you want the program to insert a number according to the position of the insertion point.

Outlining stays on until you turn it off. Here's another secret to help you decide whether to use paragraph numbering or outlining: outlining stays on until you turn it off; but paragraph numbering shuts off after you type the paragraph. If you're typing lots of numbered items and creating a list similar to an outline, you'll find that outlining (with the Paragraph style) is faster than using paragraph numbering. But if you're numbering items scattered throughout your document, either way will do, and there's a fast Alt+F5 shortcut for paragraph numbering.

Press Alt+F5 for paragraph numbering. To use paragraph numbering, press Alt+F5 when the insertion point is where you want the number to appear. You'll be asked for a paragraph level. You can just press Enter or click the right mouse button for an automatic number, or you can enter a level.

If you let the program use automatic numbering, it works like outlining: the number (or level) you get depends on the tab stop you're at. You can press Tab or Shift+Tab to change the numbering style.

The level determines the paragraph numbering style. When you use the paragraph numbering shortcut and enter a level, you'll get a number (or letter) in the *style* for that level. Confusing, isn't it? This is how it works. Say you want consecutively numbered paragraphs, but you want the numbers indented one tab from the left margin. If you let the program do it automatically, you'll get the style associated with one tab indent, which uses letters instead of numbers. But if you enter **3** as the level, you'll get Arabic numerals, even if you're not at the left margin.

Another way to make sure that you get Arabic numerals is to define a paragraph numbering style (see the next trick).

Mixing paragraph numbering and outlining. If you want to use paragraph numbering and you've used outlining earlier in your document, the paragraph numbers will be in the same style as your outline numbers. If this happens, press Alt+Shift+F5 to define a new paragraph numbering style. You'll probably want to choose Paragraph from the Predefined Formats pop-up list, too, to get Arabic numerals.

Use paragraph numbering for numbered headings. This is a neat trick. In the Define Paragraph Numbering dialog box, choose Legal or Paragraph as the predefined format and enter the headings in your document as numbered paragraphs. If you move or delete a heading, WordPerfect automatically adjusts your numbering system.

Centered paragraph numbers? Sure. In some technical documents, headings are both centered and numbered. Just press Shift+F7 for Center and then press Alt+F5 for Paragraph Number. Choose a level and press Enter.

Store numbered paragraphs as boilerplate text. It's really easy to create a test bank of numbered questions or assemble a contract from a set of numbered paragraphs if you store numbered paragraphs as boilerplate text in a separate document. You can then retrieve that document into a separate window and copy or cut paragraphs into the document you're working on, and your paragraphs will automatically be numbered correctly.

NUMBERING LINES

The Line Numbering feature is often used in legal documents, by word processors who bill according to the number of lines typed, or anywhere individual lines should be numbered.

You don't see line numbers on the screen. You don't see line numbering on the screen like you see paragraph numbering. Use the Print Preview feature on the Print menu to see line numbering. Don't be dismayed if you see every page starting with line 1, even if you've specified consecutive numbering. This is just how the program works. It will be OK when you print.

Tips for using line numbering. Position the insertion point where you want line numbering to start. Then choose Line from the Layout menu and choose Numbering. Then pick your options. You can choose whether to count blank lines and whether to number every line or to print a line number every *n* lines. (The program counts all of the lines.) You can also set a position for the number on the page, supply a new starting number and restart numbering on each new page.

Removing line numbering isn't the same as turning it off. To *remove* line numbering (remember, you don't see it on the screen), locate and delete the [Ln Num:On] code.

To turn off line numbering so that some lines in a document will be numbered and others won't, choose Line from the Layout menu; then choose Numbering and select Off.

Printing line numbers in a different font. You may want line numbers in a different, perhaps smaller, font than the document's text. The trick here is to put the font change code just before the codes that specify numbering options and then turn on line numbering. Then, just after those codes, put the font change code for the text font.

COMPARING DOCUMENTS

The Document Compare feature is another handy reference aid that lets you see the differences between the screen version of a document and a version that's stored on disk. If you've worked with several drafts of a document and aren't sure which version is the most up-to-date, use Document Compare. It's also good for seeing the changes in a document that someone else has edited.

Redlining, strikeout and document comments are handy tools you'll see tips for in this section, too.

WordPerfect uses redlining and strikeout to compare documents.   Here's how Document Compare works. Bring to the screen the document you want to compare. Choose Document Compare from the Tools menu and then choose Add Markings. Enter the name of the stored document or click on the tiny folder icon to get access to your filing system.

The phrases in the stored copy that don't exist in the screen version will be struck out, and the phrases in the screen version that aren't in the disk version will be redlined on the screen. On a color monitor, they really will be red. If text has been moved, you'll see messages telling you so.

WordPerfect compares phrases, not words.   The program considers a phrase changed if any text in it has changed. A phrase is text between commas or any other kind of punctuation mark such as semicolons, colons, question marks and so on; or between hard returns, hard page breaks and footnote/endnote codes. The screen display can get confusing if you've changed only one word in there.

Save your document before you compare it.   When you see a document that has been compared, it's easy to get lost in the system of markings that indicate what's new, what's been moved and so forth. Compare two *saved* documents so you can get the originals back if you need to.

Choose Undo to get the original document back. If you choose Undo just after making a comparison, you'll get the original document that was on the screen.

Retaining struck-out text. If you're in the legal profession, you probably use redlining and strikeout. Redlining is normally used to mark text that's added to a document, and strikeout is used to mark text that's deleted. You choose redlining and strikeout from the Font menu and apply them to the text.

When your document has been reviewed and all the changes agreed on, you normally choose Remove Markings from the Document Compare menu. But if you do, WordPerfect assumes that you want to delete all the text that has been struck out. To retain struck-out text, select the text you want to keep and then choose Normal font. Or search for and delete the [Stkout On] codes so text won't be struck out any more.

Print out document comments. If you use the Document Comment feature, you can add notes to yourself about what still needs to be done on a document, or you can have others add their comments as you work on a document in a work group and pass the file around. These comments won't print, though, unless you convert them to text, so you'll have to do your reviewing on the screen.

To print out a document with its comments, locate each comment and choose Comment from the Tools menu; then choose Convert to Text. (Hint: click Italic so comments will be clearly differentiated from text in the printed document.) You'll need to add a space before and after the comment to keep it from running into existing text.

Searching for each comment can get tedious, especially if there are a lot of them. A macro can speed things up. Record one that searches for each [Comment] code and converts it to italicized text.

Converting comments to text is a one-way street.   Once you convert comments to text, you can't unconvert them! Save under a different name the document that contains comments converted to text. That way you can get back the version of the document with the nonprinting comments. Otherwise you'll have to do more editing than you want to as you consolidate all the comments and remove the extraneous ones.

MERGING

Merging is the neat feature that lets you maintain mailing lists and create form letters.

To do merge printing in WordPerfect, you normally use three documents: a *primary* file (the form letter itself), a *secondary* file (the names and addresses in your mailing list) and the *merged document* (the form letters with the names and addresses inserted).

Because in real life you often start with a mailing list and then create a form letter, we'll look at tips about secondary files first. (You can do a merge without a secondary file, as you'll see later, but it's more common to use one.)

You can use a mailing list with more than one form letter.   A mailing list, or secondary file, can be used with more than one form letter, or primary file. For example, you can use the same names and addresses for form letters and envelopes and mailing labels.

But you don't have to use all the information in a mailing list. If there are fields that hold information you don't need to use, just don't put the codes for those fields in your primary document. You may have a field that holds a client number in each entry in your mailing list, for example, but you don't have to put that client number in every form letter you set up.

You have to get the right information in the right fields.
Setting up a mailing list is a little tricky, because you have to
get everything right, with the right codes. Each group of information, like a customer's name, address and phone number, is a *record*.
Each item of information in each record, like the street address, state
and zip code, has to be contained in a separate *field*. This is where
the codes come in, to identify each field. In the primary document
(the form letter), you put each code where you want its information
to appear. You have to make sure the codes match the fields in your
mailing list, so if you have your customer's name in field 1 and the
form letter calls for the field 1 information, you get the customer's
name, not the zip code. This may seem pretty obvious, but it's the
most common source of mistakes.

Shortcut to the Merge menus: Ctrl+F12. If you do a lot of
mass mailings, you'll appreciate WordPerfect's built-in shortcuts. Ctrl+F12 takes you to the Merge menu, where you can just type
the letter corresponding to the command you need next.

Take the time to use field names! It's worth it. Using field
names instead of numbers can save you a great deal of confusion. At the very beginning of your secondary file, choose Merge
from the Tools menu; then choose Merge Codes. Locate {FIELD
NAMES} (typing **f** takes you close to it) and double-click on it.
You'll see the Merge Field Name(s) dialog box (see Figure 7-4).

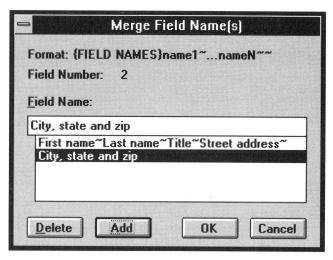

Figure 7-4: Set up a system of field names instead of numbers in the Merge Field Name(s) dialog box.

Now, name all your fields. In the Field Name box, type the first field's name and then (speed trick) type a tilde (~) and type the second field's name. You can click Add after typing each field name, but typing the tilde is faster. You can type up to 39 characters; then you have to click Add. Capitalization doesn't matter, and you can use more than one word as a field name (like *Last name* or *First name*).

If you're inserting field names with the Add button, click back in the Field Name box to type the next name. When you've named all the fields (see the next tip), press Enter or click OK. Then close the dialog box.

You'll see your field names all on one line, separated by tildes. You can fix this to make it easier to read. Go ahead and put a hard return after each field name so you can clearly see what's in each field (see the top of Figure 7-5).

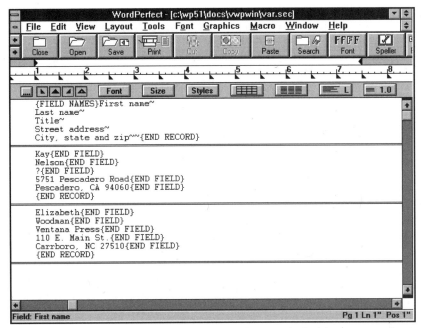

Figure 7-5: You can put hard returns after each field name at the top of your secondary file.

Think about all the ways you want to use your mailing list: they determine your fields. You could have Customer Name, First Name, Last Name, Middle Initial, Title, Company, Street Address, State, City, Zip Code, Phone—you get the idea. You *can* put the customer's name, company and address all in one field, as long as you'll always use it that way. But putting each item of information in a separate field gives you a little more flexibility for using your mailing list in other documents; you can use the customer's name, city and so forth in various places, just like those sweepstakes letters (the ones that say "Dear Mr. Rogers" in one place and "Roy" in another).

Save often as you set up your mailing list. Once you've set up your field structure, start entering records. Save your document often! Entering data in fields and records is tedious. You don't want to lose any work.

You can enter records in any order. It doesn't matter what order you enter records in. You can sort them later to put them in alphabetical order or zip code order.

Use Alt+Enter to insert an end-of-field code. As you create records, you'll see a "Field:" prompt and the name you gave to that field at the bottom of the screen. Type in your first customer name, or whatever's called for in that field. It can be longer than one line and can even contain hard returns. The field doesn't end until you press Alt+Enter or choose End Field from the Merge menu to insert an {END FIELD} code.

Be sure to create empty fields. If you don't have data for a particular field (maybe you're missing a company name, for example), just insert an {END FIELD} code for that field anyway. Otherwise you'll throw off the order; all your records have to have the same number of fields for the merge to work correctly.

Don't confuse End Record with Next Record. When you've filled out all the fields for a particular record, press Alt+Shift+Enter for End Record, or choose End Record from the Merge menu. (Don't pick Next Record, as you might think.) Then do the same for the next record, until you've finished. You can always add more records to your mailing list later.

Use an extension to identify secondary documents. The last step in setting up your mailing list is to save the secondary file. I use an extension at the end of mine, like .SEC, to tell me that these are secondary files. They aren't good for much else because of all those codes.

Creating a primary file. Now that you've got a secondary file (your mailing list), you can do a form letter, or address labels or whatever you like. To create a primary file, just type a skeleton of the document, putting the field names where you want each item of information to go (see Figure 7-6). To do this, choose Field from the Merge menu, type the field's name or number and press Enter or click OK. For a keyboard shortcut, press Ctrl+F12 and type **f**; then type the field number or name and press Enter. (Try it; it's much faster than mousing.)

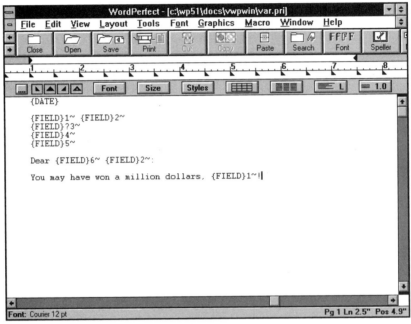

Figure 7-6: A sample primary file.

Put a question mark where a field may be blank in the mailing list. If there are places where there may not be information in a certain field because there's no corresponding information in all the records in the secondary file, put a question mark there (see Figure 7-7). All the people you're mailing to, for example, may not have a company affiliation. In the two sample records shown in Figure 7-7, my record doesn't indicate a company, but Elizabeth's does. If you don't put a question mark in that field in the primary file, you'll get a blank line where the company name was to go in the merged document.

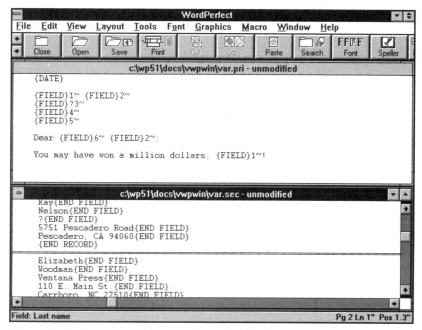

Figure 7-7: Put a question mark in fields that won't always receive information from the secondary file.

Keep your secondary document in another window. It's easy to forget exactly which field names you used, so keep your secondary file in another window (as in Figure 7-7), where you can check the field names. If you don't use exactly the same name or the right field number in the primary document, guess what? The information doesn't appear where it's supposed to.

Format your primary document just exactly as you want it to appear. Be sure to format a primary document just as you want it to look. Use spaces where spaces are to go, put in commas between city and state fields and so forth. Allow space at the top for letterhead, if you're using it. Pick the font and margins you'll use.

To see exactly how the primary file will look, turn off the display of merge codes. Use the Display Settings dialog box from the Preferences menu to turn off the display of merge codes so you can see more clearly how your primary document is formatted on the page.

Put your primary document's formatting in its Document Initial Codes. This is one time when WordPerfect's Document Initial Codes feature is useful. If you put as much of your primary document's formatting as you can in its Initial Codes window, you'll speed up your merges. You can put in the codes for tab settings, margins and paper size, among other things. (To get to the Initial Codes Window, choose Document from the Layout menu and then choose Initial Codes).

You can also format a primary document after the merge is finished by putting the codes at the beginning of the merged document, but you'll have to do it each time you do a merge.

Insert a {DATE} merge code to get the current date. If you want the date of the merge to appear in the merged documents, insert a {DATE} code from the list of merge commands or press Ctrl+Shift+F5.

But if you want the current day's date to show up in the printed merge documents, press Ctrl+F5. Otherwise WordPerfect supplies the date of the merge. Since lots of folks set up days in advance for a merge—for sending out billing notices on a certain day of the month, for example—this is an important detail to know about.

Use an extension for primary documents. Use .PRI as an extension to identify your primary documents, which aren't good for anything except doing merges, anyway.

Open a new window before you start a merge. You'll need a clear window to do a merge, because your merged document will appear in it. Shift+F4 opens a new document window.

You can see a list of your primary and secondary files. To start a merge, choose Merge from the Tools menu. Fill out the Merge dialog box with the primary and secondary file names. If you don't remember the names of those files, click on the tiny folder icon and pick the files from your directories. (This is where those .PRI and .SEC extensions come in handy.)

When the merge is done, each separate document to be printed is separated by a hard page break in the merged document. Use Print Preview to see each document as it will look when it's printed.

Don't save merged documents. Merge files are usually huge and take up lots of space on your disk. Instead of saving them, just run the merge again.

Avoiding a secondary file. You can do a merge without a secondary file if you're willing to type in the information the program needs at the keyboard. Just insert an {INPUT} code wherever you want the primary file to pause for you to enter information. Use this technique for filling out forms you use often, like memos or status reports. It's also handy for setting up a merge for others to do, since you insert a message about what they're supposed to type at each point.

Open a new window and choose Merge from the Tools menu; then choose Input. Enter the message you want to appear on the screen, such as "Type project title." Repeat this process at each place in the document where you want WordPerfect to pause for input. For example, you might want to set up prompts like those shown in Figure 7-8. Save the document that contains the prompts as a primary file. When you merge the document, WordPerfect pauses for you to enter the information at the {INPUT} codes. Figure 7-9 shows how your screen looks as you do the merge.

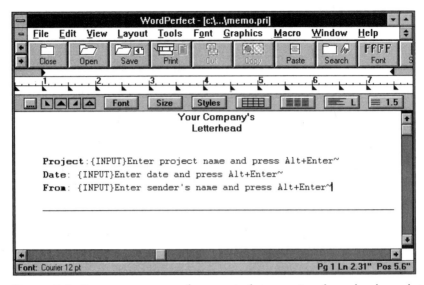

Figure 7-8: Set up a system of prompts for merging from keyboard input.

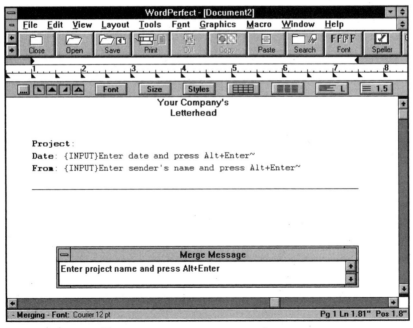

Figure 7-9: You'll see merge messages as the merge progresses.

Ring a bell to get the user's attention. To make your computer beep whenever the user has to type something, insert a {BELL} command just before the {INPUT} code. Choose it from the Merge Codes dialog box.

Run the Speller before you merge. Run the Speller on your primary document before you use it in a merge. That way you won't print 50 or 100 documents with spelling errors in them.

Running the Speller on a secondary document only wastes time. It stops at every proper name.

Stopping a merge. Sometimes you may have to stop a merge in progress. Press Esc. If that doesn't work, press Ctrl+Break. If *that* doesn't work, close the window containing the merge document. That will do it.

Doing mailing labels in a merge. Mailing labels are tricky. The first and most basic thing to remember is that you have to set up a tiny, tiny page size and then set up merge codes. Play Word-Perfect's labels macro to pick the right paper size for your labels.

Use that labels macro! The easiest way to set up a format for mailing labels is to use the LABELS.WCM macro that comes with WordPerfect. It works for both Avery and 3M labels. To use it, open a new document. Then choose Play from the Macro menu and double-click on LABELS.WCM. You can then just pick which type of label you want to use. If you don't see yours listed there, try a format close to the size you have, or go out and buy labels that WordPerfect supports. (Take my advice on this! Setting up a custom label format is very tedious.)

Depending on the type of printer you have, you may be asked for what kind of labels you're using (laser, dot-matrix and so forth). Then you can choose which label format to use. Try to find the wrapper the labels came in so you'll have the product's code number handy. Click Install to put that new paper size definition into your

Paper Size/Type list permanently. Once you've defined this label format, you can use it again and again.

Put your paper size in Document Initial Codes. If you're merge-printing labels that are two or three across, you need to put the label format codes in Document Initial Codes, not just at the top of the document, as you might think. To do this, choose Document from the Layout menu and then choose Initial Codes. Choose Page from the Format menu and select Paper Size/Type. Then select the page size you want to use (assuming you've played that labels macro so the right paper size is there in your Paper Size/Type list).

If you're not doing a merge, you can put the paper size at the beginning of the document.

You'll need to specify the fields in a primary document if you're merging to mailing labels. Setting up the label's page size is the first step in merging to mailing labels. You still need to tell WordPerfect where to put the information for the address from each field in the records. In the regular WordPerfect screen, not in the Initial Codes window, choose Field from the Merge menu and enter the field names or numbers where you want them to appear, as in this example that uses named fields:

Name~
Company~
Street Address~
City, State ZIP~

Remember to add margin changes, hard returns or tabs. They're not usually required on small labels, but you may need them on large labels that are preprinted with a return address.

Be sure to save the document with a .PRI extension so you can identify it as a primary file later. You can then merge your label primary file with your mailing list secondary file.

Sneaky trick for setting up a label primary file.   If you've already got a form letter with an address block set up, just copy the address block with its merge codes and paste it in the label primary file.

You can print mailing labels without doing a merge.   You don't have to do a merge to print mailing labels. Instead of creating a secondary file, insert the correct Paper Size code at the beginning of your document (run that labels macro if the right size isn't listed in the Paper Size dialog box) and then type the addresses, separating each one with a page break (Ctrl+Enter).

Getting one label per page?   If you're getting one label per page, read the preceding tip again. You have to put a page break between each address. Really.

Are labels getting cut off?   If the tops and bottoms of your labels are getting cut off, try entering larger top and bottom margins for the document.

Address lines overlapping?   If the address lines overlap, try using a smaller font.

Don't waste expensive labels.   Test-print one page on plain paper; then hold the printed page up to the light with a sheet of labels behind it. You'll see the label perforations around your address blocks, so you'll know whether your labels are formatted correctly. You may need to go back and add an extra hard return at the beginning of each address so the first line doesn't get cut off.

Recycle your label document.   It's tedious to get a sheet of labels printing exactly right. Once you've got a document that works, keep on using it. Copy and paste new addresses in it and save it under another name.

If you've got a sheet of labels all addressed to one company, remember that you can search and replace to quickly convert that document to a sheet of labels for a completely different company. Just replace the old company's name with the new company's name, the old street address with the new street address and so forth.

Make your own personal return address labels. You can buy tiny return-address labels and make your own personal supply. Here's a sophisticated touch to use in them: put a tiny graphic in your personal mailing labels. Make it Character type. For Size, set a tiny height, like .25 inches. Just do one, copy it and paste it in the rest of the labels. (See Chapter 9 for details about using graphics.)

Merging with plain envelopes. Don't—unless you have to. Try to use envelopes with preprinted return addresses and put mailing labels on them. The envelope macro supplied with early releases of WordPerfect for Windows doesn't always work and you can spend a lot of time trying to figure things out.

If you really have to do it, see the previous tips for merging to mailing labels and the tips on printing envelopes in Chapter 8, "Spinning Straw into Gold: Printing."

The secret of merge printing to envelopes is the same as for merge printing to labels: be sure to set up your envelope page size in the Document Initial Codes window.

WordPerfect for Windows lets you search (and replace) all codes, including merge codes. To search for merge codes, press F2 for Search (or choose it from the Edit menu). Then choose Codes and check Merge Codes. You'll see a list to choose from.

There's more to merging than meets the eye. You can do lots more with merge printing and macro language. If you're interested, curl up with one of those thousand-page books for a few hours. You'll be amazed.

SORTING

Even if you don't use mail merge and don't need to sort long mailing lists, don't overlook WordPerfect for Windows's Sort feature. It lets you easily alphabetize lists and entries in tables.

WordPerfect for Windows only sorts to the screen. If you're used to WordPerfect DOS, you probably know that you can direct the results of sorting a list to a file. Not in WordPerfect for Windows! When you sort a file in WordPerfect for Windows, your sorted items appear in the current document, replacing the original order of the items. Save your document before you sort it if you want to keep the original order intact. Then save it after the sort, under a different name, if you want to keep two versions—one sorted by zip code and another by customer name, for example.

Sorting isn't as hard as it seems. If you have a list that looks like the following example, with each item on a line by itself, it's very easy to sort it by the first word in the list. This is called a *line sort*, and you use it when the data you want to sort is on lines separated by hard returns. You don't have to change any default settings unless you've sorted a list previously and have changed any settings.

Spot Periat
Nadine Periat
Carla Periat
Renee Periat
Camille Periat

To do a line sort (sort by first name), all you need to do is select the text in the list and choose Sort from the Tools menu. Then just click OK in the rather complicated Sort dialog box that follows (see Figure 7-10), and your list will be sorted like this:

Camille Periat
Carla Periat
Nadine Periat
Renee Periat
Spot Periat

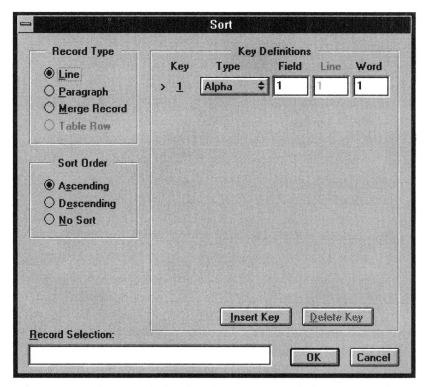

Figure 7-10: The Sort dialog box lets you specify how to sort lists.

If your list isn't sorted correctly, it probably has tabs in it.
Sometimes your list doesn't get sorted as you think it will. If this happens, it's probably because there are tabs in the list, usually preceding the entries. WordPerfect assumes that tabs separate *fields*, so the trick is to count the tabs. The field number is the number of tabs from the left margin. If your list is indented one tab from the left margin, enter **2** in the Field box.

How to sort by last name first. Have you ever sorted a list of names by last name when that list was set up with first names first? This used to drive me crazy until I saw how easy it is to do.

Say you've got a list like this (probably much longer, of course):

Hiro Sulu   ext. 6712
Ken Periat   ext. 7845
Ted Nace   ext. 9832
Ron Duarte   ext. 6734

To sort it by last name, select the list; then choose Sort from the Tools menu. Specify Word 2 as the key to sort on. Then click OK.

Remember that if there are tabs in the list, you have to count them and specify which field to sort on. If the list is indented one tab from the left margin, for example, specify Field 2 and Word 2.

 To sort an entire document, you don't have to select the list items first.   If your whole document consists of list items to be sorted, you don't have to select the items first. Just go to the top of the document and choose Sort.

 Shortcut to sorting: Ctrl+Shift+F12.   Press Ctrl+Shift+F12 to bring up the Sort dialog box.

 You can sort paragraphs, too.   Choose a paragraph sort when you're sorting paragraphs separated by two hard returns (paragraphs separated by blank lines) or separated by hard page breaks (as in a list of addresses set up for mailing labels, for example).

This is also useful for alphabetizing main index entries that have subtopics if you're compiling an index by hand instead of using WordPerfect's indexing feature. Use it to sort bibliographies, too.

 You can sort tables.   This often-overlooked feature lets you easily sort rows in tables. Say you've got a table like the one shown in Figure 7-11, and you need to sort it by last name. Select the rows you want to sort (*not* the row with the column headings) and choose Sort from the Tools menu. Then choose Cell 2 as the key to sort on. (When you sort a table, the Sort dialog box changes to show you Cell, Line and Word options instead of Field, Line and Word.) Your table will be sorted as in Figure 7-12, by last name.

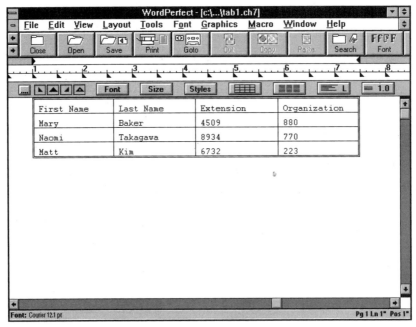

Figure 7-11: You can sort table data that's in rows.

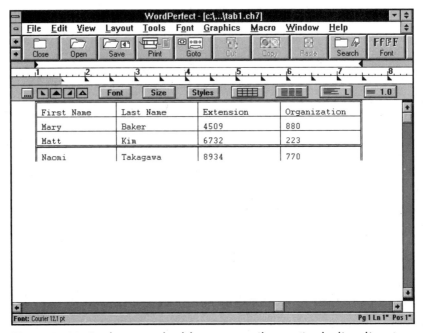

Figure 7-12: In the sorted table, row attributes (including lines) are moved along with the rows.

Traps when sorting tables. You may need to redo the lines (rules) in a table after you sort it, because WordPerfect sorts the lines along with the rows, as you see in Figure 7-12.

Don't select heading rows unless you want them sorted, too.

Don't sort a table that has cells that have been joined and that occupy more than one row.

Sorting dates. The trick to sorting dates is to format them with slashes or dashes (10/28/51 or 10-28-51). WordPerfect considers whatever is separated by a slash or a dash to be a separate word. To sort dates like these by year, enter **3** in the Word box.

Sorting lists with unequal numbers of words. Here's another sneaky trick that's often overlooked. You may want to sort by last name a list that has unequal numbers of words in it, like this one:

Elizabeth Woodman
Kay Yarborough Nelson
George Herbert Walker Bush

You can't specify to sort it on Word 2, as you normally would, because the last name is either Word 2, Word 3 or Word 4. Type **-1** in the Word box in the Sort dialog box—WordPerfect will sort each line by the last word.

Use a hard space to make the program treat multiple words as one word. If your list has entries in it like these, separate with a hard space (Ctrl+Space bar) the parts that you want the program to consider as one word.

Charles W. Stewart III
Martin Luther King, Jr.
John Dos Passos

Put a hard space between Stewart and III, King and Jr., and Dos and Passos; then the list will be sorted on Stewart, King and Dos Passos. (Sort on Word -1, as explained above.)

Use the Sort dialog box's Insert Key to specify other ways to sort. You aren't restricted to sorting on only one key. The Key Definitions box lets you set up other keys to sort on, if you click Insert Key. For example, you might want to define the Last Name field as Key 1 and then define the First Name field as Key 2: then you could sort by first name within last name (Jones, Robert would be preceded by Jones, Katherine, like listings in a phone book).

You can sort merge records. If you do complex mass mailings, you may want to sort huge lists of names and addresses by state or by zip code. Remember, fields are the parts of the record that are separated by {END FIELD} codes.

Look at the merge records in Figure 7-13. To sort them by last name first, specify a merge sort by choosing Merge Record in the Sort dialog box. Sort on Field 1, Word 2 (because the last name is the second word). To sort them by zip code, you'd specify Field 4, Word -1 because some city names (in Field 4) are more than one word long.

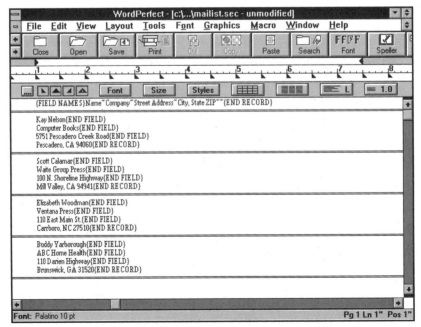

Figure 7-13: You can sort merge records.

Sorting and selecting.   You can sort merge records and, at the same time, select just the ones you want to use. Say you want to send a mailing only to customers with zip codes greater than 94000 (from our sample mailing list in Figure 7-13). For Key 1 (zip code), enter Field **4**, Word **-1**. Then enter this line in the Record Selection part of the Sort dialog box:

key1=>94000

This tells the program to sort only those records with zip codes greater than 94000. The resulting sort is shown in Figure 7-14. You can see that the records have been sorted (94060 is smaller than 94941) and selected from the mailing list at the same time.

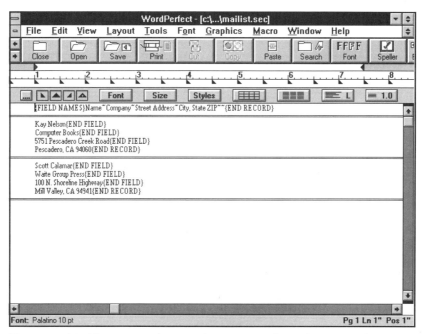

Figure 7-14: You can select and sort records at the same time.

Selecting records without sorting them.   If you want to just pull selected records from a database, click No Sort in the Sort dialog box. Then go ahead and enter the Record Selection criteria in the Record Selection box and click OK.

Use special characters to specify selection criteria. To select specific records that meet a certain criterion, use the equal sign (=). For example, look back at Figure 7-13. If you set **key1=GA**, just addresses in Georgia (with Key 1 defined as Field 4, Word -2) would be selected.

To select records that meet two criteria, define two keys and use an asterisk (*) between them. To select only the Yarboroughs in Georgia, enter **key1=Yarborough * key2=GA**. (This is, of course, assuming that you've defined Key 1 as Field 1, Word -1 and Key 2 as Field 4, Word -2.)

To select records that meet one criterion or the other, use the plus sign (+). For example, **key1=Yarborough + key2=GA** selects either the Yarboroughs or people living in Georgia.

You can also use the symbols => (greater than or equal to), =< (less than or equal to) and < or > (less than or greater than). For example, **key1>94000** pulls records that have zip codes greater than 94000.

The trick to selecting is always in getting the keys defined right before you set up your selection criteria. For example, look at why Word -2 was chosen to define Key 1 in the first example in this tip. Mill Valley is two words, so the state name can't be Word 2. Instead, you have to count back from the end of the field and use a negative number to specify the state.

Always sort alphanumerically unless you're sorting numbers of different lengths. An alphanumeric sort recognizes all the characters in a word, whether they're letters or numbers. Use a numeric sort only when you have to sort numbers of different lengths.

EQUATIONS TIPS

If you need to create mathematical expressions in your work, you'll love WordPerfect for Windows's Equation Editor. Not only does it create scientific symbols for you, but it also follows its own built-in set of typesetting rules that print variables in italics and mathematical functions in nonitalic (roman) type, so you don't have to think about these niceties.

There is a bit of sorcery involved in getting exactly what you want from the Equation Editor, though. And you can use the first two tips even if you've never done equations and never want to do them!

You can use the Equation Editor to get text effects you normally can't get from your printer. Because the Equation Editor can print text as graphics, it can create characters that aren't in any of the fonts you have. So if there's a Greek letter or a symbol you need, and your printer can't print it because it's not available in any of your fonts, use this trick: choose Equation from the Graphics menu; then select Options. Turn on Print as Graphics if it's not already on, or use the Equation Settings dialog box from the File pull-down menu. Then create the symbol in the Equation Editor, and your printer will print it as a graphic. (Use the inline macro supplied with the program to get it to appear on the same line as text, as explained in a tip below.)

Want b-i-g headings? Use the Equation Editor. You can use a variation of the previous trick to create very large headings in point sizes your printer doesn't have.

First, enter your heading into the Equation Editor as a function. (You have to do this because otherwise WordPerfect assumes you're entering variables and prints characters in italics.) In the Equation Editor, type **func**, a space, a left curly brace and your heading, with the words separated by tildes. End with a right curly brace. These weird symbols are necessary because of the way the Equation Editor works, but you don't care about all that if you're not creating real equations. Here's an example:

func {My~Own~Big~Heading}

To see how the heading will really look, press Ctrl+F3 for Redisplay. Now, choose Settings from the Equation Editor's File menu; then select Point Size and enter the big point size you want to use, such as 36 points or 48 points (see Figure 7-15). The Equation Editor sends your "equation" to the printer as bitmapped graphics.

It will be printed in Courier, Times Roman or Helvetica, not in the font in effect in your document. WordPerfect figures out which of these three fonts is closest in style to the font in effect in your document and uses that.

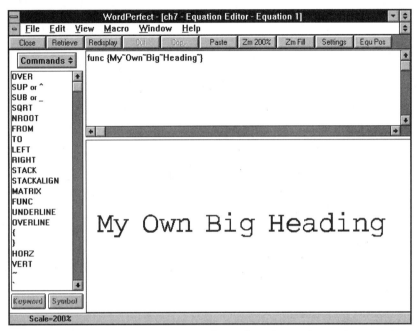

Figure 7-15: You can create very large headings through equation voodoo.

Printing equations as text versus printing them as graphics. Printing equations as graphics takes longer than printing them as text, and the quality isn't as good, either. My advice is to test print equations as text and see what your printer gives you. Then test print them as graphics and compare the results.

Flush right equations? Sure. Normally WordPerfect centers equations on a separate line. If you'd rather have them all aligned flush right or flush left, as is the style in many scientific documents, choose Equations from the Preferences menu and pick a different alignment. To change the alignment of just one equation, click the Equ Pos button in the Equation Editor and pick a different horizontal position (or choose Box Position from the Equation Editor's File menu).

Use the inline macro to get inline equations. WordPerfect normally displays equations on separate lines. If you don't want this effect, play the inline macro (INLINE.WCM) supplied with the program. It puts you in the Equation Editor, where you can create your equation, but it prints the equation on the same line as the surrounding text.

To see how you're doing, press Ctrl+F3. You'll often need to switch back and forth between entering commands and symbols for your equation and displaying the results. To see the results of what you're doing, press Ctrl+F3 to redisplay your work.

The Equation Editor has its own Button Bar. And you can customize it, too, like any other Button Bar. You just can't add macros to it. For example, if you make a button for the WP Characters command on the Edit menu, you can insert symbols easily.

You can change the size of equation text. You may want to print complex equations in a different point size than the rest of your text—perhaps larger to let you see small subscripts and super-scripts. To change the font size for all the equations in a document, use the Preferences menu and choose Equations. Then pick a point size.

To change the size of just one equation, go into the Equation Editor and display the equation you want to change. Then choose Settings from the Equation Editor's File menu and set a point size.

You can enter equation commands and key words from the palettes and from the keyboard. Sometimes it's much faster to type equations at the keyboard than to select their key words, commands and symbols from the Equations Editor's palettes with the mouse. You do need to follow a few rules if you use the keyboard, however. Refer to Figure 7-16 to see the examples given in the following pages.

◆ If you type a command, be sure to separate it from the next key word or variable with a space. Typing **xovery** gets *xovery* instead of equation 1 in Figure 7-16.

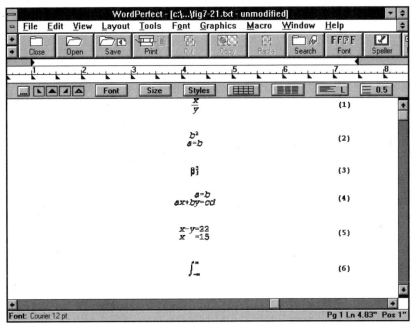

Figure 7-16: Equations created in the Equation Editor.

◆ If you type function names from the keyboard, be sure to use spaces. For example, if you enter **funccos** instead of **func cos** (for the cosine function), you'll get *funccos*, in italics.

◆ Use a tilde for spaces, not the space bar. If you use the space bar to put spaces in your equation, you'll see spaces as you type but not in the displayed or printed equation. (Try it and see.) This happens because the Equation Editor follows its own internal rules for spacing. Use a tilde for a normal space or use a single opening quotation mark (') for a thin space, which is about a fourth of a normal space.

◆ Hard returns don't work the way you think they will, either. You'll see line breaks on the screen as you type, but not when you display your results. To indicate a line break, use the pound sign (#) (or use MATRIX, MATFORM, STACK and STACKALIGN, which have their own internal alignment rules). For example, **b^2# a = b** produces equation 2 in Figure 7-16.

◆ To create a variable that has a subscript and a superscript, put the subscript first. For instance, **beta_i^3** produces equation 3.

Specifying an alignment character. This one can drive you crazy until you dig it out of the manual! Use STACKALIGN and the ampersand (&) to specify where you want equations to align (often they align on the equal sign). For example, if you type **stackalign {a &= b # ax +by &= cd}** you produce equation 4 in Figure 7-16. Notice also that the pound sign (#) indicates where to break the line.

The mysterious PHANTOM command. Aha! This arcane command simply reserves space as a placeholder. You can put it anywhere the Equation Editor expects a symbol. You can use it to stand for a nonexistent character to attach a superscript to, or to force alignment. Entering **stack {x - y = 33 # x phantom {- y} = 15}** produces equation 5 in Figure 7-16.

Notice that the characters - *y*, whose space the phantom represents, are enclosed in curly braces.

Use curly braces to group elements. This is another very basic tip that's easy to overlook. If you want characters and symbols to be treated as a group, enclose them in curly braces.

"Incorrect format?" Count those curly braces. The most common mistake anybody can make when creating equations is to have an unequal number of left and right curly braces. If you get an "incorrect format" message, count the number of left and right curly braces. If there isn't an equal number of them, that's where your problem is.

Sneaky trick for formatting limits. WordPerfect normally prints limits with the upper limit printed just over the integral sign and the lower limit printed under it. To print the limits to the *side* of the integral, use the SUB and SUP commands (or _ and ^). Entering **INT _{-inf} ^ inf** produces equation 6 in Figure 7-16.

Entering a character as a literal. If you want a word that's normally treated as a key word to appear literally as you type it instead of being interpreted as a key word, precede it with a backslash.

To use a right curly brace (}) as itself instead of as a grouping symbol, for instance, just enter it like this: **\}**.

Moving equations. More voodoo. Delete the Equation box, go to the new location and undelete it.

Setting up an equation numbering system. Many scientific journals require you to number equations in a paper that's submitted to them. WordPerfect can do that for you automatically.

The trick is to open the equation caption window (choose Caption for each equation you create); then just close the window without typing a caption. Your equations will be numbered with bold numbers in parentheses at the right margin. You can easily record a macro to search for each equation and open and close its caption window without changing anything. You don't have to do this manually.

Changing the equation numbering style. You can put equation numbers in a style other than bold. To change the style of equation numbering, go to the top of your document. Choose Equation and Options from the Graphics menu to get the Equation Options dialog box. Beneath Caption Numbering, click on the arrow and choose Italics, Small Caps, or whatever you like from the Style pop-up list.

Add text to your equation numbering system. To add automatic chapter numbering to your equations (such as 6-1, 6-2 and 6-3 for Chapter 6), use the Equation Options dialog box. Put the insertion point inside the Style box, just before the caption number but inside the parentheses. Then type in just the chapter number and a hyphen.

You can use this trick to add text to your equation numbering system, too, such as *(Chapter 6, equation I)* or *(equation I)*.

Use the Equations keyboard. There's a special Equations keyboard supplied with WordPerfect. It lets you easily type Greek letters and commonly used symbols with Alt-key and Ctrl-key combinations. Alt+A, for example, produces an alpha character, and Ctrl+B produces a bar symbol.

To put this keyboard into effect each time you use the Equation Editor, use the Preferences menu. Choose Equations; then click Select (twice). Double-click EQUATION.WWK from the list of keyboards that appears. Then click OK twice to get back to your document.

The Equation Editor won't italicize some things but does italicize others. Normally the Equation Editor doesn't italicize terms such as *cosine* and *sine*, because it considers them to be functions. But it automatically italicizes Greek letters because it considers them to be variables. If something is italicized and you want to force it to be in the normal (roman) font, precede it with **func**. Remember to put curly braces around everything that you want to be affected. (You saw an example of this earlier, with the heading trick.)

Likewise, to make numbers or functions print in italics, precede them with **ital** and surround them in curly braces. For example, entering **ital {1105}** produces *1105.*

Entering **bold** puts what follows it (in curly braces) in boldface.

The difference between LONGDIV and LONGDIVS. LONGDIV gets you a curved long division symbol; while LONGDIVS creates a square one. This is a very subtle difference.

Printing a times sign. Here's another secret you'll have to dig in the manual to find! To print a times sign (×) instead of an asterisk (*), use the TIMES command from the Equation Editor's palette. If you simply type **x**, the Equation Editor will print it italics because it assumes that it is the variable *x.*

Don't mix up OVERLINE and OVER. The OVERLINE and UNDERLINE commands put lines over (or under) whatever follows them in curly braces, so you use them to create built-up fractions and expressions. The OVER command creates a simple fraction.

Save equations as separate files. If you've slaved over getting an expression just right, save it as a separate file so you can use it again in other documents. Use the Equation Editor's Save As command. Use its Retrieve command to get the equation in another document.

Equation files all have the extension .EQN so you can identify them later.

There are lots more things you can do in the Equation Editor, but these give you a basic bag of tricks. If you create complex mathematical expressions, you're probably no stranger to those other big fat books anyway.

MOVING ON

That takes care of a lot of tricks! You may not need them very often, but they're here, waiting for you. Whenever you need to index a document, set up a table of authorities, number lines and paragraphs or create mathematical expressions, get out this bag of tricks. These are pretty complex procedures, and a tip or two may get you on your way, or help you overcome some obstacle.

In the next chapter, instead of seeing tricks for seldom-used chores, we'll look at something you do almost every day: printing.

CHAPTER EIGHT

Spinning Straw into Gold: Printing

When you installed Word-Perfect for Windows, you probably also selected a printer—most documents are printed on paper in some final form, somewhere. If everything goes right, you'll never have any printing problems. But when did everything go right? It seems like there are always problems with printing.

Although we can't get into printer problems by brand name—or this book would be huge—this chapter will give you fundamental printing voodoo, along with some arcane strategies for printing.

"WordPerfect printing" and "Windows printing." Here's the most basic consideration: which should you use, the WordPerfect printer drivers or the Windows printer drivers? If you're printing a document created in WordPerfect DOS, and you want it to be printed just exactly as it was in WordPerfect DOS, by all means choose WordPerfect printing. Printing with WordPerfect lets you choose different page sizes within a document, too; Windows printing won't let you do that. And WordPerfect printing is a little faster.

You switch between WordPerfect and Windows printing *within WordPerfect*: choose Select Printer from the File menu and then select the button next to WordPerfect or Windows in the Printer Driver box.

Print a document named PRINTER.TST to see what your printer will do. This document is in your C:\WPWIN directory. Print it to see a sample of how superscripts, subscripts, redlining, equations, footnotes and graphics will come out on your printer. Then try it with a Windows printer to see what the differences are.

Print with Windows in a system font if you print on more than one printer. If you print on any one of several different printers and want your document to come out in exactly the same way (with the same line breaks and so forth) choose Windows printing and print in one of the stroke fonts (Modern, Roman or Script).

For color graphics printing on a non-PostScript printer, use Windows printing. Print with Windows if you need to print graphics in color on a non-PostScript printer. Important: Uncheck Fast Graphics Printing in the Print dialog box in WordPerfect.

For fax or LaserMaster printing, use Windows printing. WordPerfect doesn't support these two special kinds of printers, so if you're using one of them, you have to use the Windows printer drivers.

Uncheck Fast Graphics Printing if you run out of memory when using a Windows printer. WordPerfect's graphics printing method is fast but also uses a lot of memory. Uncheck the Fast Graphics Printing option (in the Print Settings dialog box; use the Preferences menu and choose Print) if you get an "Out of memory" message when printing with a Windows printer driver.

If you can't work in WordPerfect while your document is printing, check the Print Manager.   It's sort of misleading to talk about "WordPerfect printing" and "Windows printing" when everything usually goes through the Windows Print Manager. But that's the way it is. The Print Manager lets you keep working in another document while it's printing. This is known as *print spooling* or *background printing.*

If you can't continue to work in WordPerfect while your documents are printing, maybe the Print Manager isn't on. In the Windows Program Manager, select Control Panels in the Main group and double-click on Printers. Then check the box next to Use Print Manager, if it's unchecked.

Windows lets you assign more than one printer to any port.   This can be confusing. Windows prints with the default printer. Although you can assign more than one device to any port, only one device can be active on that port. The printer that does the printing has to be both active and the default printer (use the Printers Control Panel).

You have to install a Windows printer before you can use it.   And the secret is that you have to do it *through Windows.* First, find your Windows Setup disks, because you're going to need one of them. Then double-click on the Printer icon in the Control Panel. You'll see a list of the Windows printers you've installed. Click Add Printer and select your printer from the list (just type the first letter of its name). When your printer's name is highlighted, click Install. You'll be asked to insert the appropriate Windows Setup disk that has the printer driver on it. In Windows 3.0, click Configure and tell Windows which port your printer is connected to. As the last step, click Setup and see if there are any options you need to change.

Background mumbo jumbo.   Well, we said with voodoo you don't have to understand everything! But here's a *little* background about what's going on with your printer drivers (the software that "drives" your printer), because it can really be confusing. You may see some tips later that assume you know this stuff.

When you installed WordPerfect for Windows, you probably also installed a printer or two. The program looked at a special file called an .ALL file—it contains all the information about all the printers WordPerfect supports—and created a specific .PRS (printer resource) file for your brand and model of printer. That's your *WordPerfect printer driver.*

Fonts are kept in .ALL files, too. Hewlett-Packard fonts, for example, are in a WPHP1.ALL file that contains all the fonts supported by H-P printers. As you install fonts, they're copied to your particular printer's .PRS file.

You can edit a .PRS file with a special program called the Printer program (in your C:\WPC directory) if you need to really get in there and fine-tune your fonts and other things.

Reformatting documents for your printer. When you open or retrieve a document, WordPerfect normally formats it for whatever printer is currently selected. If you've already formatted a document and then open or retrieve it while a different printer is selected, it will be reformatted for the currently selected printer unless you uncheck Format Retrieved Documents for Default Printer in the Environment Settings dialog box. If you want to keep the original formatting, uncheck that box.

Here's an example of what can happen if you have two printers. Say you have an Epson FX-1050 and a Panasonic KX-P1695, and the Epson is the default printer. The font choices aren't the same on both printers. If you open a document that's formatted for the Epson while the Panasonic is selected, WordPerfect will reformat it for the Panasonic.

This also happens if you switch back and forth between WordPerfect printer drivers and Windows printer drivers. A document formatted for one will be reformatted if it's opened or retrieved while the other printer driver is selected. Be warned.

Printing selected pages.   Yes, you can print just a few pages of a document. To do this, choose Multiple Pages from the Print menu and then use the following system:

◆ Separate single page numbers by commas. For example, to print pages 34, 77 and 120, you'd enter **34, 77, 120**.

◆ Use a dash to indicate "to the end (or beginning) of the document." For example, to print from page 20 to the end of the document, enter **20-**. To print from the first page through page 20, enter **-20**. Use a dash to specify a range of pages to print. For example, to print pages 10 through 20, enter **10-20**.

◆ Use colons to specify sections. For example, entering **2:34** specifies section 2, page 34. (You get sections when you use the New Page Number command to restart page numbering within a document.)

◆ Use Roman numerals to specify pages that are numbered with Roman numerals, such as in the preface or index of a book.

You can also combine all of this shorthand to specify several different parts of a document at once. Entering **1, 5, 10-15, 25-** prints page 1, page 5, pages 10 through 15 and from page 25 to the end of the document.

Printing a document that's not displayed.   WordPerfect normally prints the document that's displayed in the active window. To print a document that's *not* on your screen, choose Document on Disk and enter the document's name. You can also print ranges of pages and selected pages from a document on disk.

When you print just part of a page, you get weird page spacing.   When you select text and print just that selection, it's printed on the page at the place where it would fall if you printed the whole page. The last paragraph on a page, for instance, will be printed at the bottom of the page.

To avoid this, copy the text you want to print into a new document window (Shift+F4 opens a new one quickly) and print it from there.

Instant printing with Ctrl+P. To print one copy of the document on the screen, press Ctrl+P. No dialog boxes to fill out.

 Want collated copies? Let WordPerfect generate your printed document. You'll see in the Print dialog box a "Generated By" choice under Number of Copies. If you're printing several copies of a long document, leave "Generated By" set to WordPerfect: your copies will be collated. If you choose Printer or Network, your copies may be printed a little faster, but you'll have to collate them by hand.

 Nudging the Print Manager. Sometimes you'll want to change the order that your documents are printing in. This can happen when somebody yells that a certain document is needed *right now*, but you've just sent a bunch of documents to the printer, and you know that one wasn't first in line.

You can change the order that documents are printed in even after you've used the Print command on them, by going out to the Windows Print Manager (press Ctrl+Esc to bring up the Task List and choose Print Manager). Then just drag the icon of any document (other than the one that's currently being printed) to a new place in the lineup.

 If you pause the Print Manager, be sure to resume it. If you pause the Print Manager to fix a problem such as a paper jam, be sure to click Resume when you're ready to print again. If you don't, you can't print.

 Cancel printing by deleting a document from the lineup.
If you decide not to print a document that's currently in the Print Manager's lineup, highlight its name in the lineup and click Delete.

You can cancel the current print job from within WordPerfect as long as the Current Print Job dialog box is still on the screen. Otherwise, it's out to the Print Manager with you. Do it from there.

Canceling all printing (a sneaky trick). Double-click on the Print Manager's Control icon to exit from it: that will do it.

Why is the computer beeping at me? If your computer beeps and the Print Manager icon flashes at the bottom of your screen, the Print Manager wants attention. Press Ctrl+Esc and choose it from the Task List.

How to speed up printing. The Print Manager is sort of slow, but there are third-party programs on the market (such as PrintCache from LaserTools, 800/767-8004) that speed it up, whether you use WordPerfect or Windows printer drivers. You can use PrintCache with dot-matrix printers, too.

Quickly selecting a different printer. To quickly select a different printer (that you've already installed), don't bother choosing Select Printer. Instead, choose Print from the File menu and then click Select. Just double-click on the printer's name.

Printing special characters via voodoo. If your printer won't print special characters, use the Equation Editor and type them there. That way, WordPerfect tells the printer to create the character graphically, using WP Courier, WP Helv or WP Roman, whichever is closest to the font you're using in the document.

Tricks for printing envelopes and labels. WordPerfect comes with an envelope macro, but it didn't always work well in early releases of the program. Here's how to print envelopes, in general, so you can record your own macro.

Setting up to print envelopes is a two-step process. First, you specify a paper size and then you format a page for that paper size, with very small margins.

Here are all the steps involved for formatting a standard business-size envelope. Open a new document. Choose Page from the Layout menu and then choose Paper Size. Choose the 9.5-by-4-inch (business-size) envelope (see Figure 8-1).

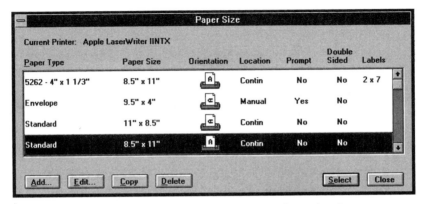

Figure 8-1: WordPerfect's Paper Size dialog box displays standard envelope sizes.

If you don't want to use a business-size envelope, click Add. Under Paper Type, choose Envelope and pick one of the other sizes listed in the pop-up list under Paper size (Legal, US Govt, A4 and so on). If you're going to hand-feed envelopes to your printer, go to Location and check Manual. If you have an automatic envelope feeder, check Continuous or Bin. Close the Paper Size dialog box and select your new envelope paper size. That's Step One.

Now you have to format your new envelope-sized page for the addresses. Use the Ruler or the Margins command on the Layout menu to set a left margin at 4 inches and a top margin of 2 inches (to print on envelopes that have a preprinted return address). If you're printing on blank envelopes and you're going to type in a return address, set a left and top margin of 0.3 inches.

If you're printing on blanks, type the return address and then press Enter until you get to Ln 2", which will be two inches from the top of the envelope. Press Tab to get over to Pos 4", which is 4 inches from the left edge of the envelope; then type the address block (or copy and paste it from the letter).

Now save this document with a name that helps you remember what it is; then you can use it again just by filling it out with a new address each time you need one. Or record the whole thing as a macro, stopping at the first line of the address block.

Are graphics printing slowly? Don't print 'em. Graphics are very slow to print. If you're proofing the text of a document, turn off graphics printing to speed things up. (Choose Do Not Print for graphics from the Graphics Quality pop-up list in the Print dialog box.) Or print text and graphics separately.

Use the Preferences menu to set your printing preferences. If there are some print settings that you always have to change (if you almost always want two copies of a document, for instance) use the Preferences menu. Or pick Draft mode for most of your printing. You can override your preferences in the Print dialog box at any time.

If you mix fonts in the first line of text, the baseline may change. Normally WordPerfect adjusts the first baseline of text from the top down—tops of letters align with the top margin. If you mix fonts on this first line, though, the baseline may change. To avoid this, check the First Baseline at Top Margin box in the Typesetting dialog box; then set a fixed line height.

Print to disk so you can print *without WordPerfect*. This voodoo trick lets you print a WordPerfect document on a computer that isn't even running WordPerfect. It's called *printing to disk* (not to be confused with saving to disk). It's a handy way to save a document so you can just take it to any computer that's running DOS and print your document, without using WordPerfect at all. Here's how to do it.

With the document on the screen, choose Select Printer from the File menu. Then select the printer you want to print the document with. The printer doesn't have to be attached to your computer, but you do need to have installed it so it appears on your list of printers. If you want to be able to print on any printer, choose DOS Text Printer.

Once you've highlighted the printer's name, choose Setup and Port. Choose File instead of a printer port and type a file name for the document. (You'll probably want to put your document on a floppy disk if you plan to carry it to another printer.) Give it a name that helps you remember what printer it's designated for, or use the .TXT extension if it's to be printed to the DOS Text Printer so it can be printed on any printer. Then be sure to switch back to a printer that's really attached to your computer.

To print your document at the other computer, use the PRINT command at the DOS prompt. For example, to print a document called REPORT.TXT on the printer attached to the first parallel port, enter **print report.txt** and press Enter. If the printer doesn't print, try putting LPT2, LPT3, COM1, COM2 or COM3 after REPORT.TXT until you find out which port the printer's attached to.

Don't try to print a document that's been saved to disk from within WordPerfect. Print it from the DOS prompt.

Keep Fast Graphics Printing on (usually). There's a Fast Graphics Printing setting in the Preferences Print Setting dialog box. Keep it on unless you're getting messages that there's not enough memory when you're using Windows printer drivers. (But turn it off for color graphics printing, as you saw in a previous tip.)

You may need to run the Install program again to install a new printer. If your printer isn't listed in the Available Printers list, click Add. Then check again to see if it's there. If it's not, you'll need to run WordPerfect's Install program again. Choose Install Printers. You'll be asked for the master Printer disks, so find them while you're hunting for the Install disk.

Use WordPerfect DOS printer drivers if you've customized a printer in WordPerfect DOS. If you've been using DOS WordPerfect 5.1, you may have added custom paper sizes and types and other things to your printer definition (.PRS) file. Instead of doing everything over again in WordPerfect for Windows, just select your WordPerfect DOS printer driver. Go to the Select Printer dialog box and choose Add. Then click on Printer Files (*.PRS), locate the printer driver you were using in WordPerfect DOS (it's probably in your C:\WP51 directory) and select it. Then it will be listed in your Select Printer dialog box in WordPerfect for Windows.

Another, sneakier, way to do this is to simply store all your .ALL and .PRS files in C:\WPC (or C:\WP51, whichever you prefer) and use the Preferences menu (it's the Setup menu in WordPerfect DOS) to specify that directory as the location of your printer files.

Text in color on the screen? Sure. WordPerfect normally displays text as black on "white," but you can use a voodoo trick to get around that if you like seeing text in color. The only other time you'll see text in color is when you open the Reveal Codes window and change the colors used there.

Here's the secret: pretend that you have a color printer. You choose Colors from the Font menu to select what color text will *print* in, but if you also uncheck the Use Windows System Colors box in the Preferences/Display menu, you'll see text in color on the screen! But unless you really do have a color printer, of course, your printer still prints in shades of gray.

You can print in shades of gray without a color printer. If you'd like gray shading in text in your document, choose Colors from the Font menu; then, in the Select Text Colors dialog box, choose a gray tone, or pick black as the color and select a higher lumination value (the greater the lumination number, the *lighter* the shading).

The general rule is not to use more than about a 15% screen if you want to read text through it, but remember that here you're shading the actual text, not a screen over it. The more lumination it has, the lighter it gets. Lumination above 50% or 60% on most printers makes text too light to read. Test print this technique on your printer; the results vary.

FONTS

Fonts cause confusion. There are two kinds of fonts: *printer fonts* and *screen fonts.* Printer fonts are the characters used for printing, and screen fonts are the characters you see on the screen. To compound the confusion, you've got WordPerfect printing or Windows printing, depending on what you've chosen in the Select Printer dialog box.

Now, the font that's actually printed on a piece of paper isn't quite the same size as the font that appears on the screen, since the screen width is smaller than the paper width. WordPerfect uses screen fonts to simulate how a page will look when it's printed. That's not so bad: WordPerfect DOS had only one screen font—12-pt. type and 36-pt. type looked the same on the screen! The problem with Word-Perfect for Windows's screen fonts is that they sometimes get too small to read. (You'll see tips for how to get around this in this section.)

Another problem is that WordPerfect has to *have* screen fonts if it's going to represent them on the screen. If you haven't installed additional screen fonts to match your printer fonts, Windows (and WordPerfect) will use a set of basic screen fonts to display the closest match of the printer font you've selected.

To get around this problem, you can get a font management program such as Adobe Type Manager (call 800/833-6687 for Adobe Systems in Mountain View, CA). Font management programs create screen fonts that look the same on the screen as they do in a printed document. Without a font management program or a complete bitmapped font (which takes up a lot of disk space), some of your screen fonts will only be approximations of the real thing. The screen font you see when you choose 12-pt. Palatino, for instance, is really Times Roman, which is very close to Palatino. (Try it and see.)

This is why people buy font management programs like ATM (Adobe Type Manager) or Fonts-on-the-Fly (from LaserTools) or MoreFonts (from MicroLogic): they create clear, easy-to-read screen fonts in the exact sizes you call for. See Figures 8-2 and 8-3 for the differences. Figure 8-2 shows various sizes of Palatino as represented by ATM, and Figure 8-3 shows them without ATM. If you look closely, you'll see that 18 pt., 19 pt. and 20 pt. Palatino are all the same size without ATM. If being able to see these differences is important to you, get one of these font management programs.

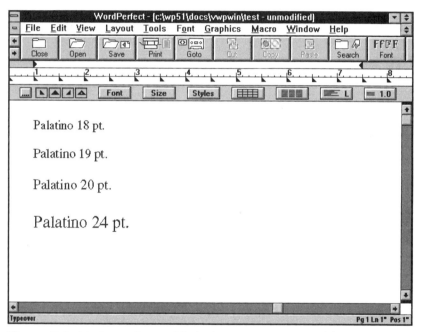

Figure 8-2: Various sizes of Palatino, as represented by ATM.

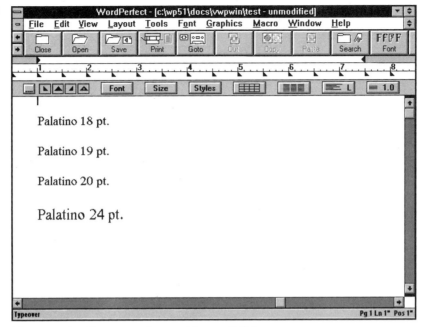

Figure 8-3: The same font without ATM.

To ATM or not to ATM? ATM (Adobe Type Manager) and other font management programs install font "outline files" to create screen fonts that look on the screen like they do in a printed document. ATM gives you PostScript fonts without your having to buy a PostScript printer, which is wonderful. It can print these fonts (actually, it "draws" them) on any printer that prints graphics, regardless of the printer fonts available in that printer. It also shows you how these fonts look on the screen. Windows, for example, shows you 10-pt. type or 12-pt. type but not 11-pt. type. ATM does. (So do Bitstream FaceLift, MicroLogic's MoreFonts, Glyphix from SWFTE or LaserTools' Fonts-on-the-Fly—they just don't use Post-Script fonts from Adobe.)

Now, here's the catch: with a PostScript printer, ATM just produces good-looking WYSIWYG screen fonts; only with non-Post-Script printers does ATM handle both screen fonts and printer fonts.

Print Preview only uses your WordPerfect screen fonts.
Even if you've installed a font management program, you won't see its pretty fonts when you use Print Preview. Only Word-Perfect screen fonts show up there. Too bad. Maybe WordPerfect Corporation will fix this soon.

Windows 3.1 adds TrueType fonts. If you're running Word-Perfect for Windows under Windows 3.1, you get the benefit of using the TrueType fonts that come with that version of Windows (see Figure 8-4). These fonts can be scaled to any size, and you don't have to store separate screen and printer versions of them or buy a font-management package to see what they look like on the screen. Windows 3.1 comes with new fonts named Arial (a sans-serif font), Lucida (in a variety of faces and styles, both serif and sans-serif), Times New Roman and Courier New.

If hard disk space is at a premium, you can choose to display only TrueType fonts (use the Windows Fonts Control Panel) and delete other fonts from your disk. This can be a great space saver if you have a laptop computer with a small hard disk.

If you delete fonts, though, don't delete MS Sans Serif, which Windows uses in dialog boxes!

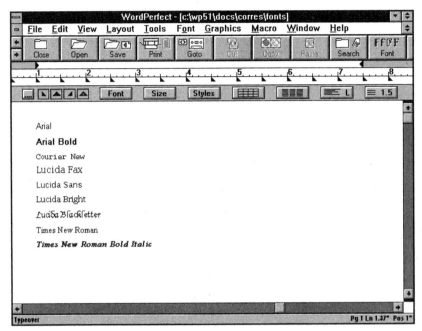

Figure 8-4: Samples of TrueType fonts provided with Windows 3.1.

Getting TrueType fonts to appear in your WordPerfect fonts list. So you're running Windows 3.1 but TrueType fonts don't appear in your fonts list in WordPerfect for Windows? The secret is to choose Windows printing in the Printer Setup dialog box. Then click Update and select.

Font substitution. If you've formatted a document to use Windows printing and a TrueType font, WordPerfect substitutes a font that's close to the TrueType font when you print with a WordPerfect printer driver or in WordPerfect DOS. New Helvetica Narrow is substituted for Arial, for example.

To tell if a font has been substituted, open the Reveal Codes window. If a font has been substituted for an unavailable font, it has an asterisk next to it, like this: [Font:*Helvetica Narrow].

What are Windows "stroke fonts"? These are also called *vector fonts.* They are, in a word, ugly. The only reasons ever to use these fonts (Modern, Roman or Script) is if you have a printer that doesn't have an equivalent sans-serif or serif font, or if you want to print the same document the same way on different printers (see an earlier tip), or if you need to print in a weird point size (Windows can scale vector fonts to any size) on a non-PostScript printer.

Vector fonts don't give very nice output. As a matter of fact, you can delete them from your WIN.INI file (or you can use the Fonts Control Panel in Windows), because they aren't used in dialog boxes or menus. Instead of using them, see the tip in Chapter 7 about using the Equation Editor to create odd-sized headings graphically ("Want b-i-g headings? Use the Equation Editor").

How to get ATM fonts to display with WordPerfect printer drivers. Edit your ATM.INI file's Synonym and Alias entries so that WP*FontName*=ATM*FontName* if WordPerfect isn't recognizing ATM fonts. For example, if WordPerfect calls a font *Garamond* but ATM calls it *AGaramond*, use this line in your ATM.INI file:

Garamond=AGaramond

If that doesn't fix it, see the next tip, which is a little more advanced.

Yucky-looking screen fonts? Change your monitor's resolution. If screen fonts aren't looking good on the screen at high resolutions such as 1024 x 768, try changing your monitor's resolution to 640 x 480 or 800 x 600. (To do this, choose Windows Setup, click Options and choose Change System Settings.)

Are you getting very small screen fonts with ATM? Turn it off. Sometimes, if you use ATM with WordPerfect for Windows, ATM's fonts appear much smaller on the screen than they actually are. If this happens, turn off ATM (there should be a control panel for it in the Windows Main or Applications group) and use the Windows screen fonts.

Screen fonts still too small? Try this voodoo. If the fonts on the screen are uncomfortably small to read, go to the top of your document (press Ctrl+Home) and set the right and left margins to one-half inch. Then select the 14-pt. Helvetica font. This corrects the problem on your screen. When you're ready to print, just delete the codes for the margin and font changes from the beginning of your document and the default settings come back into effect.

If you need to do this often, record it as a macro and make it into a button so you can quickly go into this "large-type mode" while you're working on a document.

Later releases of WordPerfect for Windows are supposed to fix this screen font problem.

Adding new fonts? New fonts usually come with both screen and printer versions and an installation program. If you don't have an installation program, install screen fonts for your Windows printer drivers with the Fonts Control Panel; install printer fonts with the Printers Control Panel.

To tell WordPerfect printer drivers that you've got some new fonts, choose Select Printer and select the printer that's going to use them. Then choose Setup and click Cartridges/Fonts and Select to see a list of the fonts your printer supports. The fonts listed there are the ones your printer can *use*. Built In fonts are built in to the printer; you install Soft Fonts. Don't mark them to be used, as described in the next paragraph, unless you've bought them and you're installing them now.

What you do in the next step depends on your printer's abilities: some printers automatically load and unload fonts during a print job; others can't. Fonts you mark with an asterisk (Present When Print Job Begins) have to be downloaded manually (these include all cartridges) by choosing Download Fonts in the Print dialog box when you turn on your printer. Fonts you mark with a plus sign (Can Be Loaded/Unloaded During Job) are downloaded automatically as WordPerfect needs them for a specific printing job. On some printers, you can mark fonts with both an asterisk and a plus sign; these fonts can be swapped in and out as the print job progresses.

There are some mouse tricks you can use to mark fonts. Double-click with the right mouse button to mark a new font (one that you've bought) with a plus sign, or double-click with the left mouse button to mark a font with an asterisk.

Change the Quantity box in the Cartridges and Fonts dialog box if you've got extra memory. The quantity of printer memory available to soft fonts is preset with your printer's factory settings. If you've added more memory to your printer, increase the quantity of memory available for your soft fonts.

Marking fonts only tells WordPerfect what fonts you've got, not where they are. There's one more step to installing fonts, and it's easily overlooked. You have to use the Printer Setup dialog box to specify the path to the directory where your fonts are stored so WordPerfect can find them.

And to use your soft fonts, you have to download them. You'll need to download soft fonts to your printer's memory when you turn on the printer. They stay in the printer's memory until you turn it off, so you usually have to do this only once before you start printing.

To download fonts you've marked as "Present When Print Job Begins," choose Initialize Printer in the Print dialog box. WordPerfect then sends to your printer all the fonts marked with an asterisk.

Pick an initial font for your printer. As long as you've just installed your new fonts, do you want one of them to be your printer's initial font, the one that's in effect when that printer is selected? If so, take one more step: choose Select Printer, highlight your printer's name, and choose Setup to specify a new initial font.

Print out CHARMAP.TST to see what symbols your fonts have. If you've got WordPerfect DOS, there's a document called CHARMAP.TST that you can use to see what's really in your font's character sets. Open CHARMAP.TST (it's probably in C:\WP51) and change to the font you want to test. Then print the document with graphics set to Do Not Print.

If you're getting really ugly "stick" figures as special characters, get a special file. If you don't have a font management program and a special character isn't in your font's character set, WordPerfect will try to create the special character you call for—and the results may not be pleasing. If this happens to you, call Word-Perfect Corporation and get the special file called the International Expanded WP.DRS file, which should solve your problem. Copy it into your C:\WPC directory.

Or get the Bitstream International Character set (Bitstream, 800/ 522-3668).

Installing Adobe fonts can sometimes be a problem. Sometimes the Adobe installer doesn't update your .ALL printer driver file, and the result is that none of the fonts you think you just installed appear in the font list. To fix this problem you need to use the Printer program, PTR.EXE, which is in your C:\WPC directory.

Run PTR.EXE, press Shift+F10 and retrieve the .ALL file that has your printer fonts. For example, WPHP1.ALL has H-P printer fonts; WPPS1.ALL has PostScript fonts. Select your printer; select Fonts and scroll until you see the Adobe fonts you've installed listed in the Soft Fonts section. Put an asterisk next to each of them. That makes them available in WordPerfect. Press F7 until you can save the document with your changes. Then go into WordPerfect, choose Select Printer and click Update to update your fonts. Then click Setup, choose Cartridges and Fonts, choose Select and mark each new font with a plus sign or an asterisk, depending on whether it's to be automatically downloaded (see "Adding new fonts?" above). Now they should be available in WordPerfect.

Call WordPerfect Corporation (800/228-1023 for laser printers or 800/228-1017 for other printers) to get a detailed manual to use with the Printer program.

If you're using a lot of fonts, the display pitch can get way off. If there are a lot of fonts in a document, WordPerfect can sometimes get confused about which display pitch to use. To correct this problem, set the display pitch to Manual and 100% (it's on the Layout/Document menu).

MOVING ON

Now that you've seen how to get a little magic out of your printer, you can take a look at how to really make WordPerfect for Windows perform its graphics sorcery.

In the next chapter, you'll see quick how-to tips for creating special effects like reversed text, pull quotes and drop caps. You'll also find revealed the mystery of getting text to appear in Graphics boxes, and you'll see the secrets of using WordPerfect's graphics editors.

Desktop Publishing Sorcery

Desktop publishing isn't exactly what comes to mind when you buy WordPerfect for Windows. But, yes, you can use WordPerfect for Windows for desktop publishing. Add just a little sleight of hand, and the biggest skeptics among you will be turned into true believers.

This chapter reveals secrets on quickly getting special effects, such as drop caps and reversed-out text—without wading through the manual, taking a tutorial (I hate "exercises") or creating a newsletter from scratch. Even if you're not interested in desktop publishing, you'll find all sorts of tricks for turning boring old word-processed things into sophisticated-looking documents that command attention.

BASIC GRAPHICS TRICKS

WordPerfect comes with more than 30 graphic images that you can use to add zip to your documents without knowing the least bit about creating graphics in a sophisticated drawing or painting program. In addition, you can use clip art, captured Windows screens and scanned images, as well as graphics created by almost any popular graphics program (if you use the graphics conversion program, that is, and you'll see how to do that later in this chapter). Tips in this section get you started with the basics of using and manipulating graphic images.

Press F11 to retrieve a graphic. Don't forget this handy shortcut. Pressing F11 puts you in the Retrieve Figure dialog box, where you can pick a graphic image to use.

Moving and resizing graphics. Press the left mouse button and drag the graphic to move it. Or click the right mouse button and choose Select Box. To resize it, move the insertion point to a corner. When it turns into a double arrowhead, move it in to make the graphic smaller or move it out to enlarge it.

Unless you want to resize a graphic, don't drag it by a sizing handle. When you click on a graphic to select it, you'll see little "knobs," or sizing handles, around it. If you drag them inward or outward, you change the size of the graphic. If you do this by mistake, choose Undo (Ctrl+Z).

You can drag a graphic to scroll a document. Here's some voodoo: drag a graphic past the window borders to scroll to a different location in your document. Then just release the mouse button where you want the graphic to be.

The Graphics box you pick determines how it looks. There are different kinds of Graphics boxes: Figure boxes, Text boxes, Equation boxes, Table boxes and "User-defined" boxes. (For hints about Equation boxes, see Chapter 7.) The type of box you use merely determines the preset options that go with it:

◆ Figure boxes have a single rule all around and no shading.

◆ Text boxes are shaded, with a heavy rule above and below.

◆ Table boxes have heavy rules above and below, but no shading.

◆ User boxes have no borders and no shading.

By choosing the Options dialog box (see Figure 9-1) for the specific type of box you're using, you can change quite a few things about a box, including borders, shading and the caption-numbering system you want to use, if any.

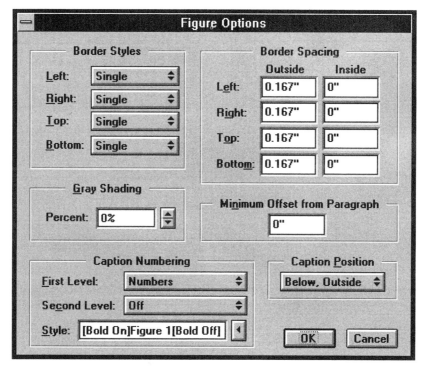

Figure 9-1: The Figure Options dialog box lets you customize Figure boxes.

The placement of the caption depends on the box type, too.
Captions for Figure boxes, Text boxes and User boxes are printed outside and below the box. Table box captions are printed above the box and to its right.

None of these boxes have a caption unless you create one.

Quickly creating a caption. To create a caption, click on a graphic with the right mouse button and choose Edit Caption from the pop-up list that appears.

 Text box tips. If you can do it to text, you can do it in a Text box. This includes using columns, tables and footnotes—which you might not normally think of as text.

To change the font in *all* your Text boxes, put a font-change code just before an Options code for Text boxes at the beginning of your document. (Always set options at the beginning of a document or before the first Graphics box, if you want them to apply to all Graphics boxes of that type.)

To change the font in an individual box, change it inside the box, before you type the text in the Text Editor.

 Undoing in the Figure Editor. Click the Reset All button to Undo in the Figure Editor.

 Test well: use the Edit All button. If you're editing a graphic image, try clicking the Edit All button. It lets you test out the effects of many things at once: moving graphics to a precise location, scaling and rotating graphics, switching to a mirror image, changing to an outline, inverting images and switching from color to black-and-white. Click the Apply box to see the effects as you create them.

You'll probably need to drag that Edit All dialog box out of your way to see its effects.

 Preview your graphics on disk. Isn't it maddening not to be able to figure out what BORD_2.WPG really looks like? No longer. You can preview graphics, including those that came with WordPerfect, by using the View button in the Open dialog box.

Click on any graphic with the right mouse button to bring up a pop-up menu. If you click on a graphic with the *left* mouse button, you can move and resize the graphic. If you click on it with the *right* button, you bring up a menu that takes you into the Position and Caption Editors.

Remember that you can bring in graphics through the Clipboard. Say that you've created some nice-looking graphs in a Windows spreadsheet or drawing program. You can copy them to the Clipboard and bring them into WordPerfect easily and quickly without worrying about what graphics format they're in. In the Windows program, just select the graph with the mouse, copy it, return to WordPerfect and paste it (Shift+Ins). WordPerfect automatically creates a Figure box for it.

If you want to capture an entire screen, press Print Screen. To capture just the active window (assuming you're running Windows in 386 Enhanced mode), press Alt+Print Screen.

You can do this in non-Windows programs, too. First, be running WordPerfect for Windows; then switch to the other non-Windows program. Display the screen you want to capture and press Print Screen (to capture the whole screen). You don't have to choose Copy if you're capturing the screen.

To capture just part of the screen, drag the mouse to select it. Then click the window's Control icon and choose Edit; then Copy. Exit from the program, return to WordPerfect and paste what you've copied. It won't be in a Figure box, but you can edit it just as you edit text in WordPerfect.

If you copy a graphic screen from a non-Windows application, it will be copied as a bitmapped graphic, so you can paste it into a program such as PC Paintbrush to edit it.

You can retrieve text into a Text box. Instead of retyping text in a Text box, copy and paste it. Or, if it's in a file by itself, retrieve that file into the Text Editor (choose Retrieve from the Text Editor's File menu).

TRICKS FOR USING THE GRAPHICS EDITORS

As you just learned in the previous tip, you can quickly get to all the graphics editors—click on a graphic with the right mouse button. This section features tricks for using those editors (Figure, Text, Equation and Table Editors) on your graphics.

Shortcuts to the graphics editors.   Double-click on a graphic with the left mouse button to go directly to the Figure, Text or Equation Editor. The program knows what kind of a Graphics box it is and opens the appropriate graphics editor.

To go to the Text Editor, click and press Alt+Shift+F11.

Hold down the Shift key while double-clicking on the graphic to open the Box Position and Size dialog box.

Shortcuts to the Figure Editor.   Of the several ways to get to the Figure Editor, the easiest and fastest one is to double-click on the graphic with the left mouse button. You can also click once and press Shift+F11; or click with the right mouse button and choose Edit Figure Box; or choose Figure and then Edit from the Graphics menu and enter the number of the Figure box you want to edit.

Shortcuts for creating Figure and Table boxes: F11 and Alt+F11.   Press F11 to create a Figure box. To create a Text box, press Alt+F11.

You can edit the Figure Editor's Button Bar.   Editing the Figure Editor's Button Bar is just like editing any other Button Bar. So if you record macros for editing graphics (e.g., rotating an image and inverting it), put them on the Button Bar.

If you want lots of buttons on the Button Bar, click on Button Bar Setup and choose Text Only. That makes room for more buttons on the screen. You can also put the Button Bar at the top or bottom of the screen instead of on the left side.

Use the Box Position and Size dialog box to wrap text around graphics.   Normally the program lets text flow around a graphic. If you don't want text to wrap around a graphic, however, uncheck the Box Position and Size dialog box. Warning: this causes text to flow *over* your graphic. So be sure this is what you want.

I really had to look for this option. Would you have expected it in the Box Position and Size dialog box? Not me.

Moving a graphic within a Graphics box.   The Box Position choices let you position the Graphics box itself. But to move a graphic image inside its Graphics box, you need to use the Figure Editor's Move button and arrow keys. Another way to do this is to choose Move from the Figure Editor's Edit menu and drag the image to the position you want.

To really fine-tune the placement of the image, click the Edit All button and enter a distance in inches to move the image up and/or to the right; to move the image down and/or to the left, use a negative number.

Use Ctrl+Right Arrow and Ctrl+Left Arrow to rotate an image.   Another neat special effect can be produced by rotating a graphic image. Just press Ctrl+Right Arrow to rotate clockwise and Ctrl+Left Arrow to turn counterclockwise. Or you can click Rotate, and a set of crosshairs representing the rotation axis will appear on the screen. To rotate the image, drag the right end of the rotation axis. Or click Edit All and enter the degree of rotation you want in the Rotate box. (Keep in mind that rotating an image 180 degrees turns it upside down.)

Your printer may not be able to handle rotated graphics.   Some printers can't rotate graphics because they can't switch from Portrait to Landscape mode on the same page. PostScript printers and some LaserJets don't have a problem with this. If you're uncertain about whether your printer can handle it, test print a rotated image.

Let WordPerfect size your Graphics boxes.   If you want WordPerfect to size a graphic in proportion with its original dimensions, choose Auto Both for the Size option in the Box Position and Size dialog box. This is particularly useful for Text boxes because the program deletes any extra white space around the text.

Choose Auto Width to specify a width. Then let WordPerfect calculate the correct height to keep the proportions of the box. Likewise, if you want to specify a height and not a width, choose Auto Height. Finally, choose Set Both to specify exactly the box size you want.

Be careful not to distort an image when you resize it.   By choosing Auto Both, you ensure that an image retains its original proportions. Otherwise, you may get some really bad distortions if you're importing a scanned image.

Cropping a graphic.   To crop a portion of an image, click the Scale button and choose Enlarge Area. Click on one corner of the area you want to crop; then drag. A little box will appear. Drag it until it covers the area you want to crop; then release the mouse button.

If you crop graphics often, make a button for it and put it on the Button Bar. It's hard (for me) to remember that to "crop" you must "enlarge."

You can change the percentage you want to manipulate graphics on the status bar.   A graphic image can be enlarged, moved, rotated or scaled by the percent shown on the status bar. Normally this is set at 10%. But you can change the percentage simply by pressing Ins and choosing 1%, 5%, 10% or 25%.

DESKTOP PUBLISHING TIPS

Have you ever dreamed of creating special effects like headings that "float" or text placed inside Graphics boxes? You probably thought you needed a desktop publishing program to do that. Not true. You can conjure up all kinds of graphic effects with WordPerfect for Windows. Read on.

Getting text inside graphics. You can put text inside a graphic image in WordPerfect for Windows (see Figure 9-2), but it's a little tricky. First, press F11 to retrieve your graphic image (this one is BORD_2.WPG); then click in the Graphics box to select it. You'll see the tiny selection "knobs" appear around it. Now, press the right mouse button and choose Box Position. The Box Position and Size dialog box appears. In Horizontal Position, choose Margin, Full. Here's the essential part: uncheck Wrap Text Around Box and click OK. Press Enter and the space bar to move the insertion point into the box and type your text. If you want to center the text, use Center Justification.

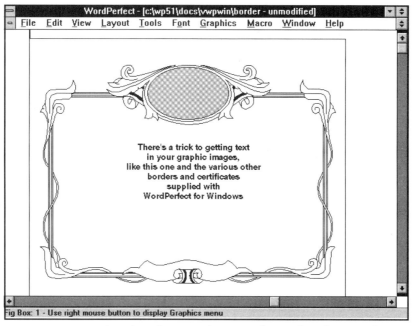

Figure 9-2: WordPerfect for Windows and WordPerfect 5.1 let you place text in graphic images.

Here's another way to do the same thing: use *two* Graphics boxes (see Figure 9-3). Retrieve the graphic image into a Figure box. Then select the box, click the right mouse button, choose Box Position and uncheck Wrap Text Around Box. Make a note of the size being used. Then create a User box (which by default has no borders or shading). In it, type the text you want to appear inside the other graphic, leaving Wrap Text Around Box checked this time. You'll probably need to press Enter a few times and use Center Justification to position the text where you want it. Or you can use the Advance command on the Layout menu to fine-tune the exact placement of the text.

Choose Box Position and Size, and make the User box exactly the same size as the Figure box by choosing Set Both and entering the width and height of the Figure box.

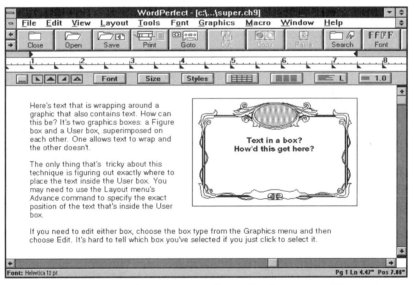

Figure 9-3: You can also use two Graphics boxes—a Figure box and a User Box—to superimpose text and graphics.

Creating drop caps and initial caps. A drop cap—a large first letter of a paragraph—is often an effective way of adding interest to a page. It earns its name because it does as its name implies—drops to the baseline of a line below the first line, as in Figure 9-4. Actually, in WordPerfect, it's hard to align drop caps with a text baseline. But try your best; purists sneer at drop caps that don't align with a baseline.

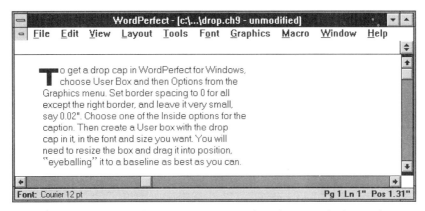

Figure 9-4: Creating drop caps in WordPerfect is a little tricky.

To get a drop cap in WordPerfect for Windows, create a User box (use a Paragraph or Character anchor type), and type your drop cap in a large font in it. However, there's always a little space left around text in a User box; so you'll need to decrease the borders around the box until your drop cap fits tightly next to your text. This involves some trial and error, depending on the font and size you use.

Taking Figure 9-4 as an example, choose User box from the Graphics menu; then pick Options. I set all the border spaces to 0 except for the right border, which I set to 0.02". I left Wrap Text Around Box checked and chose Margin, Left as the horizontal position. After I closed the Options dialog box, I created a User box that contained the letter T in 48-point Helvetica Bold.

As an alternative to creating an actual drop cap, you can simply change the size of the font for the first letter in the paragraph and then switch back to your base font after typing this ersatz drop cap. Technically, it's not a real drop cap because it doesn't drop. It's called an initial cap, aligning with the baseline of the first line of text.

Use pull quotes for a professional effect. Pull quotes (see Figure 9-5) are in vogue right now. Again, the term defines their function—they are quotes (sometimes paraphrased) "pulled" from the adjoining text of an article, newsletter or chapter. Pull quotes are usually set in a large point size (16 or 18 pts.), and may be framed with rules or a border. In addition to highlighting key points and adding visual interest to a document, they can also be used to fill up space if a page is running short.

To create a pull quote, use a Text box or a Table box. A Text box is already defined with 10% gray shading and thick borders above and below; a Table box doesn't have shading. Paste text copied from your document into it and reformat it with a different, larger font.

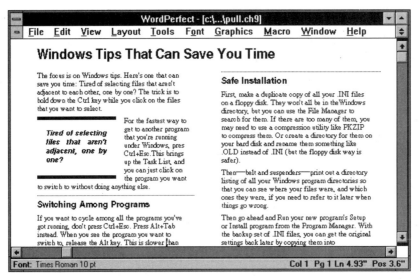

Figure 9-5: Pull quotes add interest to a page.

Reversing text. Reversed text (white on black) is another nice graphic effect for desktop-published documents. To achieve this effect (see Figure 9-6), create a Graphics box with 100% gray shading (which is black, of course), set the print color to white and type the text you want reversed.

Figure 9-6: If your printer prints shades of gray, it can reverse text.

Use a Text or User box. To specify the shading, choose Options before you create the box. Choose a font and type your text; then put the insertion point just before the text and use the Color choice on the Font menu to set text color to white. If you don't turn it white *after* you type it, you won't be able to see what you're typing! When you close the Text Editor, you'll see the reversed effect.

Test-print it on your printer. You may want to put single borders around the box to clearly define the edges.

Reversing text in tables.   If you have a PostScript printer, you can produce reversed text in tables. Use the Table Options dialog box (double-click on a column marker to bring it up) and pick 100% shading. Select the text in the cells that you want to reverse; then choose Color from the Font menu and pick White from the Predefined Colors pop-up list. Apply the shading to those cells by choosing Shading from the Cell Attributes area of the Cell Format dialog box.

Creating a shadow-box effect for tables.   This is a nice effect for tables. It makes the table seem to float on the page (see Figure 9-7). To do this, create your table. Then drag across the table to select it. Press Ctrl+F9 to open the Table menu; choose Lines. Choose a thickness for the Bottom and Right lines (such as Extra Thick) that's different from the Left and Top lines.

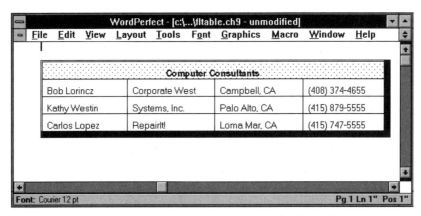

Figure 9-7: You can create a shadow-box effect by choosing thick right and bottom lines.

You also can do this with Graphics boxes; the commands are a little different but the concept is the same. Choose Extra Thick for the Bottom and Right borders and Thick for the Top and Left borders.

You can put Graphics boxes in tables, too. Here's a way to pretty up a table: retrieve a graphic image into one of its cells. There are a couple of tricks you need to know, though. First, turn off all borders to make sure that Graphics box lines don't interfere with table rules; or use a User box, which has no borders by default. You may also need to adjust the spacing around the borders. To make sure that the box stays where you want it, use a Paragraph-anchored Graphics box.

You can put tables in Graphics boxes. To put a table in a Graphics box, create the table and save it as a separate file. Then retrieve it into the Text Editor.

You can also copy a table and paste it into the Text Editor.

Your table may be too big to fit in a Graphics box. If the table you retrieve won't fit into the box you've created, Word-Perfect won't help you out by automatically adjusting the size of the box. You'll need to resize the box yourself.

Creating floating text. Here's how to create floating text, as shown in Figure 9-8. First, use the Font menu's Color command and pick a predefined color other than black or white (here, it was green). Then pick your font and point size (48-pt. Helvetica Narrow Bold Oblique is shown here). Type the word or phrase you want to float; then press Enter.

Now here's the tricky part. You need to advance up the next text you type so the first text isn't quite covered. That gives the "floating" effect. How much you need to advance the text depends on the size of the type and the font. For Figure 9-8, I chose Advance from the Layout menu, clicked Up, and entered .75 to move the second line of text up three-quarters of an inch. You'll need to experiment by following the next steps, checking the Print Preview screen and changing the amount you advance, if you need to.

The next step is to go back to black, so choose Black from the Predefined Colors part of the Color dialog box and click OK. Now, as the last step, type again the word or phrase you want to float. You won't see any spectacular results on the screen: you have to press Shift+F5 to use Print Preview to see how your floating text looks.

Figure 9-8: You can create floating text like this with a little trial and error. (Squeaker is one of my cats.)

For vertical rules on every page, create a header and hang graphics lines on it. To get vertical lines on every page of your document, hang them from a header instead of painstakingly placing them on every page. First, open the Header window; then press Ctrl+Shift+F11 (or choose Line and Vertical from the Graphics menu) to open the Create Vertical Line dialog box. Under Vertical Position, choose Full Page; under Horizontal Position, choose Left Margin (assuming you want the first rule at the left margin). Now press Ctrl+Shift+F11 again. Leave Vertical Position as Full Page, but for Horizontal Position choose Specify and enter the measurement (from the left edge of the paper) for where you want the second rule to appear. (Better get your ruler and a sheet of paper out.) Repeat these steps for all the rules you want to appear on every page.

While the dialog box is open, choose any options you want the line to have, such as gray shading. Using a gray line is a sophisticated touch that gives a watermark-like effect in your document. You might want to adjust the line thickness for a thicker rule, too.

For a horizontal rule on each page, create it in a header or footer. This adds another professional touch to your documents. A horizontal rule in a header or footer, perhaps along with a chapter title and number or your logo, can balance pages that contain text of unequal length.

Creating a page border. A page border is another snazzy effect you'll often want in your document or for presentation graphics. But you certainly don't want to create one on every page! The trick is to create a Figure box in a header and then use that header on all the pages of your document.

Here's how to create a border with a single thin rule. You can change the weight of the rule by putting a Figure Options code before the header that you'll create to hold the Graphics box.

Open a new document; then open its Header window to create a header. Choose Figure and Create from the Graphics menu. In the Figure Editor, choose Box Position from the File menu. Choose Vertical Position and Set Position, and enter the amount of space (from the top of the paper) where you want the top of the border to start. Then choose Horizontal Position and Set Position, and enter the amount of space (from the left edge of the paper) where you want the left border to appear.

Choose Size and Set Both. In the Width and Height boxes, type in the size you want the box to be. To figure out how big to make the box, subtract from the paper's dimensions the amount you specified as a top and left margin and double it. For example, if you choose half-inch horizontal and vertical positions and you're using 8.5-by-11-inch paper, you'd subtract one inch from each dimension for a 7.5-by-10-inch box.

Then be sure to uncheck Wrap Text Around Box so you can put text on the page. Close the Header window and save the document with a name that lets you remember what it is, because the page border is hidden under what looks like an empty document window.

Borders for presentation graphics use different dimensions.
If you're creating a border for presentation graphics, be aware that the proportions used for overhead transparencies and 35 mm slides are different. Use Landscape mode to orient the page sideways. Then, for overhead transparencies, use a 9-by-6.5-inch border. Use a 9.5-by-7.5-inch border for 35 mm slides.

Adding horizontal and vertical lines.   You can add horizontal and vertical lines (rules) to your documents by choosing Line from the Graphics menu. Then choose a type (vertical or horizontal) and a position. To add vertical lines between columns, choose Vertical Position and Between Columns (see Figure 9-9).

Figure 9-9: You can easily create vertical rules between columns.

Horizontal line shortcut: Ctrl+F11. Vertical line shortcut: Ctrl+Shift+F11. Use these handy keyboard shortcuts if you create lines often.

Measure positions from the top and left edges of the paper, not from the margins. If you choose Specify to enter a specific position for a line to start, remember that it should be measured from the top edge of the page (for a horizontal line) or from the left edge of the page (for a vertical line). Don't measure from the top and left margins.

Just drag lines to move or resize them. To move or resize a line, just drag it. Use the size box in the lower-right corner to make a line thicker. To place a line with fine-tuned accuracy, edit the line and then use the Edit Horizontal Line or Edit Vertical Line dialog box to place it exactly where you want it.

If you don't want black lines, choose a percentage other than 100% for the shading. This adds a more sophisticated touch to your publications. See Figure 9-5 for an idea of how to use shaded lines with headings.

Separating columns with a horizontal rule. In Figure 9-10, a horizonal rule was used to separate columns. To do this, turn columns off, add the line and turn columns back on.

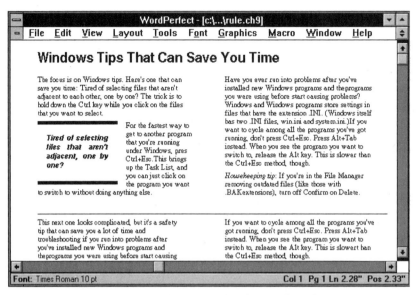

Figure 9-10: You can use horizontal rules with columns.

Wrapping text around both sides of a graphic. The trick to wrapping text around both sides of a graphic is to define two (or more) columns (see Figure 9-11).

First, retrieve the graphic; then define the columns and choose the options you want to use. Type your text. Then click on the graphic with the right mouse button to bring up the pop-up menu. Choose Box Position and Horizontal Position. Change Set Position to Column, Center. Next to Columns, type the numbers of the columns you want the graphic to be centered between. For example, type **1-2** to center your graphic between the first and second columns.

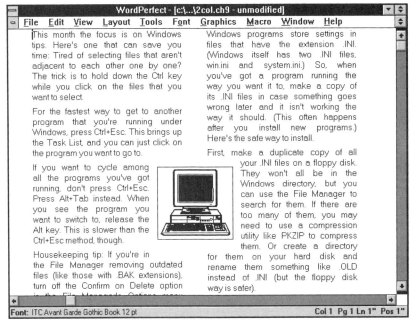

Figure 9-11: To wrap text around a graphic, define two columns of text.

Use extra space between paragraphs instead of tabs. For a more sophisticated look in your documents, add a small amount of extra space between paragraphs instead of using a tab to indicate new paragraphs. Go to the top of the document and choose Typesetting from the Layout menu; then choose Between Paragraphs and enter the extra space you want to use, such as **2p** for two points. The text in Figure 9-11 uses this effect.

Use borderless Text boxes with shading for emphasis. A screened background draws the reader's eye to text that you want to emphasize. To create a shaded borderless box with as few steps as possible, delete the top and bottom borders from a Text box.

Create a logo in a drawing program or scan existing artwork. You can create a custom logo in a drawing program, or you can scan it from a printed document. Dover Publications offers a huge variety of noncopyrighted graphic clip-art images that can be scanned and used freely. Write Dover Publications, 11 East Second Street, Mineola, NY 11501, and request the Complete Dover Catalog. Don't have a scanner? See the next tip.

Put graphics in headers and footers. You can put graphics in headers and footers, so why not put your personal logo or your company's logo in an elegant footer? WordPerfect for Windows accepts scanned files (TIFF files); if you have access to a scanner, scan your logo. Or take it to a service bureau, where for a nominal fee they will scan it for you.

Creating small ballot boxes (check boxes). If you create forms, try this: to create small check boxes (also called ballot boxes), use very small empty Figure boxes, as shown in Figure 9-12.

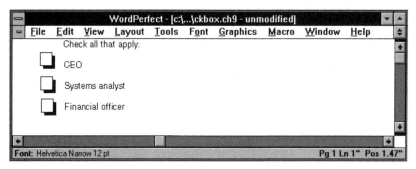

Figure 9-12: Use small Figure boxes for check boxes in a form.

Reversing an image. You can invert (reverse) graphic images, too. In the Figure Editor, choose Invert from the Edit menu. White is converted to black, and colors change to their complementary colors (blue changes to yellow, for example).

Outlining an image. To create an outline effect in a graphic image, click the Figure Editor's Outline button. Your image is displayed in outline form, as though it were a line drawing.

Colors print as shades of gray.   If you think that changing a color image to black and white (by choosing Black and White from the Figure Editor's Edit menu) changes your graphic to strictly 100% black and 100% white, think again. Colors print in shades of gray. If you have a dot-matrix printer or another kind of printer that can't handle gray shading, convert the image to an outline form for best results (see "There's a graphics conversion program you can use," later in this chapter).

Change line height under certain conditions.   In several common desktop-publishing situations, a change in line spacing gives you much better-looking results than leaving on Word-Perfect's default line height and 2-pt. leading.

Sans-serif type often looks crowded with WordPerfect's default leading. You may want to increase leading if your publication uses a sans-serif typeface such as Helvetica for its body copy. Also, increase leading if you're using wide columns. If you're using narrow columns, a reduction in line spacing often makes the text easier to read.

Change Percent of Optimal for tighter headlines.   Word-Perfect's Typesetting dialog box lets you change the amount of spacing between words and letters. For tighter headlines, select the text; then open the Typesetting dialog box, click Percent of Optimal and reduce the spacing by 10%. You won't see changes on the screen; check Print Preview for the effect.

Change Percent of Optimal and kern, too.   After you set letters and words more tightly, you may still need to adjust the spacing between letter pairs such as *Ta* and *Wo*. To do this, use manual kerning.

Kern display type (18 pts. and over).   If you use display type, especially in the larger point sizes (18 pts. and above), you may want to use this specialized typesetting feature. You can choose automatic or manual kerning.

To kern a letter pair, open a new document and type the letter pair you want to kern, such as *Wo* in *Word*. Put the insertion point between the *W* and the *o*. Then choose Manual Kerning from the Typesetting dialog box. Just press the Down Arrow key to decrease the space between the letters; press the Up Arrow key to increase the space. Click OK when everything looks right.

Sneaky trick for copyfitting.   If your newsletter page is running just a little long and you need to fit a couple more lines on the page, use this voodoo trick: decrease Percent of Optimal in the last two paragraphs of each article and squeeze them together. Nobody will notice, and you can get those last few lines on the page.

Not enough text in your newsletter? Add subheadings.   If your newsletter is short, simply add subheadings to the text instead of resetting text in a larger font or with more leading. Each subheading takes up at least two lines, maybe three, depending on how much space you leave above and below it.

Use special characters for a professional look.   Don't forget about the huge amount of special characters available in WordPerfect's character sets. There are ligatures (such as *fl*), ellipses (. . .), case fractions, curly quotes and em and en dashes, which were discussed in Chapters 4 and 5. All of these special characters can add a professional, typeset quality to your documents.

Ctrl+W is the shortcut to the universe of special characters.

FINE POINTS

The tips in this section discuss the finer points of graphics. You may find a little gem here that solves a particular problem for you.

Anchor types demystified.   A graphic's anchor type determines how WordPerfect treats it when your document is paged. A Paragraph-anchored graphic stays with the text around it.

A Page-anchored graphic stays at a fixed position on a page and text flows around it, even if it's added or deleted text. A Character-anchored graphic is treated just like a character in a line.

The preset anchor type is for Page-anchored graphics: a graphic stays on the page just where you place it, and text (normally) flows around it, changing as you add or delete text. This is the type of anchor to use if you're placing a box on a page that has columns, and the box extends into more than one column.

When should you choose one of the other types of anchored graphics? If you choose Character, the graphic stays with the text character next to it on the left. Use a Character anchor for small graphics, such as those in headers and footers.

A Paragraph-anchored graphic stays with its paragraph, even if the paragraph moves to another location. Choose this type if you're wrapping text around a graphic and you want the graphic to stay with the text.

Skipping pages?   If you use Page-anchored graphics, you'll see a mystifying "Pages to Skip" setting in the Box Position and Size dialog box. Leave it at **0** if you want the graphic to stay on the current page; enter **1** to put it on the next page, and so forth.

Positioning a Graphics box within a paragraph.   When you retrieve a graphic, it normally appears at the insertion point. You can specify *exactly* where it's positioned within a paragraph if you take a little time to figure it out. Use the Box Position and Size dialog box. Choose Paragraph as the anchor type and then type a vertical position. If you type **0"** as the position, the top of the box aligns with the first line of the paragraph.

To figure out where to position the box, measure down from the top of the first line of text. For example, if you're using 10-pt. type, entering **24p** moves the box down two lines (remember that the program automatically adds two points of leading to each line of type). You may need to experiment to get the position just as you want it.

Positioning a Graphics box anchored to a page. If you choose Set Position to specify the position of a Page-anchored Graphics box, be aware that you should measure down from the top of the page, not from the top margin.

If you choose Top as the position of the box, its top aligns with the top margin of the page.

Line height and Character-anchored Graphics boxes. If you choose Character as the type of anchor for a Graphics box, your line height may differ from the surrounding text. This happens because WordPerfect automatically compensates for the height of the Graphics box. To avoid having different line heights, either resize the Graphics box or set a fixed line height.

Default graphic sizes. You may have noticed that graphic images arrive in your documents in various sizes, unless you specify a size for them. There's a rule behind this madness: a graphic is normally retrieved at half the size of the space between the margins. So if you retrieve a graphic into a narrow column, it will be half the size of the column's width. The size of your retrieved graphic depends on where the insertion point is.

To use the same option in all Graphics boxes, set it at the beginning of the document. Say you want all your Text boxes to be reversed, or all your User boxes to be 20% gray with thick borders. Choose Text box (or User box) and Options at the beginning of your document; then specify the percentage of shading, borders or what have you. These options are then applied to all the Graphics boxes of that type in the document—although you can change options for individual boxes.

If you use Advance commands, be careful: they can add up. Once you advance a certain amount, you have to advance back by that same amount to get back to where you were. So if you advance some text up, remember to advance down by the same amount if you want the text that follows to be printed where it was. You don't see the effects of the Advance Up command on the screen, so it's easy to forget this.

Also, remember that Advance commands are cumulative: if you advance up one inch and then decide that you really should have advanced up two inches, enter **1"** as the amount to advance up to next. If you enter **2"**, you'll have advanced three inches.

Use the Advance to Position command to get to a specific location. To see exactly what a position is, move the insertion point to it and then check the Ln and Pos indicators on the status bar. Then use those coordinates to advance to that position. This is a neat trick for getting text exactly where you want it, or for returning to the position you were in before you advanced.

You can fill out preprinted forms by using Advance. If you have enough patience, you can use the Advance feature to fill out preprinted forms. Measure the distances from the top and left edges of the form for each blank you want to fill in, and then advance to the first position and type the text that goes there. Then advance to the next position.

The Advance secret: keep in mind that you're always advancing from the *current position*.

Try this on a blank sheet of paper and hold it up to the light with the form behind it until you get it right. Or use photocopies of the form. This is really a trial-and-error process.

Don't add too much text to a Text, Table or User box. If you type more text than will fit in your Text, Table or User box and still keep it on the same page, you'll get a (guess what) "Too much text" message when you close the editing window. There are a couple of things you can do, the most obvious of which is to delete text. You can also delete text around the box and make the box bigger, or you can put the text on the next page by inserting a hard page break (Ctrl+Enter) just before the box.

Convert graphics to WordPerfect format to retrieve them quicker.   When you retrieve a graphic, you often see a message like "Please wait . . . loading TIFF file." WordPerfect is converting the graphic's format (in this case, the TIFF, or Tagged Image File Format) into a format it can read. If you're going to use that graphic image again, save it in WordPerfect graphics format (.WPG format) so you can load it quicker next time.

To do this, display the graphic in the Figure Editor, choose Save As from the File menu and give the image a name. Your graphic image will be saved in its unedited form but in WordPerfect graphics format, and the original graphic file in the other format won't be changed.

Use the Graphic on Disk option to keep your document small.   Graphics files are huge. If you put very many graphics in a document, you wind up with a bloated document that can very easily exceed the capacity of a regular floppy disk, making it really inconvenient to swap files with others via floppies unless you use a compression program like PKZIP.EXE. Also, having only a few of these whale-sized documents on your hard disk eats up disk space there, too, especially when you consider that the original graphics are also stored on your hard disk.

To get around this problem, use the Graphic on Disk option in the Figure Editor so that the graphic remains neatly stored only on disk, not in your document, and WordPerfect simply retrieves it when you open or print the document.

Also use this Graphic on Disk option if you're putting a graphic image in a style.

If you transfer a document to another computer, be sure to transfer any graphic images in it, too. You can also turn off the Graphic on Disk option to incorporate the graphics into the document before you transfer it.

There's a graphics conversion program you can use.   WordPerfect for Windows comes with a graphics conversion program named GRAPHCNV.EXE. It's normally installed in your

C:\WPC directory. You can use it to convert several files at the same time to .WPG format (by using wildcards) and also to set options about how you want the resulting graphics to appear. You can specify a background color, convert colors to shades of gray or invert the images, among other things.

To run the graphics conversion program, choose Run from the Program Manager's File menu and enter **c:\wpc\graphcnv**. Add an /H switch at the end to get Help about how to use the program and the types of graphics to use it with.

Enter the path name of the file(s) to be converted and enter the name(s) you want the resulting files(s) to have. Use wildcards to specify more than one file; the program adds the .WPG extension to the converted files.

MOVING ON

This chapter has given you lots of ideas to experiment with in your documents and publications. Now, in the final chapter, "The Magic of Macros," you'll see how you can automate just about all of the techniques found in this book.

CHAPTER TEN

The Magic of Macros

Everybody seems to think macros are "hard," but they're not—not when your mojo's workin'. When you turn on the macro recorder, WordPerfect watches everything you do and plays it back when you play the macro. If you make a mistake while you're recording the macro, just correct it—the macro corrects itself when you play it, doing exactly what you did when you recorded it.

Macros are great for two kinds of tasks: things you do all the time and things you hardly ever do. A macro can automate repetitive tasks you do every day, such as typing your return address or creating a standard paragraph in a contract. But it's equally useful for procedures you rarely do that are hard to remember, such as setting up a table of contents definition or sorting and selecting records for a mail merge.

Once you've recorded a macro, you can make a button for it or assign it to the Macro menu. You hardly have to think at all about using it.

Yes, there is a complex macro language with programming rules and a universe all its own, but we won't get very far into that in this book. This is voodoo, right? So you don't have to understand everything.

When to use macros and when to use styles? Styles and macros can both make format changes in a document. Although you can use macros for formatting, remember that you can apply a style to all the different elements of your document at once and just edit it and apply it again to change the formatting. In general, use macros for keystrokes that carry out actions; use styles for formatting specific design elements in your documents.

Use keyboard shortcuts to start and stop the macro recorder. Press Ctrl+F10 to start the macro recorder; to turn it off, press Ctrl+Shift+F10. These shortcuts sure beat using the menus, especially if you're recording several macros.

Play a macro under the same conditions in which you recorded it. Whenever you play a macro, WordPerfect assumes that the conditions you recorded it under are in effect. For example, if you play a macro that copies or cuts selected text as its first step and you haven't selected any text, nothing will happen.

Record a macro under the conditions in which you expect to use it. This is the converse of the previous trap. Sometimes you'll need to have a document on the screen for the macro to have text to work on. Or you may need to have several document windows open, for example.

A macro won't record anything unless you select it. While you're recording a macro, you can open all sorts of menus and dialog boxes, but unless you actually select something, nothing will be recorded. So feel free to look in menus and dialog boxes to find the ones you need while you record a macro.

What's that "Abstract" box for? The Record Macro dialog box lets you enter a descriptive name to identify what your macro does as well as enter an abstract description that details any conditions the macro needs to run under or any steps you should take before you play it, such as opening a blank editing window, for example.

The description shows up in the File Manager (in the Description field), and both the description and the abstract show up in the Document Summary window.

 If you switch to other applications, WordPerfect suspends macro recording. WordPerfect suspends macro recording if you leave it to go out to the Program Manager or to another program. When you come back to WordPerfect for Windows, the macro recorder will still be running, where you left off.

You can't press Esc to stop recording a macro. If you press Esc, that's recorded in your macro, too. To stop recording a macro, choose Stop from the Macro menu or, for a faster stop, press Ctrl+Shift+F10.

How to stop a macro that's playing. Press Esc. If that doesn't work, try Shift+Esc.

You don't have to add the .WCM extension when you name a macro. WordPerfect automatically adds a .WCM extension when you name a macro, so you don't have to do it. You do have to follow DOS's file-naming rules, though: up to only eight characters, and no punctuation marks.

WordPerfect has to compile a macro before it can play it. The first time you play any macro, you'll see a message that it's being compiled. That's because a macro is just a mini-program, and WordPerfect has to convert it to a form it can "understand." So be prepared to wait just a bit; you won't have to wait the next time you play the macro.

The "Cinderella" bug.   Maybe they've got it fixed by now, but there's a bug in early releases of WordPerfect for Windows that won't let you compile a macro between 12:00 and 12:59 A.M. and during the first minute of every hour. Some programmer had fun with this one.

Playing a macro every time WordPerfect for Windows starts. You can have a macro play every time you start WordPerfect for Windows. This is a neat trick to use if you're sharing a computer, because your macro can set the program up with the settings you prefer to use, such as left justification, double spacing, a particular font and so forth.

First, you'll need to have recorded the macro you want to use. Then go out to Windows, select the WordPerfect for Windows icon, and choose Properties from the File menu. In the Command Line box, type **/m-***macroname* after WPWIN.EXE, as shown in Figure 10-1. Be sure to leave a space between WPWIN.EXE and /M.

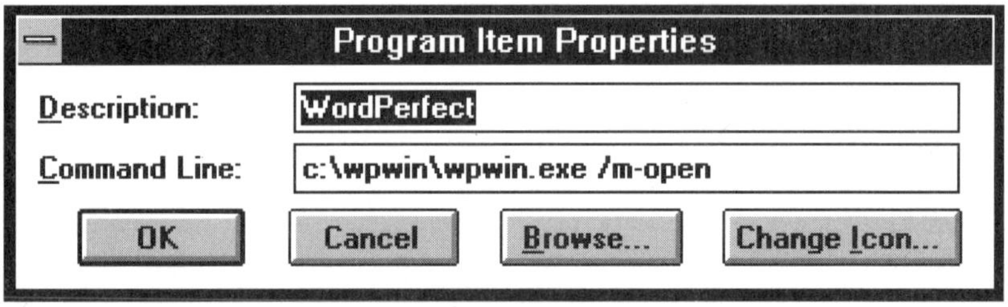

Program Item Properties

Description: | WordPerfect
Command Line: | c:\wpwin\wpwin.exe /m-open

[OK] [Cancel] [Browse...] [Change Icon...]

Figure 10-1: Set up your Program Item Properties dialog box to execute a macro at startup.

Playing a macro when you start Windows.   If you want to play a certain macro when you start WordPerfect and Windows together, give the command at the DOS prompt like this:

```
win wpwin /m-macroname
```

Put your macros on the Macro menu.   Put the macros you use most frequently on the Macro menu: you can put as many as nine macros there. Choose Assign to Menu from the Macro menu and click Insert. In the Macro Name box, type the file name of the macro you want to put on the menu. In the Menu Text box, type a descriptive name for the macro—this is the name that shows up on the menu.

That's it. From then on, you can just press Alt+M to open the Macro menu and type the number of the macro, if you don't want to take your hands off the keyboard.

Assigning macros to keys. It's a lot faster to play an often-used macro by pressing a couple of keys than by choosing it from a list. Although the manual doesn't tell you this, you can assign macros to Ctrl-key and Ctrl+Shift combinations with the letters A–Z and the numbers 0–9 while you're in the Record Macro dialog box naming your macro. For example, to name a macro *Ctrl+Shift+A*, just press those keys and CTRLSFTA appears in the Filename part of the dialog box.

Be careful if you use only Ctrl-key combinations because a lot of them (like Ctrl-C, Ctrl-X and so on) are used by the program itself.

You can't edit the Windows-style (CUA) keyboard, so you'll need to assign your macros to key combinations on a different keyboard. Select a custom keyboard (see Chapter 3 for details about how to set one up) and choose Edit. Then choose Macros from the Item Type pop-up list. Click Add, and you'll see a dialog box listing macros you've already recorded. Double-click on any that you want to assign key combinations to.

Highlight the name of the macro you want to assign the key combination to (if it isn't highlighted already). Now press the key combination you want to use to play the macro. If that combination is already in use, it will be displayed next to Current in the Change Assignment box. If you can't use an assignment, you'll hear a beep. To assign the new key combination, choose Assign.

To remove a key assignment, click the key combination and then click Unassign.

You can assign the same key combination to more than one macro. You can have Ctrl+Shift+C, for example, do two completely different things on two different custom keyboards, depending on which macro you assigned it to and which keyboard is in effect.

You can't use Alt-key macros in WordPerfect for Windows. If you're familiar with WordPerfect DOS, you probably remember that you could assign macros to Alt-key combinations; but in WordPerfect for Windows, those are reserved for menus and dialog boxes. You can use Ctrl or Ctrl+Shift and some Alt+Shift+function key combinations, though. Just be careful to use ones that haven't already been assigned. Here are some you can use:

Available Key Combinations		
Ctrl+A	Ctrl+E	Ctrl+H
Ctrl+K	Ctrl+M	Ctrl+O
Ctrl+Q	Ctrl+Y	Ctrl+T
Ctrl+Shift+Enter	Ctrl+Shift+Backspace	Alt+Shift+F10
Ctrl+Shift+F8	Ctrl+Shift+F2	Alt+Shift+F1

Not all of WordPerfect's keyboard shortcuts are listed on the menus, so here's the secret way to see which key combinations are taken. Choose Keyboard from the Preferences menu; then select a keyboard and edit it. As you pick each command, its keyboard shortcut, if there is one, is listed.

Make macros into buttons. Don't forget that you can very easily make a macro into a button. There's more on this in Chapter 3, "Customizing WordPerfect," but here's a quick how-to. Choose Button Bar Setup from the View menu; then choose Edit and Assign Macro to Button.

Make a button to take you to your macro keyboard. To be able to use your custom key combinations, the custom keyboard you assigned them to has to be selected so that it's in effect.

To switch easily to that custom keyboard, make yourself a button. Record a macro that takes you to the new keyboard; then make it into a button for your main keyboard.

You can make specialized keyboards for the different types of tasks you do, such as mail merge or typing in a foreign language with WordPerfect characters (see the next tip). Make buttons to switch to those keyboards, too.

Make yourself a macro keyboard. If there are certain sets of macros you use, such as macros that carry out specialized tasks or generate Spanish or German letters, you can make a Spanish keyboard, a German keyboard, or any other kind of keyboard for a task that requires special macros. Then, when you're ready to type, switch to that keyboard.

Keep Macro on Disk checked if you're planning to assign a macro to a button. If you think you might assign a macro to a button later, be sure to keep the Macro on Disk box checked in the Assign Macro to Button dialog box. You're telling WordPerfect to use the current version of the macro, even if you've changed it. Otherwise the macro is stored in the Button Bar file and is also separately stored on disk. If you edit the disk version, the Button Bar version won't change.

If you put macros in your Button Bar, don't display it as Picture Only. All your macros will look the same if you display the Button Bar as Picture Only. You won't be able to tell them apart.

You can use macros that are in directories other than C:\WPWIN\MACROS. Although WordPerfect for Windows creates a MACROS directory for you when you run the Install program, you can also record and play macros that are in other directories. The trick is to give the complete path name to where the macro is stored when you're asked for the macro's name. For example, I store some very specialized macros on a floppy disk; to play one of them I give its name as **a:\ch8*macro*** because the macros are stored in directories named CH7, CH8 and so forth on the floppy disk. (You don't have to use the .WCM extension.)

It's a good idea to keep most of your macros and all of your custom keyboard files in your macros directory, though, so that you (and WordPerfect) know where they are.

CONVERTING MACROS FROM WORDPERFECT DOS

You can convert WordPerfect DOS macros to WordPerfect for Windows macros, but it's often better to redo them from scratch. The WordPerfect Macro Facility (MFWIN.EXE) provided with WordPerfect for Windows has a Convert command that theoretically converts WordPerfect DOS macros to a format that WordPerfect for Windows can use. Simple macros usually convert just fine. Not everything will convert, however, and you may need to edit the converted macro.

If you have favorite WordPerfect DOS macros and you'd like to try the conversion utility on them, here's how (assuming you installed the Macro Facility when you installed WordPerfect for Windows). Go out to Windows. In the Program Manager, choose Run from the File menu; then enter **mfwin.exe** and choose OK. Choose Convert from the Macro menu. In the dialog box that appears, find your WordPerfect DOS macro directory. Select the macro you want to convert and choose Convert again. The new macro will be converted with the same name but with a .WCM extension. You'll get a message about whether your macro converted successfully or whether you'll need to edit it.

If you have to edit it, open it in WordPerfect to see if there are any commands that didn't convert. They'll be preceded by forward slashes (//). These are the things you'll need to change manually.

WordPerfect DOS macros that use Search and Replace will probably have to be edited. If your WordPerfect DOS macro uses Search and Replace and either asks the user to confirm a replacement (by typing Y) or searches for a code and changes it to another code (such as changing underline codes to italics), it won't work correctly in WordPerfect for Windows. You'll need to edit macros like these.

Macros that don't ask the user to confirm a replacement word each time it's located will work in WordPerfect for Windows (as long as everything else converts correctly, too). And macros that search for and replace a word or phrase, rather than a code, should work, too.

You'll need to rename your WordPerfect DOS Alt-key macros. Since you can't use Alt-key macros in WordPerfect for Windows, be sure to rename them after you convert them. An Alt+A macro (ALTA.WPM) from the DOS version of the program will be converted to ALTA.WCM. Rename it to use a Ctrl+Shift combination instead (see the earlier tip "Assigning macros to keys").

If you use the Macro Facility a lot, make it a program item in your WordPerfect group. If you find that you're converting macros often, install the Macro Facility as a program item in the Windows Program Manager. Highlight the WordPerfect group and choose New from the Program Manager's File menu. Then click Add Program Item and enter **macro facility** in the Description box and **c:\wpc\mfwin.exe** in the Command Line box.

Don't forget to read MACRO.DOC. A MACRO.DOC file comes with WordPerfect for Windows. If you're going to do much with converting WordPerfect DOS macros to WordPerfect for Windows macros, read it. It has information not found in the manual, such as a handy table that lists keystrokes and commands that can be converted, for example.

EDITING MACROS

In WordPerfect for Windows, you can open a macro just like any other document. This makes it really easy to edit a macro. If your macro is short, sometimes it's just as fast or faster to record it again. But if it's long and complicated, it's usually easier to edit it than to record a new one.

Opening and saving macros. You can open a macro (.WCM) file just like any other document. Choose Open from the File menu and enter the path to where the macro is stored, such as C:\WPWIN\MACROS\MYMACRO. You can choose a macro from the Open dialog box, too; if you're opening it for the first time, WordPerfect may ask whether it's OK to convert it from ASCII format. Just click OK.

To save a macro after editing it, just click Save; you don't have to do anything fancy, like converting it to another file format.

If you're typing a macro from scratch, be sure to save it with a .WCM extension—and save it in your macros directory so Word-Perfect knows where to find it when you want to play it.

It can get confusing when you're opening macros, editing them, saving them and testing them. Just remember: open and save them like regular files (from the File menu); record and play (test) them from the Macro menu.

Don't change the first line of a macro. Every macro begins with a cryptic line that identifies which WordPerfect product it's designed to be used with. For example, you'll often see something like this line for U.S. WordPerfect for Windows:

Application (WP;WPWP;Default; "WPWPUS.WCD")

If you change or delete this line, your macro may be disabled completely.

Be careful not to change punctuation marks or parentheses when you edit macros. Any text that a macro is supposed to type begins with the word *Type* and is surrounded by double quotation marks within parentheses, like this:

Type ("Kay Nelson")

If you change the text inside these punctuation marks, be sure to keep the punctuation marks just as you found them. Every opening quote needs a corresponding closing quote, and every opening parenthesis needs its closing parenthesis, or your macro won't type what it's supposed to.

There are two types of macro commands. To demystify some of the cryptic macro language (see Figure 10-2 for a sample), be aware that there are two kinds of commands that are expressed in a slightly different way. *Product commands* carry out a procedure that an application (or product) does. *Programming commands* give you control over what a macro does.

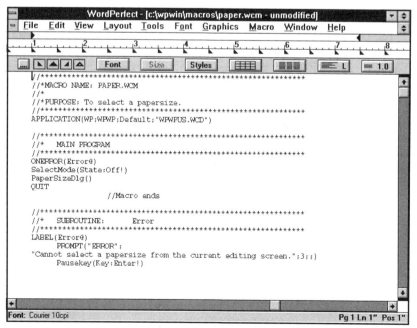

Figure 10-2: Demystifying macro language.

You can tell them apart because product commands all use parentheses. As you saw before, the Type command types whatever follows it in parentheses. Other commands produced by the editing keys, such as a hard returns, are followed by parentheses, like this:

HardReturn( )

Commands produced by selecting from menus are in parentheses and have exclamation points in them, like this:

FontItalic(State:On!)

Programming commands are the ones *you enter*, using Word-Perfect's specialized macro language. Most of them require a special syntax that tells the program exactly what to do. The macro recorder won't insert any of these special commands into a macro as you record it; you have to put them there yourself, by editing a macro or by actually writing it in the macro language. (To get a manual detailing each command in the macro language, see the tip "Order the Macros Manual from WordPerfect Corporation if you do much with macros" at the end of this chapter.)

Chaining macros.   You can make a macro start a second macro as soon as the first one finishes. This is a handy trick that keeps you from having to record an existing macro again. All you have to do is edit the first macro to include the CHAIN command, followed by the name of the other macro in parentheses and quotes, like this:

CHAIN ("*macroname*")

For example, you could chain a macro that types the boilerplate text of a letter to a macro that creates your letterhead. You can use your letterhead macro with several different boilerplate macros.

Chain a macro to itself to make it repeat.   The neatest chaining trick of all is to use the CHAIN command to make a macro repeat itself. Say you have a macro that searches for underline codes and changes them to italics. If you chain the macro to itself, it keeps on repeating until there aren't any more underline codes to find.

Nesting macros.   *Nesting* macros is different from *chaining* them. A nested macro carries out its instructions at exactly the point where it occurs in the main macro. Think of it as a subroutine that says "Go carry out these steps and then come back to the main macro when you're done."

To nest a macro, edit the main macro. Put the command

RUN ("*macroname*")

exactly at the point where you want the nested macro to run.

Nesting macros is a neat trick for making a macro move to various places in a document, carry out a sequence of commands and return to where the main macro left off.

Record macros that you want to chain or nest before you record the main macro.   The main macro won't run if the chained or nested macro hasn't been recorded; it won't be able to locate them. Record macros you're going to chain or nest (and run them, so they'll be compiled) before you edit the macro that's going to use them.

Pausing a macro.   You can also pause a macro to make it stop and let you (or another user) enter information from the keyboard. This trick is really handy for completing standard letters or filling out memo forms.

To pause a macro, you need to edit it and insert a Pause or PauseKey(0) command wherever you want it to pause. Pause makes the macro pause when it comes to that command (you don't have to use parentheses with this command); PauseKey lets you specify in parentheses the key that the user is to press to resume the macro. To specify the key to be pressed to continue, put it inside the parentheses, like this:

PAUSEKEY(Enter!)

I'm just using the Enter key as an example here—you can specify a key other than the Enter key. In fact, if the user is to type more than one line of text at the pause, you'd *better* specify another key, or the macro will start playing again when the user presses Enter for a hard return. Here's how to specify the little-used *at sign* key (@):

```
PAUSEKEY (Character!:@)
```

Now the user has to press @ to resume the macro, so it won't resume if Enter gets pressed by mistake.

The Pause command on the Macro menu isn't for inserting pauses in macros. The Pause command on the Macro menu just suspends macro recording so you can test out a technique before you record the next step in your macro; it doesn't insert a pause when the macro is played.

Sounding a beep. If you want the computer to beep each time a macro pauses (actually, it sounds more like a *tink!*), use the Beep command. For example, to sound a beep each time the PauseKey command pauses a macro for input, enter these commands:

```
Beep
PAUSEKEY (Enter!)
```

Be sure to put the beep *before* the pause, not after.

Giving the user a message. Use the PROMPT command to give the user a message as your macro plays. Here's how to type it.

```
PROMPT ("Continue";"Type the recipient's name and press
Enter to continue.";;;)
```

This line produces the Continue dialog box, which displays the message "Type the recipient's name and press Enter to continue."

Be sure to follow this command with a Pause command on a separate line. Then—belt and suspenders—to make sure the prompt message box disappears no matter what the user does, put an END-PROMPT command on a line by itself. Now what you've got is:

```
PROMPT ("Continue";"Type the recipient's name and press
Enter to continue.";;;)
Pause
ENDPROMPT
```

How to get an Open dialog box when you start WordPerfect.
Usually the first thing you do when you start WordPerfect is open a document, right? Use this macro to present the Open dialog box on startup. It's tricky, because you can't *record* it, or any other macros like it. Remember how we said earlier that WordPerfect doesn't record a step if you don't choose anything from a menu or dialog box? And what you want here is just the Open dialog box, where you can choose which file to open when you run the macro. Here's how to get around that limitation: you have to *type* the macro just like this in a new document window:

```
Application (WP;WPWP;Default)
   FileOpenDlg()
```

Then save the document (be sure to save it in your macros directory) as OPEN.WCM.

To make it a macro that executes when you start WordPerfect, exit WordPerfect, go out to Windows and highlight the WordPerfect icon in the WordPerfect group. Choose Properties from the Program Manager's File menu. In the Command Line box, go to the end of the line, type a space, and then type **/m-open**. The whole line should look like this:

```
wpwin.exe /m-open
```

Click OK. Now try starting WordPerfect by double-clicking on its icon, and you'll see the Open dialog box.

Using a macro to Search and Replace. Remember how we said in an earlier chapter that you could record a macro to go on a witch hunt for those ugly straight quotation marks and to replace them with true typesetter's quotation marks? Here's how to do it.

First create a short document on the screen (or copy part of an existing document) that has several occurrences of double quotation marks in it (or put them in, just so the macro has something to work on). The quotation marks should surround words, just as they do in a document. Now, make a copy of that text so you can test it out with the recorded macro later.

Press Ctrl+F10 to start the macro recorder rolling, and name the macro something like CTRLSFTQ.WCM (see the previous tip

"Assigning macros to keys") so it will be quick to use and easy to remember ("Q" for quotes). As a descriptive name, use something like *Curly quotes*. Click Record; then go to the top of the document (press Ctrl+Home). Open the Search and Replace dialog box (Ctrl+F2). Type a space and a double quote (") in the Search For box (because opening quotes are always preceded by a space). In the Replace With box, press Ctrl+W, insert the opening double quote from the Typographic Symbol set and close the box. Click Forward as the direction (just in case the last time you searched, it was backward). Then click Replace All. All the opening quotes will be replaced, and you'll be at the last opening quote in your document.

Now search and replace backward for all double quotes *followed by* a space (the closing quotes). In the Replace With box, press Ctrl+W and insert the closing quotes (") from the Typographic Symbol set. Close the box and click Replace All. When all the closing quotes have been replaced, close the Search and Replace dialog box and stop recording the macro.

Clear the screen and paste the copy of the original text, with the straight quotes, to test your new macro. Now press Shift+Ctrl+Q. The macro will compile and run, and then it will stop because there are no more quotes to find.

A small warning: Some printers can't produce acceptable curly quotes no matter what you do. If WordPerfect creates them graphically, they may look pretty ugly, too.

Order the Macros Manual from WordPerfect Corporation if you do much with macros. There's a specialized manual you can get from WordPerfect Corporation that deals only with macros and with macro command language. Call 800/228-1032 to order it for a nominal charge. It's worth it, and it goes into much more detail than there's room for in this book.

Increase your macro command language skills. Open some of the macros supplied with WordPerfect to get an idea of how macro command language is used in macros. Get acquainted with some of the other commands you can use. For example, you can use the command PrintFull( ) to print the document on the screen, or Speller( ) to start the Speller. A lot of the others are pretty straightforward, too, such as HardReturn( ), DateText( ) and so on. Get an idea of how the more esoteric commands are used in existing macros before you start using them on your own.

MOVING ON

We're out of room! This book, I hope, has helped you see some of the magic you can make with WordPerfect for Windows. In many areas, especially for macros, it has just scratched the surface. And because WordPerfect Corporation is constantly issuing interim releases, there may be tricks that don't work exactly as you expect them to, because your WordPerfect program disks have a different release date. Be sure to send in your card to get free updates. We'll keep you informed of more WordPerfect voodoo.

Colophon

This book was published using PC Pagemaker for Windows.
Typefaces used are Galliard, Optima and Revue.
Screen captures were produced using Tiffany Plus.

From Ventana Press . . .

More Companions
For
Creative Computing

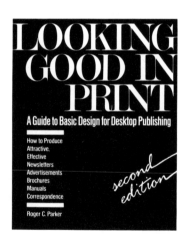

Looking Good in Print, Second Edition
$23.95
410 pages, Illustrated
ISBN: 0-940087-32-4

With over 100,000 in print, **Looking Good in Print** is looking even better. More makeovers, a new section on designing newsletters and a wealth of new design tips and techniques to broaden the design skills of the ever-growing number of desktop publishers.

Spreadsheet Publishing With Excel for Windows
$21.95
348 pages, illustrated
ISBN: 0-940087-81-2

This generously illustrated book highlights everything the Excel user needs to know about fonts, layouts and importing graphics, as well as many design features and tips that allow users to create persuasive, professional-looking documents from their spreadsheet data.

Desktop Publishing With WordPerfect — Windows Edition
$21.95
315 pages, Illustrated
ISBN: 0-940087-76-6

This example-packed book features information on WordPerfect for Windows's impressive array of typographic, graphic and page-layout capabilities. Also available for DOS versions 5.0 and 5.1.

Newsletters From the Desktop
$23.95
306 pages, illustrated
ISBN: 0-940087-40-5

Now the millions of desktop publishers who produce newsletters can learn how to improve the design of their publications. Filled with helpful design tips and illustrations.

WordPerfect for Windows Design Companion
$21.95
280 pages, illustrated
ISBN: 0-940087-90-1

This book provides readers with a wealth of ideas and tools for creating appealing, effective documents, and offers a gallery of designs created in WordPerfect to get a user up and running with the graphics features of the program.

Voodoo DOS
$19.95
320 pages, Illustrated
ISBN: 0-940087-95-2

Increase your productivity with the "magic" of **Voodoo DOS**! Packed with tricks for DOS 5 and earlier versions, this lively book offers a wide range of time-saving techniques designed for all users.

TO ORDER additional copies of *Voodoo WordPerfect for Windows,* or other Ventana Press books, please fill out this order form and return it to us for quick shipment.

	Quantity	Price		Total
Voodoo WordPerfect for Windows	_____	x $19.95	=	$_____
Spreadsheet Publishing With Excel for Windows	_____	x $21.95	=	$_____
Looking Good in Print	_____	x $23.95	=	$_____
Newsletters From the Desktop	_____	x $23.95	=	$_____
Voodoo DOS	_____	x $19.95	=	$_____
WordPerfect for Windows Design Companion	_____	x $21.95	=	$_____
Desktop Publishing With WordPerfect—Windows Edition	_____	x $21.95	=	$_____

Shipping: Please add $4.50/first book for standard UPS, $1.35/book thereafter;
$8.00/book UPS "two-day air," $2.25/book thereafter.
For Canada, add $8.10/book.   = $_____

Send C.O.D. (add $4.20 to shipping charges)   = $_____

North Carolina residents add 6% sales tax   = $_____

                                                      Total   = $_____

Name _____

Company _____

Address (No P.O. Box) _____

City_____ State_____ Zip _____

Daytime Phone _____

___ Payment enclosed ___VISA ___MC   Acc't #_____

Expiration Date_____ Signature _____

Please mail or fax
Ventana Press, P.O. Box 2468, Chapel Hill, NC 27515
919/942-0220, FAX: 919/942-1140

TO ORDER additional copies of *Voodoo WordPerfect for Windows,* or other Ventana Press books, please fill out this order form and return it to us for quick shipment.

	Quantity	Price		Total
Voodoo WordPerfect for Windows	_____	x $19.95	=	$_____
Spreadsheet Publishing With Excel for Windows	_____	x $21.95	=	$_____
Looking Good in Print	_____	x $23.95	=	$_____
Newsletters From the Desktop	_____	x $23.95	=	$_____
Voodoo DOS	_____	x $19.95	=	$_____
WordPerfect for Windows Design Companion	_____	x $21.95	=	$_____
Desktop Publishing With WordPerfect—Windows Edition	_____	x $21.95	=	$_____

Shipping: Please add $4.50/first book for standard UPS, $1.35/book thereafter; $8.00/book UPS "two-day air," $2.25/book thereafter. For Canada, add $8.10/book. = $_____

Send C.O.D. (add $4.20 to shipping charges) = $_____

North Carolina residents add 6% sales tax = $_____

Total = $_____

Name _____

Company _____

Address (No P.O. Box) _____

City_____ State_____ Zip _____

Daytime Phone _____

___ Payment enclosed ___VISA ___MC   Acc't #_____

Expiration Date_____   Signature _____

Please mail or fax
Ventana Press, P.O. Box 2468, Chapel Hill, NC 27515
919/942-0220, FAX: 919/942-1140

T O ORDER additional copies of *Voodoo WordPerfect for Windows,* or other Ventana Press books, please fill out this order form and return it to us for quick shipment.

	Quantity	Price		Total
Voodoo WordPerfect for Windows	_____	x $19.95	=	$_____
Spreadsheet Publishing With Excel for Windows	_____	x $21.95	=	$_____
Looking Good in Print	_____	x $23.95	=	$_____
Newsletters From the Desktop	_____	x $23.95	=	$_____
Voodoo DOS	_____	x $19.95	=	$_____
WordPerfect for Windows Design Companion	_____	x $21.95	=	$_____
Desktop Publishing With WordPerfect— Windows Edition	_____	x $21.95	=	$_____

Shipping: Please add $4.50/first book for standard UPS, $1.35/book thereafter; $8.00/book UPS "two-day air," $2.25/book thereafter. For Canada, add $8.10/book.   = $_____

Send C.O.D. (add $4.20 to shipping charges)   = $_____

North Carolina residents add 6% sales tax   = $_____

                                                                         Total   = $_____

Name _____

Company _____

Address (No P.O. Box) _____

City_____ State_____ Zip _____

Daytime Phone _____

___ Payment enclosed ___VISA ___MC Acc't #_____

Expiration Date_____ Signature _____

Please mail or fax
Ventana Press, P.O. Box 2468, Chapel Hill, NC 27515
919/942-0220, FAX: 919/942-1140

MORE ABOUT VENTANA PRESS BOOKS . . .

If you would like to be added to our mailing list, please complete the card below and indicate your areas of interest. We will keep you up-to-date on new books as they're published.

_____ Yes! I'd like to receive more information about Ventana Press books. Please add me to your mailing list.

Name _____

Company _____

Street address (no P.O. box) _____

City _____ State _____ Zip _____

Please check areas of interest below:

_____ AutoCAD   _____ Newsletter publishing

_____ Desktop publishing   _____ Networking

_____ Desktop design   _____ Business software

_____ Presentation graphics

Return to: Ventana Press, P.O. Box 2468, Chapel Hill, NC 27515, 919/942-0220, FAX 919/942-1140. (Please don't duplicate your fax requests by mail.)

NO POSTAGE
NECESSARY
IF MAILED
IN THE
UNITED STATES

BUSINESS REPLY MAIL
FIRST CLASS MAIL   PERMIT # 495   CHAPEL HILL, NC

POSTAGE WILL BE PAID BY ADDRESSEE

Ventana Press

P.O. Box 2468

Chapel Hill, NC 27515